KU-708-348

LEGAL SYSTEM OF ENGLAND AND WALES

The
University of

1 Royal Standard Place
Nottingham
NG1 6FZ

The University of Law, Chester

C11321

LEGAL SYSTEM OF ENGLAND AND WALES
THIRD EDITION

Frederick Price

Third edition published 2023 by
The University of Law
2 Bunhill Row
London EC1Y 8HQ

© The University of Law 2023

All rights reserved. No part of this publication may be reproduced, stored in a retrieval system, or transmitted, in any form or by any means, without the prior written permission of the copyright holder, application for which should be addressed to the publisher.

Contains public sector information licensed under the Open Government Licence v3.0

First edition published 2021

Second edition published 2022

British Library Cataloguing in Publication Data

A catalogue record for this book is available from the British Library.

ISBN 978 1 80502 000 4

Preface

This book is part of a series of Study Manuals that have been specially designed to support the reader to achieve the SQE1 Assessment Specification in relation to Functioning Legal Knowledge. Each Study Manual aims to provide the reader with a solid knowledge and understanding of fundamental legal principles and rules, including how those principles and rules might be applied in practice.

This Study Manual covers the Solicitors Regulation Authority's syllabus for the SQE1 assessment for the Legal System of England and Wales in a concise and tightly focused manner. The Manual provides a clear statement of relevant legal rules and a well-defined road map through examinable law and practice. The Manual aims to bring the law and practice to life through the use of example scenarios based on realistic client-based problems and allows the reader to test their knowledge and understanding through single best answer questions that have been modelled on the SRA's sample assessment questions.

For those readers who are students at the University of Law, the Study Manual is used alongside other learning resources and the University's assessment bank to best prepare students not only for the SQE1 assessments, but also for a future life in professional legal practice.

We hope that you find the Study Manual supportive of your preparation for SQE1 and we wish you every success.

The legal principles and rules contained within this Manual are stated as at 1 May 2023.

Author's note to the second edition

The original aim of this publication, apart from complying with the SQE1 syllabus, was to explain the fundamentals of the legal system of our jurisdiction. It is rare indeed for that system to change in anything other than a gradual manner. True, legislation can alter the tone of the overall product. An example would be the Constitutional Reform Act 2005 which carved out a Supreme Court from what was previously the House of Lords. But the overall landscape tends to be consistent in its geography, altering only marginally as the decades roll by.

There were no substantive changes to the text of this book for 2022. The reader, however, needs to exercise a certain amount of judicial discretion when it comes to data and statistics. So, for instance, at 4.7.2.2, we should not expect the number of MPs chosen for Private Members' Bills to remain at 20. Then, in Chapters 6, 7 and 8, we should not expect information on court workloads, officeholders, diversity matters, court closures and the like to remain the same. But the underlying message continues unchanged. So the generalised conclusions, and accordingly the learning points, remain as stated in the current edition.

One area could be subject to change in due course. The current Conservative Government has indicated a desire to revisit the Human Rights Act 1998. At the time of writing, some sort of review is in process. But the Act for the moment maintains its current appearance. We should keep an eye on this for the future.

Author's note to the third edition

The passage of time has required some generalised updating throughout for this third edition. The broad principles, analysis and culture described in the first and second editions, however, remain unchanged.

Author acknowledgments

Thanks to colleagues who facilitated the creation of this Manual, provided critical readership, gave encouragement, provided ideas, or generally helped finesse it into a finished product. I am grateful to them. They are: Sarah Corbett, Nick Ross, Fabio Smith, Jo Ballard, Jill Howell-Williams, Russell Binch, Salome Verrell, Stephen Illingworth, Paula Fentiman, Sean Hutton, Martin Norris, Peter Goodchild, Jacqui Kempton, Alison Smith, Valerie Vickery, Farhana Begum, Kevin Browne, Gary Atkinson, David Stott and the editorial team, the design and production team, and the review team. Any errors and omissions are, however, entirely mine.

I would also like to acknowledge the efforts of the authors of The University of Law's *Legal Method* manual from earlier years, ie Peter Goodchild, Timothy Hawkins and colleagues. This publication has referred to and adapted material from that manual at Chapters 4 and 9. It has relied heavily on material from that manual at Chapter 5.

Love and hugs to Beverley, Hal, Sam and Alex who encouraged me through the process.

This book is dedicated to my dad, Christopher Price, who inspires everyone he meets.

Contents

Table of Cases

Table of Statutes

1 Introduction to the Legal System of England and Wales and Sources of Law

SQE1 syllabus

This chapter will enable you to achieve the SQE1 assessment specification in relation to functioning legal knowledge concerning an introduction to the legal system of England and Wales and its sources of law.

Note that, for SQE1, candidates are not usually required to recall specific case names or cite statutory or regulatory authorities. Cases are provided for illustrative purposes only.

Learning outcomes

By the end of this chapter you will be able to apply relevant core legal principles and rules appropriately and effectively, at the level of a competent newly qualified solicitor in practice, to realistic client-based and ethical problems and situations in the following areas:

- what constitutes a legal system;
- the rule of law;
- the role of EU law within the legal system of England and Wales;
- sources of law;
- legislation;
- the distinction between civil and criminal law;
- the role of the Crown, Parliament and the judiciary in the development of the legal system of England and Wales;
- other influences on the functioning of that legal system; and
- the link between a sustainable democracy and the balance of powers.

Overview of this publication

This publication begins by setting the scene, moves on to case law, deals with legislation and statutory interpretation, discusses the judiciary and finishes with an analysis of the court hierarchy, appeals, jurisdiction and case law.

You should be aware some of the subject matter mentioned in this summary of chapters might be a little alien on first reading. But don't worry. As you progress through the material we hope things will become clearer on provision of more details.

Here is a summary of each chapter.

Chapter 1: this chapter introduces the legal system and sources of law, mentioning some fundamental starting points such as the role of the monarch, the development of Parliament as a legislative body, and some seminal historical developments such as the Magna Carta.

Chapter 2: this delves into more detail of the various sources of law inherent in our legal system. It mentions the monarchy (again – it keeps cropping up), nobility, church and other influences. It also pays heed to some important legal commentators and philosophers.

Chapter 3: this chapter deals with the development of case law. It looks at important concepts such as basic freedoms, including habeas corpus, and the development of other areas of law which we today take for granted. It looks at certain developments in terms of social equality. It also alerts us to the fact sometimes the law has perpetuated inequality, which serves as a reminder lawyers should be eternally vigilant as to the operation of law and society.

Chapter 4: here we deal with the format of an Act of Parliament (primary legislation), the legislative process, Private and Public Acts, and types of Act.

Chapter 5: here we discuss statutory interpretation, ie what Acts of Parliament intend and mean. This involves important matters such as the literal rule, the golden rule, the mischief rule, the purposive approach, certain rules of construction, aids to statutory interpretation and certain presumptions.

Chapter 6: this chapter discusses the judiciary and other personnel of the legal system. It mentions magistrates and other figures within the criminal justice world. It deals with juries and their role in deciding innocence or guilt of defendants charged with more serious crimes. It also mentions judicial figures within the civil justice arena.

Chapter 7: in this chapter we consider the civil court hierarchy, plus appeals and jurisdiction within this area. The chapter looks at the geography of the court system, the route to be travelled from inferior courts upwards when there is an appeal, and related matters. We also discuss rights of audience.

Chapter 8: this chapter is a close relation to Chapter 7 in that it deals with the criminal court hierarchy, appeals and jurisdiction. It deals with magistrates, the Crown Court and appeals. It also chooses as a case study the death of a young man in south London in 1993, which has served as something of a running commentary ever since on the nature of criminal justice within our society.

Chapter 9: here we discuss civil case law and precedent. We look at various examples of judicial decision-making to gain an insight into the nature of case law. We look at *ratios*, obiter statements and the various techniques open to courts when dealing with previous cases, such as distinguishing, reversing and overruling (note to puzzled readers: don't worry, all these terms will be explained in the fullness of time).

Chapter 10: this deals with criminal matters as a variation on the theme of Chapter 9 relating to the civil area. Here, we consider case law from the criminal courts, together with certain pertinent and interesting areas of criminal practice. These also press on the interaction between criminal legislation and the interpretation of it by the courts.

Chapter 11: this is a review chapter, with numerous tables and charts, to provide in a compact manner some essential learning points from the subject as a whole.

How this publication sits within the SQE environment

This text has four purposes.

- First, and crucially, it prepares students for SQE1. It aims to provide the necessary learning to deal with questions on the legal system of England and Wales and sources of law.

- Second, it acts as a gateway publication for other topics within the SQE1 environment. For instance, as part of the discussion of the legal system it might discuss constitutional matters, which then lead to further learning in relation to constitutional law. Similarly, when discussing case law it might mention well-known decisions in the field of contract, or alternatively tort, or business law and so on. This should then encourage a reading in more detail of those areas of law for other aspects of SQE1.

- Third, it represents a launchpad for the rest of the SQE journey. You might find some aspects of it helpful when preparing for SQE2 and the practical aspects of the law contained there.

- And fourth, for everyone interested in the legal system and sources of law, whether intending to attempt the SQE or not, it provides an introduction to the wonders of the England and Wales jurisdiction. It seeks to provide an initial understanding of various areas: the legal system, sources of law, the rule of law, constitutionality, personal freedoms, criminal law, contracts, other civil law obligations, business matters, the place of the EU within our world, even institutions such as the BBC, and much more. In that sense, don't feel obliged only to read it as part of preparation for an exam. It serves as a generalised text to stimulate further interest in the law.

1.1   Introduction: what is a legal system?

A legal system could mean a variety of things. To a judge it might represent the ability to resolve differences within society. To a politician it could be a vehicle for assisting in the allocation of resources. A scientist would regard it as a means of enabling and protecting research. For businesses it could be a means of ensuring fair play between government, free enterprise and the individual. To ordinary people it represents the protection of freedoms.

These are important but somewhat nebulous concepts. For a more specific definition we can refer to a wealth of textbooks and academic publications. For instance, Slorach, Embley, Goodchild and Shephard, *Legal Systems & Skills*, 3rd edn (Oxford University Press, 2017) at chapter two offers the following:

> The legal system describes the body of institutions that make, execute and resolve disputes on the law of the jurisdiction, together with the law they deal with. You may encounter the term legal system in a narrower sense, meaning the courts of a jurisdiction.

The authors then go on to state that:

> a jurisdiction is most commonly used to refer to a political entity where a particular law has application.

1.2   What a legal system is not

Let's speculate as to what a legal system is *not*. It is not a thing of pleasure, where everyone obtains unlimited enjoyment from it, because it invariably involves hard choices. It is not optional in the sense that people can pick and choose as to its extent. It is not ethereal and temporary.

Let's give a few simple examples. Children play in a street. Two of them get fed up and play elsewhere. There is no legal element to this, although there may be a system of sorts. The activity and the decision to cease it is entirely voluntary, it was essentially pleasurable and it was a temporary event.

A family sits down to breakfast one morning. This is a demonstration of community, perhaps even tribalism, but there is no legal system governing the process. Breakfast is a primary need, one could say, but it is essentially pleasurable, voluntary and transient.

John goes to work in a factory. He performs his duties for eight hours a day, five days a week. He may or may not find it a pleasurable activity, but it is essentially voluntary in that he is not forced to do that job. It is also temporary in the sense that at the end of every day he leaves it behind. His work is governed by safety considerations, but it is not a legal system as such.

So activities, obligations, social interactions and business commitments, although they may take place within a legal framework, are not themselves, alone, examples of legal systems. As part of establishing what we mean by legal systems, let's travel the globe.

1.3   Examples of legal systems around the world

This is not a comparative text, but before we examine the legal system of England and Wales, and exactly what it is, it is useful to consider other such structures around the world. From this exercise we can compile a template of characteristics that accrue to a typical jurisdiction.

There are many ways of defining and explaining a legal system. One approach is to break the construct into three essential components. First, there is the *constitution* of the country in question. Second, we can consider the *contributing cultural and historical factors* to that constitutionality. Third, there are the *unofficial and often popular elements* which influence that society's conventions, customs and principles.

- Let's start with *India*. This is the most populous democracy on the planet and thus a good starting point.
    - A question and answer document by Ashish Bhan and Mohit Rohatgi entitled *Legal Systems in India: Overview* (Practical Law – Thomson Reuters, with the law stated as at 1 January 2020) is helpful here. The constitution dates from 1950 and comprises over 450 articles and 12 schedules. It has a parliamentary tradition with strong federal instincts to ensure unity within the numerous states.
    - Its contributing cultural and historical factors include influences from the British Empire, trade links with countries as far flung as Australia, the varied cultures of its 29 states and seven union territories, the mutiny – or maybe freedom struggle – against British rule of 1857–1858, the various religions of the nation, and the process of partition from what became Pakistan in 1947.
    - The unofficial and popular elements of the legal system would be represented by the geographical remoteness of its far-flung areas, the significance of its railway system, its street and urban panoramas, its agricultural diversity, and of course cricket.

- What about *China*?
    - The China Legal Information Centre website states the country's current constitution was promulgated by the National People's Congress in 1982. It has been amended several times since.
    - As you would imagine for such a noble and enduring culture, its cultural and historical antecedents are many and varied. These include the events of its various dynasties and kingdoms going back 2,000 years or so, religions such as Buddhism, the more recent influence of Chairman Mao and the Long March, its border ties with other powers such as India, the contribution of its various regions, its new and uneasy relationship with Hong Kong since that territory reverted to Chinese sovereignty from Britain in 1997, and the role of its ancient philosophy and literature. Confucian thought would be an example of Chinese philosophy, and the 14th-century novel *The Water Margin*, with its story of banditry and themes of abuse of power by officials, an example of its stimulating literature.
    - Unofficial and popular influences on the development of its legal system would include modern architecture and technology, particularly in terms of the internet and commerce; the somewhat uncomfortable relationship between city and countryside; and the popular thirst for educational improvement.
    - Clearly the Communist Party, and its controlling elite, is also a key continuing driver of the legal system. We should therefore note that a fully functioning system of law does not necessarily guarantee a pluralistic democracy, however desirable that would be.

- The *United States of America* (USA), popularly referred to as just the United States (US), has a legal system often considered approximate to, and derivative of, that in England and Wales.
    - The US constitution was formulated in 1787 by a select body of opinion formers and endures today with 27 amendments. This is therefore the pillar of its legal system.
    - Its contributory cultural and historic elements include the governance and presence of France and Spain in the growth years of the current nation state, the opening up of the West, the role of its indigenous peoples, the institution of slavery, the right to bear arms, its growth as a global trading power, its role as international policeman, a 'frenemy' type relationship with the United Mexican States, the many labour riots of the late 19th and early 20th centuries, its tolerance of multiple religions and ethnicities, and the development of its cities.

○ Unofficial and popular elements contributing to the legal system would include the country's intense focus on frontier individualism, its adherence to immigrant traditions and culture, its fondness for elections (including sometimes of judges, something unheard of in England and Wales), the national love of baseball and other sports, the link between popular media and consumerism (walk-in fridge, anyone?) and even the national tendency to measure distances not in miles but time taken in an automobile – an ever-present reminder that cars are the royalty of travel in that vast continent.

○ All in all, this is a truly diverse collection of influences.

1.3.1 Conclusion on components of a typical legal system

We can therefore conclude that some common elements for a legal system, based on this superficial survey, would be as follows:

- the existence of a constitution;

- a relationship between central and local government;

- the leadership of a dominant body of people who control the levers of power, and who set the agenda for the operation of the system;

- the influence of geography, military events, and neighbouring states;

- invariably the impact of religion;

Figure 1.1 Three aspects of a typical legal system

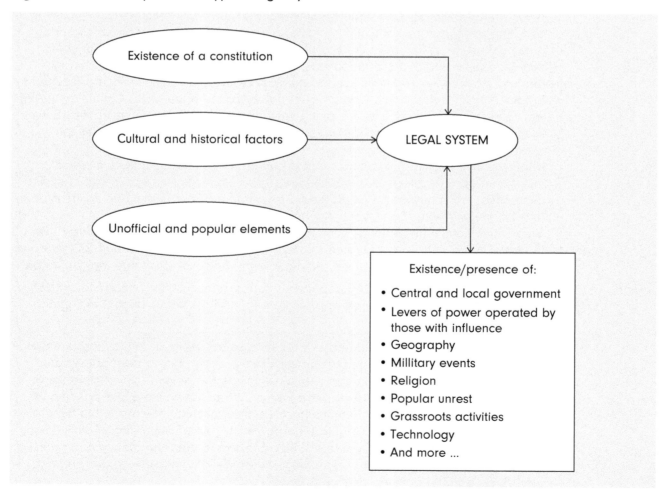

- some element of the popular will, involving the influence and expectations of the ordinary population, and often popular unrest;

- grassroots activities, such as leisure pursuits, trade and travel; and

- the growth of technology.

Let's consider now the legal system of England and Wales.

1.4 The rule of law and its place in our legal system

Lord Bingham in his seminal work *The Rule of Law* (Penguin paperback, 2011) said:

> all persons and authorities within the state, whether public or private, should be bound by and entitled to the benefit of laws publicly and prospectively promulgated and publicly administered in the courts.

This is a definitive modern definition of the rule of law. It means every person, whether born in a cardboard box or a country mansion, should be governed by, and benefit from, the laws of the land. Further, those laws should be clearly stated, understood and administered.

Lord Bingham went on to outline a number of principles which he believed to be essential components of this concept. By way of paraphrasing his excellent thoughts, some of these requirements include:

- the law must be clear and predictable;

- the exercise of discretion should be subordinate to the exercise of law;

- we should all be equal before the law;

- the state should provide an essential safety net for the settlement of matters which private parties and individuals were unable to resolve; and

- the state should adhere to its international as well as national obligations.

1.4.1 A case illustrating the application of the rule of law

Any number of court cases could illustrate the operation of these basic principles. Let's take one as an example. Imagine you are a foreign national who comes to work in the UK. You are employed in an embassy of an overseas state. You then think you are treated badly, alleging discrimination, harassment, unpaid wages and unfair dismissal. Should you be allowed to progress a case in an Employment Tribunal (a specialist court dealing with dismissal and related claims by employees)?

These were the outline facts in Benkharbouche and Janah v Secretary of State for Foreign and Commonwealth Affairs *[2017] UKSC 62. The two employees were Moroccan nationals working at the Sudanese and Libyan embassies in London respectively. They alleged various employment-related injustices. The embassies argued, amongst other matters, they had immunity from prosecution by virtue of their status as emanations of foreign governments. The UK Government's involvement in the case stemmed from its interest in the state immunity principle.*

The Supreme Court decided the claims against the embassies should be allowed to progress. The court acknowledged the concept of state immunity but ruled it should not apply to these claims. It concluded the provisions of the Human Rights Act 1998, enacting the European Convention on Human Rights 1950 (ECHR), and the European Union (EU) Charter of Fundamental Rights 2000 should take precedence.

This case incorporates a number of the elements inherent in the rule of law. It prioritises law over discretion, placing considerable weight on the interplay of the various pieces of legislation relevant to the dispute. One of its conclusions was the need for equality before the law, placing the interests of the two employees on an equal footing with the entitlements of the embassies and, indeed, the UK Government. The case demonstrated the need for the judiciary to step in when individuals were unable to resolve their differences. And it indicated that the legal system takes an interest in the affairs of non-nationals, thereby emphasising its international outlook.

1.4.2 Some thoughts on the rule of law

The rule of law in the legal system of England and Wales is integral to the effective governance of the UK. It provides certainty for both nationals and foreigners, thus underpinning the UK's status as an international centre for democratic principles, trade and justice. It purports to treat people equally, whether you are rich or poor, or part of the 'establishment' or not. It proceeds by way of reference to rules, precedent and law.

Any number of countries have legal systems. How effective those systems are, however, depends on the existence and application of the rule of law. Not every jurisdiction is lucky enough to have a rule of law as effectively developed as that of the UK.

Figure 1.2 Some components of the rule of law

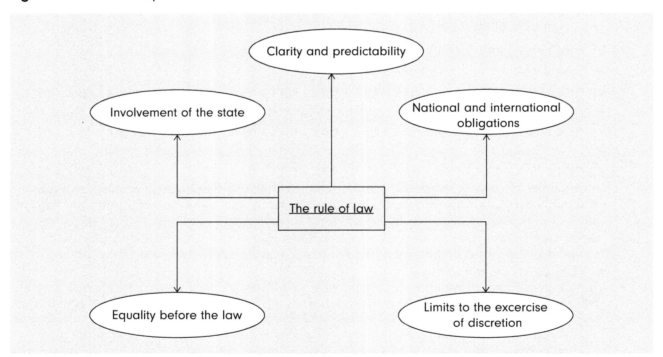

1.5 International law

This leads us to the topic of international law. It is not the aim of this book to deal with this interesting area, but a brief reference is helpful in establishing the context of the UK in the wider world. The UK, and hence the jurisdiction of England and Wales, takes note of and is subject to international law principles. A glance at Malcolm Evans (ed), *International Law*, 5th edn (Oxford University Press, 2018), for instance, indicates the vastness of this subject. Hundreds of international instruments and other documents are listed there.

The UK subscribes to a considerable number of treaties and conventions. Equally there are others it declines to recognise. The important points to note for our purposes are:

- the UK takes pride in its position in the world, and its legal system reflects that;

- international law should be considered an adjunct to the legal system of England and Wales, rather than something superior;

- international agreements often promise more than they deliver. One thinks of the League of Nations, formed in 1920, which lamentably failed to maintain peace in Europe in 1939–1945; and more recently the Kyoto Protocol 1997 on climate issues, which has struggled to gain traction in environmental matters; and

- the rule of law must remain paramount, regardless of the international perspective. Sometimes the UK courts find themselves in the position of reaffirming key legal principles in the face of tension with other states.

1.6 1066 and all that

The current legal system is a product of much strained compromise. When William the Conqueror arrived at Pevensey in 1066 he brought with him more than bloodshed and the customs of his native land. Having defeated, and killed, Harold at Hastings he introduced presumptions that quickly found their way into a system of rule. First he re-allocated resources, something that most obviously manifested itself in the distribution of land grants to his supporters. So from an early stage in the legal history of the nation the primacy of ownership of land was firmly established.

Next, William and his Norman successors set about legitimising the power they wielded, and that came through a system of control, which grew in sophistication over time. That system has little resemblance to the institutions and practices that exist today. But they do provide an insight into what we mean by a legal system.

- There were rules and customs.

- There was chain of command, which was essentially hierarchical in nature. Participants submitted to a jurisdiction – here, usually, the King, or his officials, or those representing his inner circle.

- Records of decisions were sometimes kept and in time these would be referred to as reports.

- The process also orientated itself around not just people and rules but also time and place. Time became apparent through the regularity and timetabling of hearings, and place expressed itself through the venues – sometimes imposing and impressive ones – where decisions were made.

Throughout this structure those at lower levels of society frequently bridled at abuses of power. That was as much the case for nobility who perceived themselves to be excluded from the fruits of economic success as it was for, in time, the peasantry and the emerging middle classes.

The system of rule and society imposed by the ruling elite in the early centuries after William's invasion laid the foundations for today's legal system.

1.7 The Magna Carta 1215

King John and his nobility, who were in dispute, built upon those foundations in an agreement called the Magna Carta reached at Runnymede, Surrey, in 1215. Pretty much immediately after the signing of the document its signatories lost interest in both the letter and the spirit of the agreement. But a number of its provisions, designed at the time to regulate relations between king and nobility, retain their significance. Society today would frown on various clauses of this document, which have prejudicial elements to them, but other parts of the Magna Carta endure in one form or another today.

At clause 12 there is a loose reference to the concept of taxation involving consent. Clause 13 doffs its hat to the commercial primacy of the City of London – an insight into the perennial role of commerce, and wealth, in developing the law. Clause 17 mentions 'law suits' being held in a fixed place. This combines with references to assizes, in other words travelling courts, and inquests, ie investigations into deaths. Both these forums exist today, albeit in a modified form (and neither are perfect).

Perhaps the most significant parts of the document, as we look back with the benefit of hindsight, are clauses 38, 39 and 40. Clause 38 states that no official shall put a defendant on trial on the basis of an unsupported self-incriminatory statement alone. This can plausibly lay claim to the sentiment that it is for officialdom, not the defendant, to make the running when presenting a prosecution – and that the burden of proof in a criminal matter lies with the prosecutor.

Clause 39 states that there shall be punishment only within the law of the land. Clause 40 says that justice shall not be sold, delayed or denied. These last two provisions represent concepts particularly dear to modern democracies – namely, that everyone is equal before the law, legal decisions should be made on the basis of consistency rather than whim, and justice should be conveyed swiftly, without heed to the highest bidder.

Following the Magna Carta the legal system in our country adopted in embryo important concepts which are still pertinent. These can be summed up as follows:

- the involvement of the monarch and other elite elements in society;

- the acceptance, sometimes gradually, often in the face of conflict, of the rule of law;

- the importance of commercial interests such as those represented by the City of London;

- the existence of courts and their officials; and

- the presence of simmering, and frequently overt, dissatisfaction amongst key elements of the population, in this instance the barons and higher nobility. As we shall see, social unrest among those lower down the socio-economic ladder was also significant in the sprouting of the legal system we enjoy today.

1.8 Legislation – the new normal

As the centuries rolled by, the forces shaping legal society adopted a more assertive form. In particular Parliament grew in importance. Not only did it represent the will of ruling society, working in an occasionally uncomfortable partnership with the monarch, but it also started to affix its name to laws relating to governance.

By way of example, one of the earliest recorded Acts of Parliament is from 1497 and relates to the taking of apprentices for wool-making in Norfolk. There is evidence of it being approved by the Lords, with the then King Henry VII endorsing his monogram. At this stage in its development what we now call the House of Commons had yet to establish itself as a legislative player. But even so this Act show-pieced a basic template for the creation of legislation. Representatives of classes of society would gather in Parliament, a discussion of sorts may or may not take place, laws would be drafted and those laws would be approved by the monarch. This final step of course is what we now call 'Royal Assent', the customary endpiece to the creation of an Act, even in today's modern world. The idea that governments can simply create law with the stroke of a pen, without involving Parliament, was swiftly discounted by our constitution. Government by decree is considered something entirely un-British.

1.9   How the judiciary found its voice

Just as the nobility and the emerging classes had, in their own ways, wrestled influence from the grip of the Crown, so the judiciary began its own, somewhat uncomfortable, journey towards self-assertion. During the reign of Henry VIII the King brought upon himself the increased significance of judicial pronouncements through his desire to divorce his first wife. He also needed to put some distance between himself and the Catholic establishment in Rome.

The legal advice he received was not always welcome. An early casualty of tension between monarch and the law was Sir Thomas More (1478–1535), whose tenure as Chancellor (then a lawyer's post, not the Treasury role it is today) to Henry VIII ended in More's execution. Even so, with an admirable determination to separate the judicial process from that of executive authority, law officers and the courts continued to make decisions which indicated that there were limits to governmental power.

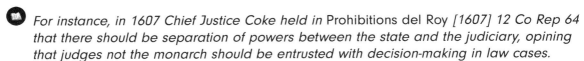 *For instance, in 1607 Chief Justice Coke held in* Prohibitions del Roy *[1607] 12 Co Rep 64 that there should be separation of powers between the state and the judiciary, opining that judges not the monarch should be entrusted with decision-making in law cases.*

This principle holds good today. Even those with only a rudimentary grasp of constitutional matters understand that judges should be independent of Parliament and the executive. Some commentators believe this is more akin to a balance, rather than a strict separation as such, of powers, and that is something to ponder as you read this book and progress your legal studies generally.

Another, even more impressive, example of lawyerly muscle would be the Case of Proclamations *[1610] 12 Co Rep 74. There, Coke gave a ruling on new buildings in and around London. In the case report the following statement appears:*

> *The King has no prerogative but that which the law of the land allows him.*

This is an admirably brief and indeed blunt statement on the limits of Crown power. It reinforced the notion that decisions have to be made, and adhered to, according to rules rather than the caprice of government functionaries.

More recent cases have continued to repeat this theme. During the Second World War, in Liversidge v Anderson *[1942] AC 206, the House of Lords (now the Supreme Court) was called upon to consider the competing demands of the executive as against the individual. In a time of crisis, to what extent can the Government restrict freedoms? The majority favoured the Government but it is the dissenting judgment of Lord Atkin which is still held dear today:*

> *In England, amidst the clash of arms, the laws are not silent. They may be changed, but they speak the same language in war as in peace. It has always been one of the pillars of freedom, one of the principles of liberty for which on recent authority we are now fighting, that the judges are no respecters of persons, and stand between the subject and any attempted encroachments on his liberty by the executive, alert to see that any coercive action is justified in law.*

What does this statement mean? Set against the backdrop of war, it was then, and remains today, a striking reminder of our entitlement to personal freedom. Lord Atkin believed the executive, no matter how powerful, and no matter what the circumstances, should expect its actions to be checked by the judiciary when considering individual liberties.

A thoroughly modern twist on the need for the executive to recognise limits on its powers is the case of Miller v Secretary of State for Exiting the European Union [2017] UKSC 5. *There, the Supreme Court held that there was an obligation on the Government to involve Parliament before triggering the Article 50 process for leaving the EU. In its own way this was the judiciary repeating the message from the* Case of Proclamations: *the executive cannot be allowed to over-reach its powers. Whatever your views on the EU and the United Kingdom's departure from it, one of several conclusions to be drawn from this case is that there are limits to the royal prerogative and executive power.*

There is thus a consistent line of reasoning from ancient times to the present that the separation of powers between the executive, the legislature and the judiciary – or the balancing act inherent in their relationship – is a cardinal principle of the legal system.

1.10 Bill of Rights 1688

The Bill of Rights is considered an important part of the UK constitution and a foundation stone of the legal system. It represents a further restriction on the power of the monarchy and as such contributed to the development of Parliament and the courts.

It sets the tone in its preamble by stating it was an Act 'declaring the rights and liberties of the subject'. It includes references to freedom of speech, the existence of juries, the undesirability of cruel and unusual punishment, and the requirement for free elections to Parliament. It also stated, crucially,

> That the pretended Power of Suspending of Laws or the Execution of Laws by Regall Authority without Consent of Parlyament is illegall.

We have kept the old English spelling here, and what this last provision reinforces is the restriction on the Crown's powers to suspend or make laws without the involvement of Parliament.

The Bill of Rights therefore reinforces basic principles of the rule of law and continued the gradual development of the legal system we recognise today, namely the involvement of the Crown (albeit with increasingly limited powers), Parliament and the courts.

1.11 Extending the franchise

As time passed the legal system continued to develop its own distinct character. One of its early hallmarks was a reluctant sharing of power between those in the ascendancy and those seeking more influence. An early example of this would be the Magna Carta. The principle was then taken to extremes in 1649 when King Charles I lost his head during the Civil War period.

By the 1800s a new constituency was agitating for influence: the growing alliance between property owners and the merchant classes. At the same time industrialisation created seething social discontent amongst the poor. At Peterloo near Manchester in 1819 a crowd formed to protest against poverty and proclaim the benefits of voting reform. The authorities used force against those present and 18 died.

This heavy-handed reaction could not quell the fervour of reform. Together, the growing sophistication of the mercantile classes and the physical muscle of the underclasses prompted the reform of representative democracy, in the form of the Representation of the People Acts of 1832, 1867 and 1884. These Acts extended the franchise to an increasing number of people (well, men; votes for women came later). This meant a greater proportion of the population were electing Members of Parliament and, by implication, contributing in some way to the creation of legislation in Parliament.

Ever since these Acts the ability of the general public to influence the operation of Parliament, and hence a key aspect of the legal system, has grown considerably. With the growth of the internet and social media that trend has naturally accelerated in the last few decades. Not all popular involvement in the parliamentary process is dignified: the House of Lords Select Committee on Communications Report, 'Regulating in a Digital World' dated 9 March 2019, noted that one female Labour MP received 8,121 abusive Twitter messages in 150 days in the run up to the 2017 General Election.

1.12 The place of EU law within our legal system

The United Kingdom joined what is now the EU on 1 May 1973. That decision was confirmed with a 67% vote in favour through a referendum on 5 June 1975. The European Communities Act (ECA) 1972 anticipated the UK's membership and provided for the UK's institutions taking note of EU law.

For instance the ECA 1972, s 2(1) states as follows:

> All such rights, powers, liabilities, obligations and restrictions from time to time created or arising by or under the Treaties, and all such remedies and procedures from time to time provided for by or under the Treaties, as in accordance with the Treaties are without further enactment to be given legal effect or used in the United Kingdom shall be recognised and available in law, and be enforced, allowed and followed accordingly ...

There is some tortured syntax in the middle of this section but the sentiment is clear. Obligations created under EU laws, in particular the Treaty of Rome 1957 (hence the reference to 'Treaties'), shall be 'given legal effect' and 'enforced'. Politicians and the courts took a while to embrace this concept but what is now acknowledged as the supremacy of EU law, so long as the UK remains within the EU, was considered in the House of Lords (now the Supreme Court) in 1990.

 In R (Factortame Ltd) v Secretary of State for Transport *[1990] 2 AC 85, Lord Bridge of Harwich discussed the impact of the Treaty of Rome, as updated, on UK law, and the role of the European Court of Justice (the ECJ) in deciding on the scope of European Community law. Towards the end of his judgment Lord Bridge made the sensational statement that:*

> *I do not think that it is open to your Lordships' House to decide one way or the other whether ... Community law overrides English law and either empowers or obliges an English court to make an interim order .... It follows, I think, that your Lordships are obliged under ... the Treaty to seek a preliminary ruling from the ECJ.*

In other words, the highest court in the land was unable to confirm it could rule on a UK provision which involved EU law. On the contrary, it considered itself obliged to refer the matter to the ECJ. This judicial deference to EU legal structures caused some heartache. Large numbers of people, not just lawyers, took the view the UK's way of life was threatened by such an intrusion.

This no doubt contributed to the referendum decision of 2016 in which a slim majority voted to 'leave' the EU rather than 'remain'. By that time EU law concepts had taken a considerable hold on England and Wales and its sources of law, and one interesting aspect of future developments is the extent to which EU influences will continue to hold sway over our own jurisdiction.

Divorce from the EU remains somewhat challenging. In 2023 the Conservative Government proposed to do away with a substantial element of historic EU influence through the Retained EU Law (Revocation and Reform) Bill. Supporters hoped to achieve two outcomes. First, it would represent a symbolic coda – ie endpiece – to what is popularly dubbed 'Brexit'. Secondly, it would allow the replacement of EU legal principles with something more obviously national. At the time of writing, there is a degree of uncertainty as to the Bill's provisions, detail and timescale.

The EU and United Kingdom have also experienced difficulty in maintaining what all parties hoped would be frictionless trade between the parties. The Northern Ireland Protocol, which aims to maintain North–South cooperation across a range of activity, has proved hard to facilitate. On 27 February 2023, the UK and the EU announced the agreement of the Windsor Framework, which intends to alleviate areas of trade tension and other matters of potential and actual dispute.

The flowchart in **Figure 1.3** illustrates the development of the legal system. It is somewhat subjective, picking and choosing its landmarks. We've called it 'a sideways glance', meaning it doesn't pretend to be comprehensive, or even balanced. Some of the commentary is a bit tongue in cheek. Hopefully you get the idea.

Figure 1.3   A sideways glance at the development of the legal system

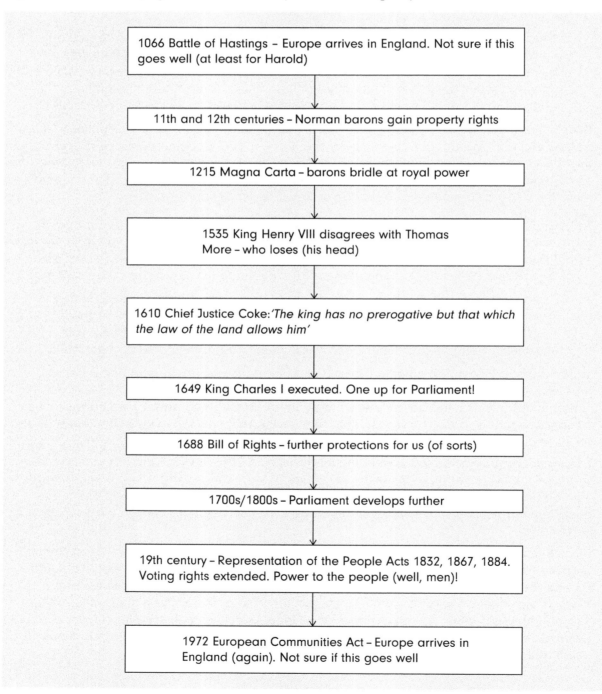

1.13 Why England and Wales (but not Scotland)?

You might be wondering why there is a combined legal jurisdiction for England and Wales but not for Scotland or Northern Ireland. We can leave Northern Ireland to its own particular history. But what about Scotland? After all, the Stuart King James I reigned over both his own country and England from 1603. So how come the legal systems are procedurally distinct?

The answer lies principally in history. There has always been compelling neighbourhood between England and the principality of Wales. In strategic, tactical and administrative terms England in the 1400s and 1500s saw Wales as pleasingly subordinate. Geography also played its part: the proximity of mercantile centres at Gloucester, Tewkesbury, Worcester and Chester to the Welsh borders meant the two countries had frequent interactions in trade, cultural and commercial terms.

The reigns of Henry VII (1485–1509) and his son Henry VIII (1509–1547) were significant in that those kings had a historical and familial attachment to Wales, symbolised by the landing of Henry VII at Pembroke prior to his defeat of Richard III at Bosworth Field. Naturally the Welsh were not always compliant with the concept of greater unity, but legal juncture was set through the Acts of Union 1536 and 1543. These established administrative and legal institutions which in turn led to enduring links between the two countries.

Scotland by contrast sent King James and his successors to England in 1603 without wishing to compromise its own customs, which it guarded with considerable success. It then waited until 1707 for its own Act of Union with England. By that stage Scotland was comfortable in its own legal culture. The English establishment was sufficiently sage to allow the distinctiveness to remain.

This explains why we talk of the jurisdiction of England and Wales rather than one which includes Scotland or, for that matter, Northern Ireland.

1.14 Differences between civil and criminal law

There are many different areas of law, and at this introductory stage of learning about legal systems it is a good idea to be clear about one stark distinction: that between civil and criminal law.

Curiously, what you may have thought as being something very obvious can in fact be somewhat opaque. Take these examples:

- Albert rushes into Brian and knocks him over, injuring Brian's shoulder. Albert is accused of assault occasioning actual bodily harm under the Offences Against the Person Act 1861.

- Charles rushes into Donald and knocks him over, injuring Donald. Charles has committed no offence, and indeed is congratulated by those around him.

Why the difference in approach to these two apparently similar events? The context is all important. Here, the distinction is one of consent. Assume Brian is walking down the street and did not agree to being attacked. Contrast that with Donald – assume he was playing rugby, a sport where violence is effectively legalised. Charles no doubt did not intend to injure Donald but either way there would be no suggestion Charles has done anything wrong. Albert, however, would face criminal sanctions.

Here is another example.

- Edward walks onto Frank's land without permission. He has committed a civil wrong called trespass, for which there may be only a nominal result in something called 'damages' (compensation) in a limited sum;

- Further down the road Gary walks onto land owned by the Ministry of Defence without permission. Gary is charged with a criminal offence under the Serious Organised Crime and Police Act 2005 and could be in deep water, receiving a stiff fine or imprisonment in jail or both.

The distinction here stems from the activities of the armed forces. Frank's land needs no security. But a military base, if that is what it was, needs close protection. This explains why Edward's act is not a crime but Gary's is.

Civil law involves agreements and mainly private resolutions. Criminal law involves punishment. Here is a brief and somewhat global list of the differences between the two areas.

- Civil law deals with contracts, disputes and differences where the outcome is measured in remedies or the payment of monies. In the event of the courts having to make a decision, a matter must be proved on the balance of probabilities.

- Criminal law imposes restrictions and obligations on the population, where the outcome is measured in punishment for transgressions, with the public taking an interest in both the offence and the punishment. The ultimate penalty is the loss of one's freedom through imprisonment.

Criminal matters must be proved beyond reasonable doubt, and the 'golden thread' of justice as stated in the case of Woolmington v DPP *[1935] AC 462 is that the accused is innocent until proven guilty.*

1.14.1 An early example of a criminal case

To illustrate the operation of the criminal law within the legal system, let's take an early example. Here is one of the first reported cases from London's Central Criminal Court, the Old Bailey. You can find more such cases at oldbaileyonline.org. We have kept the original language for colour.

This case involved the theft of a mirror from a property owner. The thief pretended at one stage to be a member of the public pursuing the perpetrator, and as you can see the ruse was ineffective.

> *Theft Grand Larceny 29 April 1674*
>
> *Also there was another Tryed for stealing of a Looking-Glass from one Oliver Smith. The manner was thus, there did a great Looking-Glass stand in the window of the said Mr. Smith, valued at nineteen shillings, and he one Evening hearing a crackling of the Glass of the Window, went to look to see what the matter was, but could see no person. Presently after going again, he found the Glass gon, and the Thief running away, who immediately following him, and crying stop Thief, he threw down the Glass, and in making hast away dropt of his Hat, crying himself, stop Thief, but being most suspected himself, he was taken and his Hat carried to him, which he owned. And Committed to Newgate, and from thence to Justice-Hall, where his Indictment being read, he pleaded not Guilty, but the Evidence coming against him, he was found guilty by the Jury and had Judgement to be hanged, being burnt in the hand before.*

Here, the defendant stole a mirror. The owner chased the thief who was eventually detained.

Did you detect the punishment given to the accused? He actually received two: being branded, or burnt, in the hand, and then being hanged from the neck. Today the state cannot sentence someone to death, incidentally.

Note the role of evidence in a court case illustrated here. The defendant dropped his hat, which linked him to the scene of the crime.

This vignette thus offers an insight into key ingredients of the criminal law process, and these remain integral to prosecutions today. They can be summed up as follows:

- there must be an action which is forbidden by society, usually through a statute or other law. We say 'usually', because sometimes (although rarely these days) there are customs which are influential;

- there will be a victim (occasionally you hear of a 'victimless crime', but judges don't recognise this slogan);

- the importance of evidence, such as items or possessions, and also the personal testimony of both the victim and the accused;

- the requirement of proof;

- a finding of guilt; and

- some form of punitive resolution, which most typically involves unwelcome consequences for the guilty, and often an element of retribution to give satisfaction to the victim and society.

Criminal procedure operates as a microcosm of the rule of law, and reflects the requirement of the legal system to embrace transparent standards.

The operation of the criminal law is a subject that can be developed in your other studies.

1.15   The role of the police

To the extent the police are crucial in arresting suspects, bringing them before the courts, and facilitating the withdrawal of liberties, they are an essential component of the legal system.

Policing in the UK is by consent. The police operate with the agreement and support of the general population. Although they wear a uniform, they are ordinary citizens in the same way as you or me.

Policing in London, which is generally considered the brainchild of Sir Robert Peel (1788– 1850), was given official form through the Metropolitan Police Act 1829. It is subject to the jurisdiction of central government and the Home Office. Outside London, police activities are controlled by local authorities.

It is an important principle that police actions should remain within the law. If constables act outside the law, there are both civil and criminal penalties. There is a host of legislation governing the behaviour of the police, some notable instances of which include the Police and Criminal Evidence Act 1984, the Criminal Justice and Public Order Act 1994, and the Policing and Crime Act 2017.

In Mohidin v Commissioner of The Police of The Metropolis *[2015] EWHC 2740 (QB) the court reviewed an interaction between police and youths in June 2007 on London's Edgware Road. Officers stopped, arrested, handcuffed and removed to a police station various individuals. The case involved allegations of assault, racial aggravation and gross misconduct.*

This incident impacted on many parties:

- *the complainants made claims, among others, for false imprisonment and assault;*

- *police officers were arrested and tried for misfeasance in public office;*

- *medical evidence was called to assess the impact of events on the health of individuals involved;*

- *there were investigations by the Independent Police Complaints Commission (IPCC), now the Independent Office for Police Conduct; and*

- *the innocent parties received damages.*

The conclusions we draw from cases such as this is that the police must act within the law, they are as equal as the rest of us before that law, and courts are assiduous in providing remedies in the face of wrongful acts by the police. This is a powerful reminder of the rule of law within the legal system of England and Wales.

1.16   The British Broadcasting Corporation (BBC)

Not everyone would agree a broadcaster should feature in a book on legal systems. The BBC is, however, unique. It began life in its current form by way of Royal Charter in 1927. The Charter is periodically subject to renewal. The BBC remains today admired for its journalistic prowess, its place within the national identity, and its ability to hold the Government to account through media scrutiny. A licence fee payable by households throughout the UK provides finance for it. It is thus (at the moment) publicly funded but not through conventional taxation, and this lack of direct fiscal control by the Government means it is able to maintain independence of a sort from Westminster politicians.

One of the recitals to the original Royal Charter states as follows:

Whereas In view of the widespread interest which is thereby shown To be taken by Our People in the Broadcasting Service and of the great value of the Service as a means of education and entertainment, We deem it desirable that the Service should be developed and exploited to the best advantage and in the national interest.

The last two words are significant. The concept of broadcasting in the national interest has developed into a principle of scrutiny of not just the executive but also Parliament and the courts. One could say the BBC therefore acts as an important additional check and balance within the legal system. Other media bodies also do this, but none with the reach, funding, influence and power of the BBC.

The Beeb, or Auntie, as it is sometimes patronisingly called, has its critics and is no longer held in the universal affection that accompanied it during, for instance, the Second World War. But it remains an important representative of popular culture, plays its part in scrutinising officialdom, abides by strong principles and rules – for instance through its editorial guidelines – and maintains an international outlook. As such it pays close heed to certain aspects of Lord Bingham's analysis of the rule of law.

Like the courts, the BBC also has a duty to be impartial. This reinforces its role within the UK's bicameral and judicially influenced democracy.

Its impartiality, as stated in the First Public Purpose of Article 20 of its current Charter, was reviewed in the somewhat oddball, and one off, case of Keighley v BBC *[2019] EWHC 3331 (Admin). There, the High Court stated that:*

> *The BBC should provide duly accurate and impartial news, current affairs and factual programming to build people's understanding of all parts of the United Kingdom and of the wider world ... so that all audiences can engage fully with major local, regional, national, United Kingdom and global issues and participate in the democratic process, at all levels, as active and informed citizens.*

The court then added:

> *it is clear that the BBC has adopted performance measures to assess its performance in promoting its First Public Purpose (ie impartiality), and that there is no proper basis for the contention that the BBC has acted irrationally or otherwise unlawfully in adopting the framework that it has.*

You should not get the idea that judicial review of the BBC is a regular event. This case does, however, confirm the view of the courts that the BBC is essentially an independent body, a perspective almost certainly echoed by the vast majority of the UK population.

The BBC has a number of attributes that reinforce its importance. It:

- has a commitment to impartial broadcasting;

- regularly reports events in Parliament; and

- through its news reporting and current affairs programmes, holds to account both the Government and His Majesty's Official Opposition.

As such it plays an important role in scrutinising the acts of officialdom, and therefore playing its part in the fine-tuning of our legal system and its constitution.

1.17 The UK constitution

These points beg the question: what is the UK constitution? The answer to this is more properly located in a book on constitutional and administrative law, but a simple response can be provided here. The constitution guides the interplay between the various elements of society. The monarchy has its role. So do you and I, in our own simple way: by voting, complying with laws, paying taxes, appearing before the courts when required and so on.

The constitution is uncodified in that it is located across different sources, only some of which are written. So we start with declarations such as the Magna Carta, progress through the Acts of Settlement for Wales and Scotland, include the Bill of Rights 1688, and refer to any number of compromises between the Crown, nobility, Parliament and the people.

The levers of constitutionality are then operated through a combination of the monarch, Parliament and the courts. Often constitutional steps involve not just the written word but also precedent, custom, prerogative and convention. To this we can add the occasional roles of the Church of England and the Armed Forces, who would consider themselves as friends to the constitutional process. This is in both a broader societal manner and a narrower legalistic form. In broad terms both these institutions have strong links historically to the Crown and the landed classes. In a narrow sense they have their own courts where decisions are made, which occasionally still create jurisprudence of benefit to society as a whole.

We should also acknowledge the semi-constitutional role of the Civil Service within our society. The Civil Service is the administrative arm of the executive. It is non-political, and its senior officials are responsible for enacting business – and of course a winning party's campaign pledges – within the various government departments. You often hear of the exercise of 'soft power' within our society, meaning that people exert influence in an almost invisible manner. The Civil Service represents a significant source of 'soft power', offering guidance and advice to our elected leaders, and at the same time providing continuity between administrations over long periods of time.

Figure 1.4 Overview of influences on the constitution and legal system

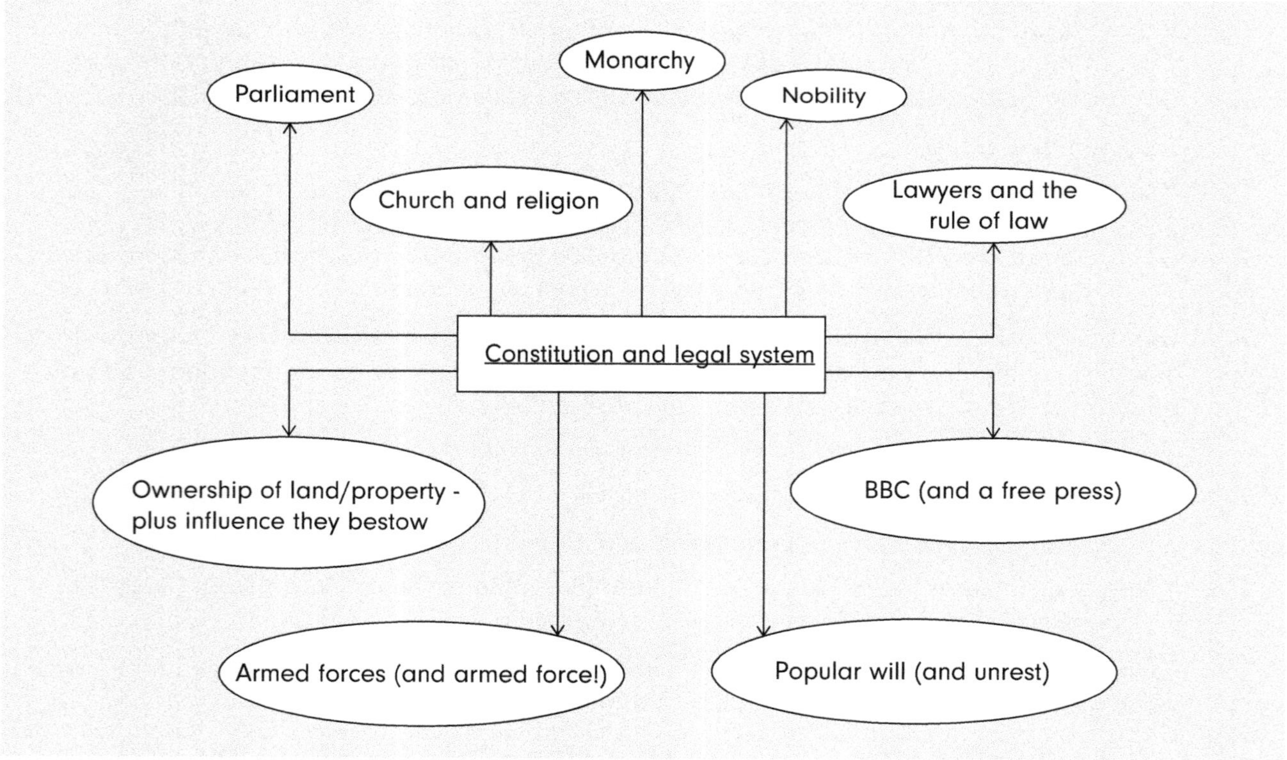

Summary

This chapter has travelled from the days of William the Conqueror to the era of the internet. It has discussed the nature of the legal system of England and Wales. It has also touched on the sources of law inherent in that system.

The key characteristics of the legal system of the jurisdiction can be summed up as follows:

- the involvement, actual or symbolic, of the monarch;
- the election and/or involvement of individuals in the two Houses of Parliament;
- the complicity, support and/or involvement of society in the law-making process, often as a result of protest or violence, in order to assert their entitlements;
- the creation of legislation by the executive and the legislature;
- the continuing scrutiny of legislation as part of the process of resolving disputes through the courts;
- the insistence by lawyers and judges on their independence;
- public support for the separation, or balance, of powers as between the executive, the legislature and the judiciary;
- the continuing influence of other organisations within society, such as the media and the police; and
- last but not least, an adherence to the rule of law.

The sources of law for our jurisdiction include the following, and you can see that this is a combination of the general and the specific:

- parliamentary legislation;

- case law formulated by judges when making decisions in court;

- external agencies such as the EU;

- the gradual growth of a fully functioning, pluralistic and participative democracy; and

- the ability of the governing elites – whether that be monarchs, nobility or the mercantile classes – throughout the centuries to share power as an alternative to having their privileges removed by force.

Sample questions

Question 1

A student is reviewing the operation of the legal system of England and Wales. She has read about the influence of the monarchy, and its relationship with the aristocracy and nobility. She has also studied the history of riots and popular unrest. She has noted the role of the judiciary and read much case law.

Which of the following has contributed meaningfully to the development of the legal system in England and Wales?

A   The monarch, the Church of England and the nobility, but not the general population.

B   The nobility, the landed gentry and trades unions, but not the monarchy.

C   The general population, the nobility and the armed forces, but not the judiciary.

D   The judiciary, the nobility and the monarchy, but not the Church of England.

E   The monarchy, the nobility and the judiciary, but not the trades unions before 1800.

Answer

Option E is correct. The monarchy, the nobility and the judiciary were and continue to be vital influencing factors. But there were no trades unions before the end of the 19th century, so they had no influence before 1800.

Option A is wrong because all four of the monarchy, the Church of England, the nobility and the general population have contributed, in their own way, to the development of the legal system. Option B is wrong because the monarchy has had, and continues to maintain, an important role in the legal system. Option C is wrong because the judiciary was and is key to the legal system. Option D is wrong because the Church of England historically has played an important role, although currently its official constitutional influence is much diminished.

Question 2

A solicitor works for a firm that deals with parliamentary and constitutional matters. A client would like her to give a talk to junior employees on the role of the legal system and constitution within England and Wales. She is preparing her talk and is pondering the impact of the European Convention on Human Rights (ECHR), the place of the monarchy, the significance of the Magna Carta, the role of Parliament, and the importance of the rule of law.

Which of the following statements relating to constitutional matters within England and Wales is correct?

A   The European Court of Human Rights law can compel Parliament to pass legislation.

B   The rule of law means that the monarch is treated the same as everyone else.

C   The Magna Carta is part of the UK's written constitution.

D   Parliament is subordinate to the executive, ie Government.

E   The rule of law states that everyone is equal before the law.

Answer

Option E is correct. As Lord Bingham stated, the principle of being equal before the law is an essential pillar of any reputable legal system. Equality before the law does not mean that everyone has the same choices or level of wealth. But it does mean the law should operate on essentially objective principles, according to established rules.

Of the other answers, option A is wrong because, although ECHR law remains important to UK law, there is no mechanism for ECHR provisions forcing Parliament to act against its will. Option B is wrong because self-evidently the monarchy has privileges beyond those afforded the rest of us. Option C is wrong because the UK has no written constitution. It is uncodified, although the Magna Carta is important of course. Option D is wrong because Government and Parliament operate jointly, and neither can claim complete dominance over the other in their relationship.

Question 3

A Government wants to deal with an unexpected event. There is no law allowing the necessary steps to be taken. Newspapers, social media and the majority of the population appear to support immediate imposition of a decree, ie an executive measure, even if there is no legal basis for it.

Should the Government issue the relevant decree?

A   Yes, because this is written into the constitution.

B   Yes, because the Magna Carta allows executive decrees.

C   Yes, because otherwise elements of the population will riot.

D   No, because the monarch will refuse to give Royal Assent.

E   No, because 'the King has no prerogative but that which the law of the land allows him'.

Answer

Option E is correct. Chief Justice Coke made the statement in 1610 that the Crown, and thus Government, is bound by the law and cannot act outside it. It would not therefore be possible for a Government to take action, or pass a law, without the necessary legal basis. This is a good example of how judicial statements can be an important source of law.

Option A is wrong because there is no written constitution for the legal system of England and Wales. There are elements that are written, such as the Parliament Acts and the Bill of Rights, but otherwise the constitution is uncodified, and operates according to precedent and the law. Our constitution frowns on the concept of government by decree.

Option B is wrong because the Magna Carta says no such thing. Option C is wrong because there is no evidence a riot will result, and in any event the threat of a riot would not be reason for a law to be passed (even if rioting has at times in the past led to the creation of laws). Option D is wrong as Royal Assent is the final step in the passage of an Act of Parliament, which is not what is being proposed here. Incidentally, it is a long-standing convention the monarch never refuses Royal Assent. Equally, it is a convention no Acts are provided for Royal Assent without having passed through the necessary earlier steps.

2 Sources of Law of England and Wales

SQE1 syllabus

This chapter will enable you to achieve the SQE1 assessment specification in relation to functioning legal knowledge concerning the sources of law of England and Wales.

Note that, for SQE1, candidates are not usually required to recall specific case names or cite statutory or regulatory authorities. Cases are provided for illustrative purposes only.

Learning outcomes

By the end of this chapter you will be able to apply relevant core legal principles and rules appropriately and effectively, at the level of a competent newly qualified solicitor in practice, to realistic client-based and ethical problems and situations in the following areas:

* the creation of statute by Parliament, the legislative process in the Houses of Commons and Lords, and Parliament's importance as a source of law;
* the role of judges as a source of law, through their decisions in court;
* common law and equity;

- the role of the monarchy, nobility, armed forces and religion as sources of law, and their influence today;

- the place of constitutional reform within the legal system, and some relevant provisions of the House of Lords Act 1999 and the Constitutional Reform Act 2005;

- the place of academics, jurists and legal commentators in the legal system;

- principles and philosophies that impact on the practice of law today, such as the doctrine of habeas corpus, the sovereignty of Parliament, the separation (or balance) of powers, and utilitarianism;

- the place of the EU as a source of law; and

- the significance of the internet in today's legal world.

2.1 Introduction

Few of us would think a storyteller from the late Middle Ages could be a source of law in the 21st century. But Geoffrey Chaucer (1340s–1400) in the *Man of Law's Tale* refers to an aspect of court procedure current today. The *Tale* involves a trial of a woman accused of murdering another. A knight is called to give evidence and the *Tale* states:

> Now hastily do fetch a book, and if this knight shall swear how she slew this woman, yet will we advise ourselves whom that we wish to be our judges. A Briton book written in evangelical terms was fetched and on this book he swore anon she guilty was ...

> Middle English Text from Larry D Benson/Houghton Miflin. This version of paragraphs 662–668 translated by Frederick Price.

The reference to 'evangelical' means the Gospels. So here we have an instance of a witness swearing an oath on a religious book prior to giving evidence in front of a judge. Today, witnesses at trial are required to swear an oath, or provide an affirmation as to the truth of their story, or to give a solemn promise. In the *Man of Law's Tale* the knight apparently lied and was struck dead by a divine hand. Chaucer thus reinforces the correctness of honesty in court, with a suitable punishment for perjury, which is the legal name for lying in front of a judge. The sanction today is not so terminal, of course, but there are still consequences for misleading a court.

You can therefore see that modern law can derive from ancient roots. But it is not all about old 'stuff'. It is constantly self-generating, for instance a statute receiving Royal Assent last week, or a judgment given in court yesterday.

2.2 Scope of this chapter

This chapter will explore the many different sources of law for the legal system of England and Wales. We have mentioned some in our first chapter, and we can expand on the topic here. The two most obvious sources are Acts of Parliament and decisions made by judges in court – ie case law. There are also influences stemming from the operation of society over the centuries, through the Crown, nobility, church and armed forces. We also have principles articulated by academics and jurists from long ago. Then there are more modern sources, such as the EU, and perhaps the internet. Apart from the last two, these have ancient origins. Yet they all remain important today. Indeed, collectively they represent a patchwork, of constitutionality, the sum total of which is a concordat of legal concepts essentially practical, popular, democratic and fair.

We will begin with Acts of Parliament.

2.3   Acts of Parliament

Acts of Parliament, or statutes, are everywhere. If we intentionally injured a wild bird the Wildlife and Countryside Act 1981 would apply. When we drive cars we should note the Road Traffic Act 1988. If we injure someone in a brawl we might be punished under the Offences Against the Person Act 1861.

Statutes are just one sort of legislation. Other types include secondary legislation such as the statutory instrument (SI); byelaws for local councils and authorities; and more obscure edicts such as Church of England Measures, the last of which we will return to in a moment. None of these match Acts of Parliament for importance, scope and judicial relevance. Statutes:

- are *important* because they convey in their purest form the will of the people, who have elected the House of Commons to run Government on their behalf;

- have *scope* through their impact on society; and

- have *judicial relevance* because the courts take delight in interpreting them.

Statutes have been in existence since Norman times. The oldest statute still in force is the Statute of Marlborough of 1267, relating to the judicial nature of damages. This set the trend: as the years rolled by, it became established precedent that monarch and Parliament had control of the law-making process. Over time the volume of legislation has increased significantly. In 1911, for instance, Parliament passed 760 pages of legislation, according to statistics from the House of Commons library. In 2006, 14,580 pages were added to the law books.

Acts of Parliament range across the widest possible landscape. For instance, you would probably expect to receive a fine for dropping litter somewhere, but you can also be made to pay a fixed penalty for putting rubbish out on the wrong day. The offence is envisaged by the Clean Neighbourhoods and Environment Act 2005. You might also expect nuclear fission to be closely regulated, but even so it is surprising that legislators anticipated you and me setting off a neutron bomb. Just in case we do, the Nuclear Explosions (Prohibition and Inspections) Act 1998 makes it an offence to cause a nuclear explosion.

2.3.1   Creation of Acts of Parliament

AV Dicey, a celebrated Victorian thinker and generally recognised as a constitutional guru, said Parliament passes Acts, and those Acts can make, change or repeal law. We call this *'sovereignty'* – a vital aspect of Parliament, and a key part of our constitution. We will return to the various nuances of this principle later. They can also be explored in more detail when you study constitutional and administrative law. For now, let's look at how legislation is made.

Parliament consists of the Monarch, the House of Commons (which is democratically elected) and the House of Lords (which is not). Both Houses are involved in the process of creating Acts of Parliament. Before this occurs, the Government usually (but not always) publishes a Green Paper, which is a consultation document on possible new law, and a White Paper, which incorporates the Government's firm proposals for the new law.

An Act will then begin its life as a document known as a Bill. Only when it has passed through a series of stages, involving scrutiny and debate, will it eventually become an Act of Parliament. Debate is an essential aspect of democracy, and indeed the word 'Parliament' comes from the Norman French term meaning 'talking shop'. Whether you believe this is a relevant definition for the two chambers of Westminster today is a matter for you.

2.3.2   Acts of Parliament – the process

Here is a summary of how an Act is created, and the stages it goes through.

- First, the Bill is drafted and given a first reading in the House of Commons. Bills normally commence in the Commons as an acknowledgement of that body's elected status. The Commons consists of 650 or so Members of Parliament (MPs), sent to Westminster by voters in their constituencies. In the eyes of MPs, and possibly most constitutionalists, this gives them the upper hand in the legislative process. The argument that the House of Lords is equal to the Commons is certainly hard to sustain in today's modern world.

- Next, there will be a second reading, where there is a detailed debate in the chamber of the Commons on the various sections of the Bill. MPs are called to make contributions by the Speaker of the House, ie the person who controls debates and ensures fair play between the Government and His Majesty's Official Opposition. A Government minister will be responsible for the Bill, open the debate, listen to contributions by MPs, and oversee the Bill's passage through the various stages. The House will vote on parts of the Bill as necessary.

- Next there will be committee scrutiny. This could be by way of a Committee of the Whole House, or a dedicated committee with an interest in the underlying subject matter. Here there is further detailed scrutiny on a clause by-clause-basis. This is detailed, grinding and often gruelling work. It is not a spectator sport. But many reputations, and careers, are made during this process.

- Then the Bill will return to the floor of the House for the Report Stage. Here, the House will vote on any proposed amendments suggested in committee.

- Next, there will be the third and final reading of the Bill, representing the final version as approved by the Commons.

- The focus then moves to the House of Lords, which follows the same various stages. The Lords will scrutinise, vote on and agree the final version. The Lords is free to adopt the Bill as provided by the Commons, or it can vote on amendments to it. At the Third Reading stage it must return to the Commons for any amendments to be approved.

- NB: If the Lords rejects a Bill twice it is possible for the Commons to bypass the Lords by way of the provisions of the Parliament Acts 1911 and 1949. This prevents what is seen as the undemocratic Lords blocking the will of the democratically elected Commons.

- The final step in this, usually lengthy, process is provision of Royal Assent by the Crown. At this stage the Bill becomes an Act, ie becomes law. We say 'usually' because ministers can, if they pull the correct levers, expedite the process massively. Legislation touching on both Brexit and coronavirus occupied considerably less time, for instance.

- Occasionally, opponents of a Bill attempt to delay it by talking at length, either in committee or debate. This is called 'filibustering' – deliberately, but in a procedurally allowable manner, wasting time through verbosity. Governments have the answer to this, however: the imposition of a timetable, called a 'guillotine'. As you can imagine, many MPs are wary of curtailing the entitlement to a filibuster. It represents an important weapon of the legislature, ie the Houses of Parliament in the ever-present tussle for power and influence between it and the executive, ie the Government of the day.

- In the absence of provisions to the contrary, statutes apply to all the UK. A specific statement should accompany Acts that do not apply to Wales, Scotland or Northern Ireland.

You will note the involvement of the Lords, and the curtailing of their influence through the Parliament Acts. LTC Rolt in *Isambard Kingdom Brunel*, Fifth Impression (Longman, 1964) provides a vivid illustration of the need for restraint in the second chamber. Brunel, one of the most important infrastructure engineers in UK history, sought an Act of Parliament to enable the London–Bristol rail route. In 1834 the Commons, at the second reading, passed the Great Western Railway Bill by 182 votes to 92. The Lords then rejected it 47–30. Even in the Hanoverian era, where we were all expected to doff our caps to the ruling classes, such aristocratic interference could only endure for so long. The Bill eventually became law in 1835. Today, that rail journey remains one of the most significant inter-regional transport links in the nation.

2.3.3 Flowchart on creation of Acts of Parliament

Figure 2.1 summarises the process of a Bill becoming an Act. At each step there is a brief summary of the detail involved.

Figure 2.1   Overview of creation of an Act

> **House of Commons**
> **First Reading**
>
> This stage is purely formal. The title is read out and the Bill is printed and published.

> **Second Reading**
>
> At this stage, the main debate by MPs on the principles of the Bill takes place.

> **Committee Stage**
>
> Bills may be referred to the Committee of the Whole House or a standing committee (reflecting the division of parties within the House). The committee scrutinises the Bill clause by clause and considers any amendments.
>
> Opponents sometimes deliberately cause delays by discussing matters at length in committee. However, the Chairman has power to decide which amendments should be discussed and a business sub-committee allocates time for discussion.

> **Report Stage**
>
> If any amendments have been made by the Committee of the Whole, or if the committee stage was taken in standing committee, a report stage is necessary. The House votes on any amendments. The debate on the report stage is similar to that at the committee stage, ie each part of the Bill is considered with a view to amendment or addition. The Speaker can select the amendments to be debated.

> **Third Reading**
>
> The purpose of the third reading is to consider the Bill as amended but usually the debate is brief. This is the final opportunity to vote, although MPs often do not do so.

> **Proceedings in the House of Lords**
>
> Proceedings in the Lords do not begin until after the third reading in the Commons.
>
> Procedure in the Lords is the same as that outlined above for the Commons, so the Bill will go through all the stages again.

> **Amendments by Lords**
>
> When the Bill has reached its third reading in the Lords, it must be sent back to the Commons if any amendments have been made.
>
> Theoretically, the Bill can go backwards and forwards an infinite number of times until the proceedings on it are terminated. In practice, if the Commons disagrees with the Lords' amendments and restores the original wording, the Lords usually accepts it.
>
> Under the Parliament Acts 1911 and 1949 the Commons can in extreme situations bypass the Lords if the latter blocks the will of the former. For this to happen the Speaker of the Commons – ie the referee between the parties – must certify the conditions of s 2 of the 1911 Act are met.

> **Royal Assent**
>
> The final stage is where the monarch formally gives approval to the Bill and it becomes an Act of Parliament. Royal Assent is now a formality – an example of constitutional and legal convention.
>
> Once a Bill has received the Royal Assent, it becomes 'law' and takes effect immediately on that day, unless there is a contrary provision in the statute.

2.4   Case law

Case law is one of the main sources of English law today, in addition to Acts of Parliament and secondary legislation.

2.5   Common law

Common law is the original and traditional mode of decision-making by judges. Historically, it involved decisions on contracts and the payment of damages. It provided remedies for disputes involving the letter of the law.

 An early example of this is Pinnel's Case *[1602] 5 Co Rep 117, where it was held that 'the gift of a horse, hawk, or robe' would be sufficient to allow one contract to replace another.*

Over time, the exercise of the common law on its own proved somewhat inflexible and other principles developed to make the delivery of justice overall more flexible and fair.

2.6   Equitable principles

The desire for flexibility and fairness led to the creation of the court of Chancery and the use of equity. The word 'equity' in the legal context means arriving at a resolution that is fair to all parties, taking into account a mix of considerations such as the facts, the behaviour of those involved, and the respective situations of the parties. The court of Chancery was presided over by the chief law officers of the time, called Chancellors, and adopted the approach that certain disputes needed resolution in a different manner.

Initially, there were few guidelines for the Chancellors to use, but as time passed, judges developed a set of equitable principles or maxims. These were applied by the court of Chancery and are still relevant today. Set out below are some examples:

(a) Equity looks on that as done which ought to be done. This means that equity will enforce the intention of the parties, rather than allowing something to founder because of a failure to conform to rigid procedure.

(b) He who comes to equity must come with clean hands: accordingly, an equitable remedy will not be granted to a claimant who has not acted fairly.

(c) Delay defeats equity: as a consequence, a claimant cannot wait too long before making a claim, as this may prejudice the other party.

(d) Equity will not suffer a wrong to be without a remedy. This means what it says: under equitable principles, if a court decides there is a wrong, a solution beneficial to the injured party should result.

Equity allows various useful remedies to the innocent party. Equitable remedies include the following:

* injunctions, ie a requirement that something be done or not done;

* specific performance, ie the carrying out of an obligation, usually in relation to land;

* recission, in other words confirming that a contract no longer exists;

* rectification, ie correcting a wrong; and

* an account of profits, ie allowing an innocent party an appropriate share of a wrongdoer's gains.

You can explore these in detail elsewhere, but to gain a flavour of their nature we can expand on specific performance. In somewhat simplistic terms, this compels the wrongdoer to complete whatever it was they started but failed to finish. For instance, if you contract to purchase a delightful cottage overlooking the sea, and the vendor refuses to complete the sale, you might use specific performance to force the transaction to its conclusion. You should remember, however, specific performance has limited application. You cannot use it, for instance, to force a builder to finish constructing your house, or a lawyer to complete drafting that much promised contract, or the gardener to clip your roses.

2.7 The combined concept

The Supreme Court of Judicature Acts of 1873 and 1875 created a single court structure and merged the separate court systems of equity and the common law. For the first time, court procedure as a whole adopted a common approach rather than being left to individual courts.

As a consequence, all civil courts can now grant both common law and equitable remedies in the same proceedings. For example, an injunction to stop continuing unlawful behaviour can be ordered in addition to damages for loss.

2.7.1 An example

Let's illustrate the way in which equity and common law can combine to arrive at an appropriate result. Let's imagine that you are a jobbing builder, in other words something of a sole operative, perhaps occasionally combining with someone else to work effectively on a construction project or other contract. You do a splendid job of building a client's home. The client refuses to pay. You suffer financial stress as a result, and are at risk of going out of business as a consequence of cashflow problems. The client knows you have financial issues and takes advantage of this by offering to pay a proportion of the debt in full and final settlement. In desperation, you accept. You then seek to claim the balance later.

 These were the facts in D & C Builders Ltd v Rees *[1966] 2 QB 617. Here, Lord Denning held the client's behaviour was somewhat dubious, and pronounced that there was no equitable bar to the builder recovering the balance owed. The court did not state which equitable maxim applied here, but one could speculate the client through her behaviour and attitude had failed to show clean hands. This would be the second of the four points mentioned above. Courts today often refer back to previously decided cases and the* Rees *case is no exception, in that it was mentioned in an approving manner in the 2016 case of* Stevensdrake v Hunt *[2016] EWHC 111 (Ch).*

2.8 Civil law

Civil law is a code-based system derived from traditional Roman law concepts. Examples of countries with codified constitutions include France and Germany. The jurisdiction of England and Wales draws on few codified concepts, as common law and equitable notions have overtaken them somewhat. The European tradition of civil law is, however, important to the culture of EU law and hence lawyers here should be aware of them.

2.9   How these principles dovetail today

We have considered the development of English law, the place of Acts of Parliament, and the nature of common law and equity. Their relationship to each other, and other sources of law, is summarised in **Figure 2.2**.

Figure 2.2   Parliament and the courts

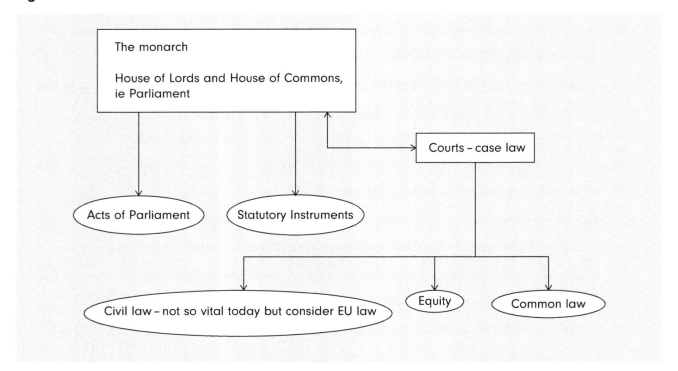

2.10   Case law in action

There are examples every working day of case law being created. To take but one interesting case, in the decision of *Wednesbury* [1948] 1 KB 223 the Court of Appeal gave impetus to a new area of law in the field of judicial review. There, in declaring local authorities should act reasonably, the courts placed limits on the way in which councils conduct themselves. As Lord Greene Master of the Rolls (MR) stated:

> The court is entitled to investigate the action of the local authority with a view to seeing whether they have taken into account matters which they ought not to take into account, or, conversely, have refused to take into account or neglected to take into account matters which they ought to take into account.

This decision led to the growth of an entirely new branch of constitutional and administrative law. From this point on, individuals and businesses could expect administrative decisions by public bodies to be governed by due process. The *Wednesbury* ruling illustrates the flexibility inherent in a court system that combines different attributes with an ability to stay relevant to the issues of the day.

In addition to Acts of Parliament and case law, the legal system also defers to other influences from long ago. We will consider these now.

2.11 Traditional sources of law

Our core sources of law took shape long ago. By this, we mean before parliamentary democracy took meaningful shape. We are being deliberately vague: cautiously, we are talking about the period before 1600–1700.

2.11.1 The Crown

The key source of law for this period was the Crown. The monarchy dominated society. Monarchs devised and passed laws, and in the 12th and 13th centuries the process involved little or no collaboration with other branches of society. Creating law was essentially a despotic act. In subsequent centuries royalty took a marginally more consensual approach, as indicated by the various proclamations issued by the Tudor dynasty. Paul L Hughes and James F Larkin in their three-volume *Tudor Royal Proclamations* (Yale University Press, 1964 and 1969) mention a series of laws reinforcing royal sovereignty. Some reflected the predominant religious thinking of the day. Others met the needs of contemporary society by dealing with pressing economic and social issues: the coinage, wool trade, wages, insurance rates and wine prices. Either way, they represent the singular influence of the Crown. This is something that endures today, albeit in a different form, for instance in the convention that the monarch must give Royal Assent to any Bill before it becomes an Act.

2.11.2 The nobility

The next, traditionally crucial, source of law was the nobility. They gained this role by flexing their military muscle. As part of the feudal system they controlled apportionment of land, gathering of taxes and dues, and raising of armies. They naturally expected their say in the formation of laws, something realised through the Magna Carta 1215, and their increasingly formalised presence as advisers within the royal household, and in bodies such as the Privy Council. These days the Privy Council is somewhat honorific, but in the past it was the premier body advising and guiding the Crown. Today, the nobility has a constitutional presence through the House of Lords, the second chamber of Parliament, with a crucial role in the creation of legislation.

2.11.2.1 The House of Lords

The House of Lords is a favourite topic of the popular press, as it largely consists of individuals who arrive there by virtue either of their birth or appointment by governments. It is an unelected chamber, although some members, as we note below, do submit to a quasi-electoral process. Occasionally journalists lampoon members of the House for falling asleep during debates, or turning up for five minutes purely to claim their daily allowance, and so on. Indeed it does appear somewhat anachronistic within a democratic setting. Its supporters, however, would say it is an integral part of our bi-cameral society, acting as a counterweight to the overt populism, and perhaps short termism, of the House of Commons.

2.11.2.2 Hereditary peers

For many years the peerage, through its hereditary members, dominated the House of Lords. But their parliamentary role has diminished recently. The House of Lords Act (HLA) 1999 abolished the automatic entitlement of all hereditary peers to sit in the Lords, leaving just 90 members at any one time to co-exist with life peers. Any hereditary vacancies are filled through a by-election process amongst the hereditaries themselves. There is therefore the curious process of ancient bloodlines jockeying for position by way of electoral preference in a second chamber, which regularly receives criticism for being undemocratic.

Those interested in the position – or it might just qualify as a 'job' – must declare themselves available for election. The authorities keep a register of hereditary peers who wish to stand for election under the obscure Standing Order 10. At the end of 2019 the list began with the Marquess of Abergavenny. It proceeds in alphabetical order to the Earl of Yarborough. In the middle we have a host of colourful and historic names such as the Duke of Buccleuch and Queensberry, Lord Cochrane of Cults, the Earl of Iddesleigh, Viscount Runciman of Doxford and more. You should note hereditary peers still have a role in local and national society, living busy lives up and down the country. But their parliamentary profile is much lower. Such is the price of progress in a modern democratic culture.

2.11.2.3 Life peers

The HLA 1999 also impacted on the role of life peers, who since the Life Peerage Act 1958 have provided considerable numbers of the House of Lords. Traditionally they are a mix of eminent achievers from all walks of life, MPs from the Commons who have retired or lost their seats, and (controversially) sometimes donors to, and key supporters of, political parties. Usually, life peers display considerable knowledge and wisdom in their main role of scrutinising and debating legislation. Even so, the body politic decided there were too many peers overall, and the HLA 1999 reduced their number to approximately 660 at the time of writing. The Government of the day refreshes the head count through regular appointments, most notably in the annual New Year's honours process. The convention is the Prime Minister makes recommendations to the monarch who confirms the appointments.

2.11.3 Judges and Parliament

Constitutional changes have also altered the role of judges within the Westminster 'bubble'. For many years the House of Lords included top justices, known as the Law Lords, within their ranks. They rubbed shoulders with the other characters inhabiting that House: blue-blooded hereditaries, failed MPs, millionaire widget manufacturers, windy academics and the like, nodding sagely throughout debates. Occasionally they spoke, especially when laws relating to, well, the law, came up for discussion. But they generally kept a low profile, avoiding any suspicion of taking sides. They had a parallel status to the Lords Spiritual, ie the archbishops and senior bishops of the Church of England, who also had, and indeed today still do have, seats in the Lords.

Many traditionalists saw nothing wrong in this arrangement, relying on the fabled sense of British fair play for these senior legal figures to act in an appropriate manner when present in the House. The argument was they provided gravitas, common sense, perspective and so on that might have been lacking in other members of the Lords. But their involvement was something of an anomaly. How could judges sit in, and engage with, a body whose laws they were meant to interpret in court? The whole arrangement seemed contrary to the balance of powers, whereby the judiciary held itself above the hurly burly of Parliament.

Section 23 of the Constitutional Reform Act 2005 addressed this issue. It removed the top judges from the House of Lords. Instead, the 2005 Act created a Supreme Court, and sited the Law Lords there, on the western side of Parliament Square. The House of Lords now is a term, and body, referring purely to the legislature. It is no longer permeated – or infected, depending on your view – with a judicial presence. Our top judges, bearing in mind their geographical proximity to our law makers, remain very much at the centre of the Westminster culture. But they now have a more clearly defined role as interpreters of the law rather than participating, however peripherally, in its legislative creation.

The 2005 Act also reformed the role of the Lord Chancellor, so that the post no longer exercises judicial functions, and is more obviously a holder of political office within the Government as Secretary of State for Justice. They, along with other Secretaries of State, attend Cabinet, which is the inner circle of Government, for regular meetings chaired by the Prime Minister.

2.11.4 Religious influences

Religion also has an ancient role in the creation of law. This originally stemmed from papal decrees, whereby popes provided centralised instructions to monarchs on various aspects of doctrine and observance. The influence of the pope in terms of applicable law diminished considerably in England when Henry VIII reformed the church during 1509–1547. But whether driven by popes or royal families, religious observance resulted in a body of ecclesiastical, or canon, law that had a significant influence on early society. This is something made clear by RH Helmholz in his article ([1997] 75 *Texas Law Review* 1455–70), on Norman Doe, *The Legal Framework of the Church of England: A Critical Study in a Comparative Context* (Oxford University Press, 1996). Church law embraces a blend of divine concepts, doctrinal matters and practical control. The last is illustrated through edicts on finance and property, a reminder that these two elements are routinely wrapped up with legal principles. Other areas of early legislation covered marriage and the use of Latin in holy texts.

If you believe Church law is an outmoded relic, think again. The Church of England (CoE)'s governing body, called the General Synod, passes laws on a regular basis. There are three sorts:

- Measures, which are the equivalent of Acts of Parliament;

- Canons, which are of more limited scope; and

- Subordinate legislation in the form of statutory instruments.

Church law impacts on our daily lives in relation to births, baptisms, weddings and, as you would expect, deaths. As with more general Acts of Parliament, some of these are from long ago but still in force. For instance, the Ecclesiastical Dilapidations Measure 1923 is still relevant to the finance of dioceses, ie local administrative areas of the CoE. Moving to the modern day, s 3 of the CoE (Miscellaneous Provisions) Measure 2020 allows authorised lay workers to perform funerals in places other than a church or churchyard. This sort of thing has an impact on a great number of us.

2.11.5 The military

We should also consider the role of armies and the use of armed force. Until the 1700s, society implicitly accepted regime change through violence. William the Conqueror set the tone in 1066; Cromwell confirmed the process during the English Civil War. The military establishment, through the growth of armies and their generals, became a source of law through their ability to support and sustain the victors. Essentially, legal influence stemmed from the point of a gun and the tip of a sword. Perhaps inevitably from their position as power brokers, generals developed a commanding presence within society and thus the legal system.

JV Capua, in 'The Early History of Martial Law in England from the Fourteenth Century to the Petition of Right' (1977) 36(1) *Cambridge Law Journal* 152–73, discusses the significance of the military in our history. In particular he mentions martial law, which is defined as 'a summary form of criminal justice, exercised under direct or delegated royal authority by the military or police forces of the Crown, which is independent of the established processes of the common law courts ...'. In other words, it is a form of dictatorship, and the armed forces had a developed role in facilitating it at various stages in our history.

Fortunately for society as a whole this hasn't happened within our living memory. A form of it occurred in Ireland early last century. The Civil Contingencies Act 2004 allows the exercise of emergency powers in the interests of civil protection and welfare. So traces of this flirtation with military rule exist today, and at times of national crisis there is often talk of using the army to ensure the effective operation of society as a whole. It is clear the army has a key role in the history of democracy, and hence the law, within British society.

In practical terms, military law remains relevant today, albeit within a narrow frame of reference. The Armed Forces Act 2006, for instance, makes provision for the discipline of service personnel through various means, including the court martial process, whereby wrongdoers can be reduced to the ranks, discharged without honour and imprisoned. The Service Civilian Court has powers to try the civilian relatives of those in the armed forces, and also civilian contractors. Section 359 of the 2006 Act allows for pardons for those executed for cowardice, throwing away arms, sleeping on duty or similar infringements during the First World War. All these measures remain of relevance and comfort to the civilian population today.

The flowchart in **Figure 2.3** illustrates some traditional sources of law and their inter-relationship. Note we start with the monarchy – you might think its role is largely honorific, but you simply can't ignore it. Everything seems to flow from, and indeed back to, it.

Figure 2.3 'Traditional' sources of law and their inter-relationship

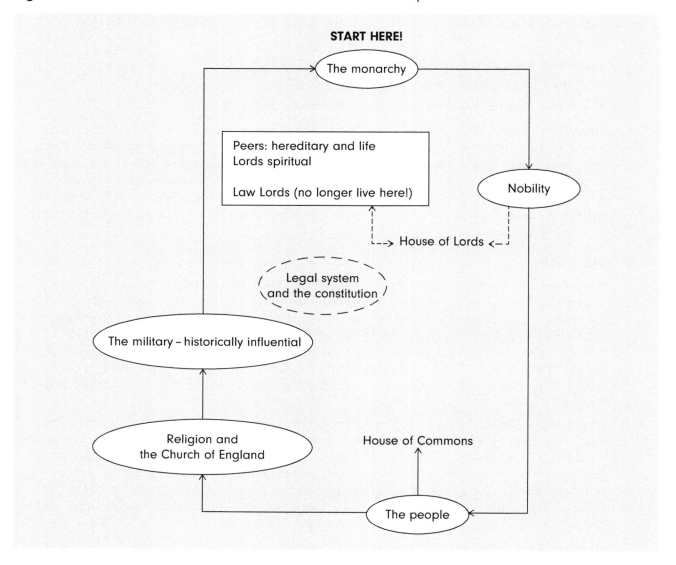

These, then, are some institutional sources of law with continuing relevance today. We also need to consider the role of legal academics, commentators, philosophers and those in related areas. We will do that now.

2.12 Legal academics, commentators and philosophers

Lawyers have a long tradition of deferring to academic commentators. You could if you wish trace the starting point for this practice to Alfred the Great and earlier, but we shall concentrate on trends since the 16th century. We shall mention individuals, briefly explain their philosophy and confirm their continuing significance.

2.12.1 Sir Edward Coke (1552–1634)

Coke, pronounced 'Cook', was Chief Justice of the Common Pleas. He was influential in the late 1500s and early 1600s. He pronounced on matters such as habeas corpus and freedom of the individual. The doctrine of habeas corpus, traceable to 1305, means literally 'you shall have the body'. It is the principle someone should only be arrested and imprisoned with lawful reason. Consequently, an arrested person should be given their freedom unless there is justification for them to be imprisoned.

This judicial reasoning is crucial to the operation of a free society, and its tenets are applied up and down the land today.

 In Jalloh [2020] UKSC 4, the Supreme Court illustrated the principle. Ibrahima Jalloh was granted asylum and then ordered to be deported following conviction for a criminal offence. He was subject to a curfew at night in his home city of Sunderland between February 2014 and July 2016. He was electronically monitored by way of tagging. Lady Hale on behalf of a unanimous majority held the curfew to be unlawful, a deprivation of liberty, and false imprisonment. This is an instance of policy colliding with law, and it is a current example of the principle that freedom should only be withdrawn in accordance with the law.

2.12.2 John Locke (1632–1704)

Locke was one of the leading philosophers of his day. As the Stanford Encyclopedia of Philosophy suggests in *Locke's Political Philosophy* (9 November 2005), he made a key contribution to the place of property within the law. He applauds the accumulation of property, but not without restrictions. He advocates taxation by consent of the majority. He discusses the role of labour in the economic cycle, indicating that its value inevitably diminished when property values rose. Locke's contribution to our sources of law endures today. Whether you like it or not, the ownership of property is a central part of British life, and much law stems from it. One thinks of landlord and tenant legislation, laws relating to commercial property ownership and tax reliefs, initiatives concerning affordable housing, and planning law generally.

2.12.3 Charles-Louis de Secondat, Baron de La Brede et de Montesquieu (1689–1755)

Montesquieu, as we simplify him, pronounced on the separation of powers, believing it was essential the executive, legislature and judiciary perform distinct functions, and that they should not trespass on each other's areas of operation. So, broadly, these bodies should have the following roles:

• The executive should formulate policy and initiate legislation;

• The legislature should scrutinise laws and pass them; and

• The judiciary should interpret those laws.

Without this separation, Montesquieu stated, there can be no liberty. His views were embraced with gusto in the USA when drafting their constitution, and have endured in this jurisdiction too.

 The case of Miller v Secretary of State for Exiting the European Union [2017] UKSC 5 provides a good illustration of the impact of this principle. Here, the Supreme Court, in its role as interpreter of laws, said the Government, in its policy role relating to departure from the EU, was obliged to consult Parliament, in its legislative role, on the exit procedure from the EU.

2.12.4 Jeremy Bentham (1748–1832)

For someone active as a jurist and political reformer so long ago, Bentham's views have astonishing relevance today. He is famous for the philosophy of utilitarianism, articulated in his 1776 pamphlet 'A Fragment on Government'. Utilitarianism broadly means government has a duty to the 'fundamental axiom' that 'it is the greatest happiness of the greatest number that is the measure of right and wrong'. He realised that good rule depended on the support of the majority, a partnership if you like between the governors and the governed.

He finessed this philosophy into a great number of areas. He opined on economic, political, educational, legal and religious matters. In his writings he explored the nature of legislation, the virtues of the rule of law, and the need for penal reform. He was an early advocate of principles of international law, and of what we would today call comparative law, ie the study of different jurisdictions. He was sceptical as to religion's place in effective governance – a further aspect of the doctrine of separation of powers, in a way. He also found time to discuss judicial administration and welfare reform. Bentham's philosophy is a true cornerstone of the modern legal system.

You may think his writings have no place in the administration of today's law. But let's consider one scenario involving the welfare state. Imagine you married someone in a foreign country. You arrived in the UK and became absorbed into society. Your spouse died. Under welfare legislation certain widows are entitled to a bereavement payment. Your application for such a payment is rejected by the authorities. The reason? You were not a spouse in the proper meaning of the word because your marriage was polygamous, ie your husband had another wife, something allowable in the jurisdiction where you originally married, but illegal in the UK.

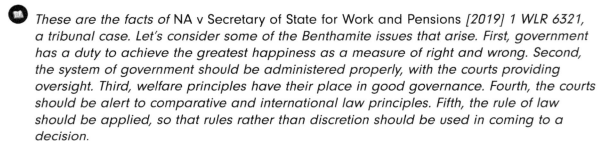 *These are the facts of* NA v Secretary of State for Work and Pensions *[2019] 1 WLR 6321, a tribunal case. Let's consider some of the Benthamite issues that arise. First, government has a duty to achieve the greatest happiness as a measure of right and wrong. Second, the system of government should be administered properly, with the courts providing oversight. Third, welfare principles have their place in good governance. Fourth, the courts should be alert to comparative and international law principles. Fifth, the rule of law should be applied, so that rules rather than discretion should be used in coming to a decision.*

In the NA *case, a widow claimed bereavement and related benefits under the Social Security Contributions and Benefits Act 1992. The Secretary of State had refused the application on the grounds that the relationship with the deceased was polygamous. A First Tier Tribunal refused her appeal. The Upper Tribunal found she was indeed 'married' and as such qualified for the payments. It allowed the widow's appeal.*

The culture of this decision illustrates the link between centuries old thinking and modern jurisprudence. The Tribunal embraced the idea there should be the maximum happiness for the population, within a simple administrative setting. This is shown at paragraph 77 of the judgment where the judge states that: 'Claimants necessarily apply for bereavement benefits at a difficult time and the system needs to be straightforward and non-intrusive to administer so as to minimise distress'. Note the implication that the Government needs to do good in order to provide happiness, and that the administration of welfare should be as simple as practicably possible.

The Tribunal then discussed the different marriage ceremonies in the respective jurisdictions, observing UK concepts were not necessarily superior. The judge went on to allude to Bentham's concept of partnership between Government and people, particularly in welfare matters, saying at paragraph 81 'that furthermore, I suspect that most passengers on the upper deck of a Birmingham bus, whether or not they are of Bangladeshi or Pakistani heritage, would regard the appellant as a "lawful" (rather than a polygamous) widow'. The Tribunal here is paying considerable heed to the will of the populace, and the requirement of Government to be alert to it. The Tribunal also provided a forensic analysis of the relevant rules, basing its decision not on whim or discretion but the strict application of the law. It did what courts up and down the country do every day – apply the rule of law.

The judge concluded by expressing a more generic principle, namely the ability of the judiciary to comment on executives failings. At paragraph 116 of the judgment the Tribunal expressed 'concern at the apparently glacial pace of the Secretary of State's consideration' of matters involving widow's allowances in similar situations. The coda, therefore, of this judgment is a reminder of the separation (or balance) of powers, and the importance of an independent judiciary.

We can therefore see Bentham's views absorbed into today's courts. Many cases illustrate this. When next reading a court report, you should see what influences from past thinkers are detectable today.

2.12.5 AV Dicey (1835–1922)

Dicey was a renowned constitutional author from Victorian times who wrote the *Introduction to the Study of the Law of the Constitution* in 1885. He says at chapter two of his work:

> There is no law which Parliament cannot change, or (to put the same thing somewhat differently), fundamental or so-called constitutional laws are under our constitution changed by the same body and in the same manner as other laws, namely, by Parliament acting in its ordinary legislative character.

This is a simple statement of parliamentary sovereignty – the idea that only Parliament can make and change laws. Dicey is considered somewhat 'alpha male' today by some commentators, as since the 1880s the constitution has subtly evolved beyond the bare bones of his analysis. But his central thesis remains sound, and his views carry weight today.

By way of illustration, imagine you work for an organisation devoted to individual privacy. You are sceptical at the operation of secret state organisations. You wish to challenge the legality of security services such as the Government Communications Headquarters (GCHQ) engaging, without a warrant, in computer network exploitation (CNE). To you and me this is computer hacking, albeit on an official basis. You apply to a body called the Investigatory Powers Tribunal (IPT) for a ruling. You then wish to judicially review the decision of the IPT. The matter is disputed all the way to the Supreme Court.

 These are the outline facts of R (on the application of Privacy International) v Investigatory Powers Tribunal *[2019] UKSC 22. In their ruling, their Lordships by a narrow majority ruled the IPT's action was subject to judicial review. In so doing they gave consideration to Dicey's view, and they were aware that they were in no position to thwart the will of Parliament. Lord Sumption noted an earlier Supreme Court decision stating that parliamentary sovereignty was 'a fundamental principle of the UK constitution'. The Court had adopted, and Lord Sumption repeated, Dicey's view that such sovereignty comprised*

> *the right to make or unmake any law whatever; and, further, that no person or body is recognised by the law of England as having a right to override or set aside the legislation of Parliament.*

In this case the Court was concerned with the interpretation of a particular section of the Regulatory and Investigatory Powers Act 2000 allowing CNE. It is, however, interesting that it saw the need to quote, and embrace, Dicey's long-established view. This decision is thus another reminder of the currency of old concepts.

2.13   Reflection on jurists and academics

We have looked at some ancient commentators who remain important sources of law. There are other people too who could be considered – Thomas Paine and his *Rights of Man*, Thomas Hobbes and *Leviathan*, and more – the list is quite long. But the point of this chapter is to give a flavour of the influences on our society today, not a discussion of every contributing individual. You can find out more through your own reading as your studies progress.

These thinkers as individuals are highly important to our legal culture. Collectively, they become even more significant. Either directly or peripherally, they belong to the same culture – that of a legal system paying homage to a combination of individual freedoms, parliamentary dominance, property entitlements and lawful outcomes. Diagrammatically they could perhaps be linked as in **Figure 2.4**. Note we've created a 'sweet spot' where they all meet, indicating the sum of their collective parts is far greater than their individual contributions. Of course there are other thinkers and philosophers too.

Figure 2.4   Academics and thinkers as source of law with in the legal system

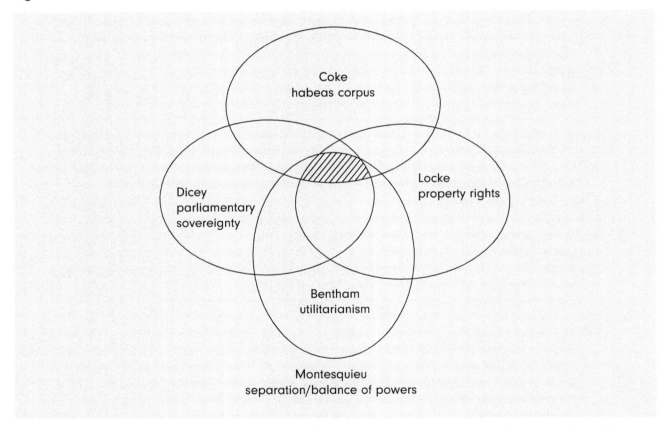

The shaded area indicates the 'sweet spot': when all four of these coalesce you have the essence of English law. For example, imagine you fall on hard times and are provided with social housing. A government official believes, without evidence or substantiation, you are dealing in drugs and enters your home in breach of legislation and attempts to detain you.

A court ruling would embrace:

*   property rights (Locke)
*   the importance of legislation (Dicey)
*   unlawful detention/habeas corpus (Coke)
*   the separation/balance of powers (Montesquieu)
*   social entitlements (Bentham).

Two other subjects deserve mention: the EU, and the growth of modern technology in the shape of the internet.

2.14 EU law

The United Kingdom voted by a slim majority to leave the EU in a referendum in June 2016. Departure legislation has since passed through Parliament. Since the 1970s, when the UK joined what was then the European Economic Community, EU law has gained a significant role within our jurisdiction. You can study EU law further when considering constitutional and administrative matters elsewhere. For our purposes here, it is sufficient to note that:

- it is currently part of our legal system;

- it is a relevant source of law; and

- it will be fascinating to see how in the future it will impact on our lives, if at all, and in what form.

2.15 The internet

You could have quite a debate as to whether the internet is merely a reflection of the law or a source of it. We will let you ponder this distinction, and you will have the chance to explore the internet's impact on contract, tort, land law and business transactions elsewhere.

For the moment we should note the enormous influence the internet has over legal issues and practice. One obvious area is in the field of social media, which is little short of a minefield for the unwary. If you are wondering about the impact of it on the legal profession, the Law Society – the body representing solicitors in England and Wales – issued a Practice Note on 5 December 2019 with the following passage on client matters:

> Even if you do not have a relationship with clients via social media, you should take account of the fact that your presence on social media channels, like weblogs and micro-blogging sites, may accidentally impact on your professional obligations towards your clients.

> For example, if you comment on Twitter that you're in a certain location at a certain time, you may unintentionally disclose that you're working with a client and breach the requirement on confidentiality that 'you must keep the affairs of clients confidential unless disclosure is required or permitted by law or the client consents'.

This excerpt serves as a reality check for those of us who obsess about selfies or are compulsive tweeters. It suggests you can't just blithely publicise your fascinating train journey to Stevenage or somewhere similar in case you tip off the world at large you are about to visit your biggest client. You could be betraying a key confidence. The Practice Note also demonstrates the perils of using social media as part of your law firm strategy.

These issues are of course magnified throughout society, and invariably find their way into the courts, and as such have increasing significance in our legal system.

2.16 Review of what we have done in this chapter

In this chapter we have pondered the following:

- the creation of Acts of Parliament. These days our legislators are keen creators of laws, reflecting both their desire for votes, and society's belief that difficult questions deserve a solution in law;

- decisions of judges in the courts. This happens any time a court rules on a dispute. These decisions have attracted a collection of terminology. You might see them described as case law, or precedent, or common law. Whatever the exact description, the important thing to know is that judicial rulings – or at least those that are reported (and, oddly, even some that are not) - are exceptionally influential in the law today;

- custom and procedures that have evolved over time. We have mentioned the Royal Assent. Another example might be a prime minister visiting the monarch to be invited to form a new Government. The idea of being invited is a fiction: backstage manoeuvring amongst politicians will have cemented the decision before any royal involvement;

- foreign influences, treaties and other events – for instance, joining the EU, and following EU laws and the decisions of the Court of Justice of the EU (the CJEU, or ECJ). We joined the EU in the 1970s following the Treaty of Rome 1957. Leaving the EU means the significance of decisions of the ECJ will change;

- early influences in society, such as the nobility and the armed forces;

- the significance of religion. When discussing this, you should remember that, many centuries ago, the distinction between church and state did not exist, or at least manifested itself differently to that experienced today;

- writings of legal philosophers, academics and jurists. The views of some of these remain vitally important to the freedoms we enjoy today; and

- storytelling (and maybe even myth) from ancient times, such as Chaucer's tales.

Summary

There are, as you can see, many sources of law for England and Wales. Parliament has a key role today, and so do judges. The legal system has, however, grown over centuries, and the modern process is laced with ancient origins, so there is more to the system than immediately meets the eye. History and philosophy play their part.

The actions of courts and politicians today inevitably impact, for better or for worse, on our lives. Those actions stem from a combination of old concepts and new procedures, and are still evolving. Directly or indirectly, these sources of law rule our lives.

Sample questions

Question 1

The Protection of Animals Bill (fictional) is progressing through Parliament. It has many sections and requires much scrutiny. There is considerable interest in the Bill within both the House of Commons and House of Lords.

At what stage will the Bill become an Act?

A   At the Second Reading in the Commons.

B   At the Committee Stage in the Commons.

C   At the Third Reading in the Commons.

D   At the Third Reading in the Lords.

E   On Royal Assent.

Answer

Option E is correct. It is a long-standing convention that a Bill only becomes an Act once it receives Royal Assent.

Option A is wrong because the second reading in the Commons is important for debate but does not represent finality in the passage of a Bill. Option B is wrong because the Committee Stage is where the detail of the Bill is considered, and at this juncture it is not ready to become law. Option C is wrong because after the Third Reading in the Commons the Bill must then go to the Lords for their consideration. Option D is wrong because, although the Lords must deal with the Bill, it should return to the Commons if there are any amendments, and even if there are no amendments it will only become law on Royal Assent.

Question 2

A man buys some shares in a technology company. The shares are held, for entirely legitimate tax reasons, by a trust company on the man's behalf. No one other than the man or the trust company has an interest in the shares. The trust company encounters financial problems and goes into liquidation. The liquidator (a court appointed official whose job is to distribute the trust company's assets) is deciding what to do with the man's shares.

Which of the following is most likely to apply?

A   Common law principles mean the shares can be sold by the liquidator to someone else.

B   As a matter of parliamentary sovereignty the shares would now be owned by the Government.

C   As a matter of equity the shares would need to be returned to the man.

D   As a matter of common law the shares would remain with the defunct company indefinitely.

E   As a matter of equity the shares would be sold and distributed to creditors.

Answer

Option C is correct. This is because the man has 'clean hands' and it would be fair and equitable for his shares to be returned to him. Indeed, this is a classic equitable solution to what would otherwise be a knotty problem.

Option A is wrong because common law would require a contractual or similar legal basis for a liquidator to act in this manner, and as no one other than the man and the trust company have an interest in the shares this is not the case. Option B is wrong as parliamentary sovereignty applies to the making of legislation, not the resolution of individual matters such as an insolvency. Option D is wrong as it would be deeply unfair for the shares to be in limbo. Option E is wrong because it would also be unfair and inequitable for creditors to take shares that are not rightfully theirs.

Question 3

A woman was appointed a peer by the monarch, on the recommendation of the prime minister, in the New Year's honours list three years ago. She is an active and diligent participant in Parliament. She is not a minister. A Bill is progressing in the normal way and the woman would like to make her views known, and vote, on various aspects of the proposed law.

In which of the following ways will the woman be allowed to contribute?

A She can make a speech during the First Reading of the Bill in the House of Lords.

B She can vote in the House of Lords as a life peer.

C She can vote in the House of Lords as a hereditary peer.

D She can speak in the House of Commons at the Second Reading.

E She can speak at a meeting of the Cabinet.

Answer

Option B is correct. As the woman has been appointed, this means she is a life peer. As such she is entitled to vote during the various stages of the Bill as it passes through the House of Lords ('the Lords').

Option A is wrong because there are no speeches during the First Reading of a Bill, whether in the Lords or the House of Commons ('the Commons'). This is because the First Reading is a brief formal process where the Bill is introduced, with no opportunity for a speech. Option C is wrong because the woman is not a hereditary peer. There are only 90 of these, they are not appointed as such, and if a vacancy occurs it is filled by way of an election of other hereditaries. Option D is wrong because a peer is not a member of the Commons and accordingly cannot speak during a Commons stage of a Bill. Option E is wrong because the woman is not a minister and would not be invited, or entitled, to attend Cabinet.

3 Development of Case Law

SQE1 syllabus

This chapter will enable you to achieve the SQE1 assessment specification in relation to functioning legal knowledge concerning the development of case law.

Note that, for SQE1, candidates are not usually required to recall specific case names or cite statutory or regulatory authorities. Cases are provided for illustrative purposes only.

Learning outcomes

By the end of this chapter you will be able to apply relevant core legal principles and rules appropriately and effectively, at the level of a competent newly qualified solicitor in practice, to realistic client-based and ethical problems and situations in the following areas:

- views by certain commentators on the role of judges in creating case law;
- the making of sometimes difficult judicial decisions relating to morality and taste;
- decisions on essential freedoms;
- cases relating to individual entitlements, such as remedies for breach of contract;
- cases on constitutional matters;
- some aspects of the relationship between Parliament and the courts;
- judgments on matters relating to the development of society;
- decisions on certain aspects of business law, and the link to political and economic matters; and
- instances where judicial rulings reflect, perpetuate or even create unfairness.

3.1   Introduction

What is the role of judges? One influential figure thought he had the answer. Judges should allow:

> Flexibility of law ... which always had to uphold the regime's interests as a top priority, so laws could not be allowed to restrain the leadership's room to maneuver.

> From an article by Robert Argenbright (2002) *Russian Review* 249

In other words, judges should be compliant, to allow the state and a country's leadership to pursue their policies unhindered. A judge's top priority is to sustain a regime's interests. These are the views of Vladimir Ilyich Lenin (1870–1924), the famous Bolshevik and early leader of the Soviet state, and a man not known for supporting democratic principles.

Francis Bacon (1561–1626), in his *Essay of Judicature* (1625), took a different approach. Bacon was a leading jurist and Lord Chancellor during the Tudor and Stuart periods. He thought a judge's main job should be to tackle inequality:

> The principal duty of a judge, is to suppress force and fraud ... A judge ought to prepare his way to a just sentence, as God useth to prepare his way, by raising valleys and taking down hills: so when there appeareth on either side an high hand, violent prosecution, cunning advantages taken, combination, power, great counsel, then is the virtue of a judge seen, to make inequality equal; that he may plant his judgment as upon an even ground.

We have kept the original language, so 'useth' means 'uses', and 'appeareth' means 'appears'. Bacon sees judges as champions against violence and falsehood. Their primary role, he says, is to discount the prejudices of competing elements of society, with the aim of arriving at a just outcome. A judge should not be swayed by over-eloquent speeches, powerful people or heavy-handed behaviour. Judges can then plant their judgment 'on an even ground', ie make a decision that has firm foundations, is essentially fair and will stand the test of time.

These two very different views have one point in common. They imply the central role of the judge in making decisions in court. In the jurisdiction of England and Wales we call this case law. This is something infinitely varied. Generally, court judgments are carefully reasoned, sensible and consistent. But that is not always the case. Judges, like the rest of us, can make mistakes, or indulge in misplaced nuances. The process of arriving at a decision is a very human matter. We will now look at the development of case law as a key influence on the operation of the legal system.

3.2   Law, morality and ethics

When discussing the legal system we need to distinguish between law on the one hand, morality on the other and ethics somewhere in between. We can accept the three are indeed distinct, but need to appreciate the first has jurisdiction over the other two. Judges have generally accepted they should rule on moral and ethical matters. This is a natural extension of the concept of the rule of law, as it would be inappropriate for a judicial system to decline to rule on tricky matters. Morals involve a basket of issues including personal choice, matters of taste, agonising dilemmas, freedom of action, unpleasant trade-offs and the like. Are judges meant to ignore these? Of course not. People come before the courts in order to receive an unbiased resolution of intractable differences. And where morality stumbles, the law steps in.

3.2.1 Murder, morality and case law

Imagine the following scenario. You are a seafarer, working on a large yacht. In bad weather the vessel founders. You jump into a small lifeboat with three other people. You are castaways. You drift. The days pass. After 12 days of minimal rations you have no food or water. You all become desperate. One castaway, a young boy, becomes noticeably weaker than the others. In desperation on day 20 you decide to kill him and eat him in order to survive. This nourishment, if it can be called that, sustains you for a critical period. Four days later you are rescued.

In normal circumstances this would be what lay people call an 'open and shut case'. Killing someone, and eating them, would constitute the most heinous crime imaginable. The charge against the defendant would be one of murder (cannibalism is wrapped up in the original offence). If you were the judge, or the jury, what would you decide?

These were the facts, and the issue confronting the court, in R v Dudley and Stephens *(1884) 14 QBD 273. The court needed to decide whether it was justifiable to murder someone to save your own life. The defendants faced a terrible dilemma: should they spare someone who quite possibly was about to die anyway, and in so doing risk death themselves; or should they, in the words of the case report, offer a prayer asking forgiveness, go to the boy, tell him that his time was come, and put a knife into his throat and kill him? By deciding on this latter course, they saved their own skins.*

The court found the defendants guilty of murder. It gave considerable thought to the facts and the jurisprudence. It stated:

> *law and morality are not the same and many things may be immoral which are not necessarily illegal, yet the absolute divorce of law from morality would be of fatal consequences ...*

As part of its judgment the court said that 'it is not the law at the present day' that a man may save his life by killing 'an innocent and unoffending neighbour'. It discussed the defence of necessity and decided it did not apply, in part because the victim was 'the weakest, the youngest, (and) the most unresisting'.

The court condemned the defendants to death. Afterwards, the sentences were commuted – in other words, changed for something more lenient. The men were imprisoned. This is called clemency – a form of sympathetic leniency in recognition of the circumstances of the crime. Nowadays the concept doesn't exist in its pure form, but advocates are allowed instead to enter a plea in mitigation after a guilty verdict. Mitigation offers reasons – of a sort – as to why a client committed the crime, in the hope of achieving a lesser sentence.

We can draw certain conclusions as to the nature and development of case law from this sad tale.

* The court took great care to consider previous decisions by judicial authorities. Some of these were from other jurisdictions, and some were in the nature of academic or philosophical declarations. This reinforces the international nature of the legal system, and the occasional relevance to judges of foreign sources of law.

- In discussing necessity the court referred to a defence that has relevance today. This illustrates the continuity of case law decisions, and the way in which judgments endure over many years, and sometimes centuries.

- The court was well aware of the human element of the case, and the terrible circumstances of the decision to murder the boy. It was prepared to consider the moral and ethical aspects of the defence.

- Even so, the rule of law prevailed, in that murder could not be countenanced. It would be different if killing someone was required as a matter of self-defence.

- You will note the reference by the court to 'neighbourhood'. This word, and concept, took on a different nuance in the House of Lords (now the Supreme Court) in 1932 in a famous case in the area of tort, ie civil wrongs. That case is *Donoghue v Stevenson* [1932] AC 562. This is therefore confirmation that case law can involve the transfer of concepts from one field to another. Indeed, this is an essential aspect of a legal system retaining its relevance.

- The court stated 'there is no safe path for judges to tread but to ascertain the law to the best of their ability and to declare it according to their judgment'. This is a classic statement of the role of judges, and the part they play in developing case law. It is the job of judges to 'ascertain the law', ie to interpret and declare it, not to put themselves centre stage in seeking to change it. But as we shall see, some judges seek to push the boundaries of this principle through broad interpretation, a sense of justice or stubbornness.

3.2.2 Public taste, morality and case law

Courts occasionally deal with tricky matters of public taste and what the law calls decency. Imagine someone has a business in adult entertainment. They wish to import into the UK films of a salacious nature. The ECJ says the import of these videos is unlawful. The business then wishes to import into the UK blow-up dolls. The ECJ says this is allowable.

You might think that this is a somewhat inconsistent approach. The business wishing to import the items in question is entirely lawful, even if the items themselves are questionable. The products are lawful in their country of origin, even if some of us might be a little puritanical in our view of them. It might appear odd, therefore, that one sort of material is allowable for import, but the other is not. In the eyes of most people the underlying need – to exercise some form of control over trade in 'dubious' goods – is the same.

But the court was being consistent, and reinforcing the rule of law, and the role of courts in developing the law. The key factor was whether the goods were legal in the UK. The videos at the time were not. The dolls at the time were.

The first of these cases, involving the videos, was Case 34/79 *Henn and Darby* [1979] ECJ. The doll case was Case 121/85 *Conegate* [1986] ECJ.

There is an EU angle to these cases but, putting that to one side, you should note for our purposes the following points:

- Matters of morality often require decisions by courts. Those decisions are made according to the governing law, which in this instance was tinged with EU concepts.

- Law stems from the will of society, either through legislation passed by the authorities or perhaps custom, both of which involve the prevailing views of the population. Those views may well change over time, in which case the approach of the governing classes, and the courts, will usually adapt. If they don't, that is a recipe for social unrest.

- You can see the central role of courts, in this instance the ECJ, in embracing the need to rule on matters of morality and at the same time maintain the rule of law.

Figure 3.1 Overview of the role of judges and courts in developing case law

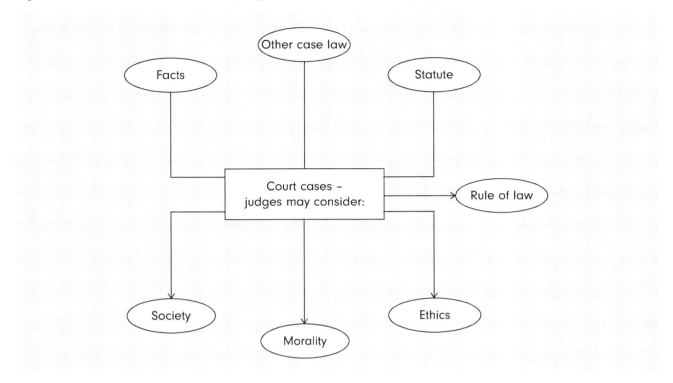

3.3 Types of case law

We have looked at the role of case law in declaring courts have status when ruling on matters of a moral or quasi-moral nature. We now turn to the foundations of case law. There are a number of categories worth considering and some relevant ones are:

- cases relating to essential freedoms. In many ways these are the bedrock of our judicial process, as they go to the heart of a free society, and the democracy inherent in it. This sort of thing would include the requirement that no one should be imprisoned on a whim, and that an accused should be innocent until proven guilty;

- decisions relating to entitlements. You can see this as an extension of democratic rights. For instance, you might wish to claim compensation for a civil wrong, ie a tort as mentioned above. Alternatively, you might wish to enter into a contract. In both these instances, it would be impossible to progress very far without having basic freedoms in the first place;

- court cases relating to constitutionality. These might involve decisions confirming the supremacy of Parliament, and the operation of conventions;

- matters relating to the changing nature of society. These could be decisions which nudge the executive towards passing legislation in subsequent years. Topics could include ownership of property, social relationships, environmental issues or welfare law;

- cases relating to the operation of business. The presumption here is that businesses should benefit from the same protections as individuals. Business law covers a wide field, and we will look at just one area, involving companies that wield too much power at the expense of their rivals and consumers; and finally

- to counter any suggestion that the law is perfect, there are decisions that protect privileges and perpetuate injustice. In the past courts have reflected the attitudes, and, yes, prejudices, of society. They came to decisions that might not be considered healthy today. In an attempt to put a positive gloss on these rulings, perhaps we should try to see them as part of a continuum leading, ultimately, to better outcomes.

Figure 3.2 summarises these in diagrammatic form.

Figure 3.2   Six areas of case law

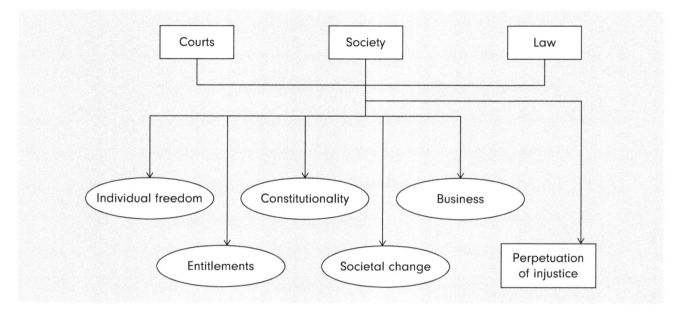

Let us now look at these six types of case law. There are other categories too – as part of your learning, you should see if you can spot, catalogue and discuss others as well.

3.4   Cases relating to essential freedoms

We should never take for granted the right to go free. Captain Renault, played by Claude Reins, in the movie *Casablanca* directed by Michael Curtiz (1942), says towards the end when investigating a crime: 'Round up the usual suspects'. That is not allowed in the jurisdiction of England and Wales. The police must have evidence and good cause before arresting someone. Likewise, you cannot be stopped and asked to prove your identity without good reason.

3.4.1   Habeas corpus

Most importantly of all, you cannot be detained, and deprived of your freedom, unless the law allows it.

The suggestion that the state can remove someone's liberty without due cause was negated early on in the relationship between courts and the executive. The case of *Zadig and Halliday* [1917] AC 260, HL reviewed the matter. There, the House of Lords discussed the Government's powers of internment during the First World War. The law then allowed arrest and imprisonment 'of any person of hostile origin or associations, where the authorities believed such internment would secure public safety or the defence of the realm'. Internment, then as now, is a form of summary imprisonment, with limited, or sometimes no, judicial oversight. The Lord Chancellor, Lord Finlay, referred to *Darnel's Case* (1627) 3 St Tr 1 128. He mentioned the views of Lord Justice Coke, a hugely significant legal figure of the early 1600s. Coke in *Darnel's Case* set out the key concepts of individual freedom. In particular he mentioned 'habeas corpus', the doctrine that imprisonment without suitable justification was unlawful:

> I. No man can be imprisoned upon will and pleasure of any but a bondman or villein.
> II. If a freeman of England might be imprisoned at the will and pleasure of the King or by his command, he were in worse case even than a villein ... and III. A freeman imprisoned without cause is civilly dead.

This statement by Coke, as borrowed by Lord Finlay in 1917, can be summarised as follows. First, we cannot be imprisoned unless by an official having the appropriate 'will or pleasure', ie authority. Second, someone imprisoned by the executive without the relevant authority would be automatically reduced in status to the lowest level. Third, and most crucially for our purposes, a free person imprisoned without due cause is as good as dead. This last point emphasises the vital importance of personal freedom. In effect, Coke is saying you are better off deceased than falsely imprisoned.

Incidentally, the word villein in those days meant a feudal servant of the landed gentry. It does not mean the 'villain' or 'baddy' of today.

3.4.2 'Maybe it's because I'm a Londoner ...'

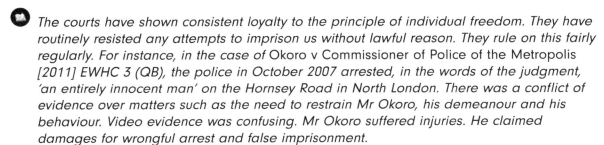

The courts have shown consistent loyalty to the principle of individual freedom. They have routinely resisted any attempts to imprison us without lawful reason. They rule on this fairly regularly. For instance, in the case of Okoro v Commissioner of Police of the Metropolis *[2011] EWHC 3 (QB), the police in October 2007 arrested, in the words of the judgment, 'an entirely innocent man' on the Hornsey Road in North London. There was a conflict of evidence over matters such as the need to restrain Mr Okoro, his demeanour and his behaviour. Video evidence was confusing. Mr Okoro suffered injuries. He claimed damages for wrongful arrest and false imprisonment.*

The court found the use of police computer procedures were inadequate; officers had exaggerated their accounts of Mr Okoro's behaviour; and certain testimony could not be accepted. At paragraph 106 of the judgment the court stated: 'I am not persuaded on the evidence laid before me that the Commissioner has discharged the burden upon him of justifying the arrest of Mr Okoro'. At paragraph 115 the judge concluded: 'Consequently I find that the arrest was wrongful and the ensuing detention unlawful'. The court then awarded the claimant damages of £13,000.

3.4.3 Case law and religious tolerance

Courts can sometimes subtly adapt legal principles to ensure optimal outcomes. Imagine you are a Quaker in the 18th century. The establishment frowned upon, and tended to discriminate against, Quakers. Then as now, Quakers have a particular religious philosophy, much admired today, not so much then. Imagine you object to payment of a particular church tax. The authorities take action against you. A court makes a ruling on the matter that is not in your favour, suggesting the refusal to pay was merely a result of your scruples, in other words your personal preferences.

These are the facts in R v Wakefield *(1757) 1 Burr 485. There, the Court of the King's Bench disagreed with the court below. Lord Mansfield said the ruling 'ought not to stand in the way and prevent our coming at the real justice and merits of the case', even if the original ruling was apparently conclusive. This decision is not of the same calibre as ones involving habeas corpus, but in its own way it is equally important, hinting at the development of jurisprudence supporting religious tolerance. As such it can be seen as another example of the courts demonstrating backbone in the face of executive pressure, even perhaps laying foundations for subsequent case law on civil disobedience.*

3.5 Decisions relating to entitlements

Avoiding imprisonment has little meaning if we are unable to act on the freedoms we take for granted. It is a basic aspect of life that we may wish to enter into contracts, or claim compensation for a wrong. As you would expect, the courts are active in these fields.

 In Slade's Case *(1602), the court touched on a matter that remains relevant today. The case stretched over five years, and involved much debate by the judiciary, but the nub of the issue can be found deep into the judgment where it is stated:*

> *Although an action for debt lies upon the contract, the bargainor may nevertheless have an action on the case or an action of debt at his election ...*

Put into plain English, this means that the innocent party in any breach of contract is entitled to 'an action on the case', ie more than the simple basic act of repayment of a debt. This might seem an unremarkable statement to us today. It confirms that payment or repayment of a sum of money may in some instances be inadequate. It does not, for instance, take into account further losses suffered as a result of the breach, or inconvenience, or the knock-on effects of an obligation being ignored. But this statement was somewhat innovative. It represented the early stages of a process that developed contract law principles, and those relating to recovery of damages, to their current maturity.

Case law has developed tort too, although this has more recent roots. We have already mentioned the 1932 case of *Donoghue v Stevenson* and that is a good place for you to begin when reading further on this subject.

3.6 Cases relating to constitutional matters

The United Kingdom constitution, which is uncodified in that it cannot be found written down in one place, has many sources and has developed over time. It is a blend of many different influences. One thinks of the tussles between the Crown and nobility resulting in the Magna Carta of 1215. There is the growth of parliamentary sovereignty. There is the balance of powers between executive, legislature and judiciary. We can also add to these matters the following: constitutional conventions, electoral reform, the growth of a civil service, popular discontent and demonstrations that put pressure on rulers to make changes, and the influence of the church.

3.6.1 Parliamentary sovereignty

Courts have naturally played a part in confirming the operation of the constitution. To give but one example, judges have from an early stage deferred to the sovereignty of Parliament. You will not find a statute or a rule book that says: 'What Parliament wants, Parliament gets'. But that is in effect what our constitution says. Parliament is supreme. It can pass whatever laws it likes. This is of course subject to the recent intervention of European Union law, but we can put that to one side for the purposes of this discussion, especially as the UK voted to 'leave' in 2016. Subject to that, courts have confirmed parliamentary sovereignty and, in so doing, made it quite clear that they cannot thwart Westminster's will.

 We can see an instance of this in Brass Crosby's Case *1771 [1558–1774] All ER Rep 586. This is a case about parliamentary privilege – the ability of Parliament to control its own affairs without external interference – and is illustrative. Here, an official of the Tower of London arrested the Lord Mayor of London and detained him. The official was acting on the authority of the Speaker of the House of Commons. The Speaker alleged that the Lord Mayor, who was himself a Member of Parliament (MP), had abused his privileges as an MP. The underlying issue, which today's observer might find singularly uncontroversial, was over the publication of parliamentary debates by an independent printer.*

3.6.2 The courts and parliamentary privilege

In making its decision the court declined to look into the substantive issues. It found by a clear majority it had no status to contradict Parliament's wishes, in this instance revolving around its particular Westminster privileges. This therefore illustrates what happens when different principles appear to contradict each other. On the one hand Lord Mayor Crosby suggested he was being detained unlawfully in breach of the principle of habeas corpus. On the other hand, the detention, even if it lacked an element of certainty in law, was authorised by the supreme legislative body of the jurisdiction, namely Parliament. Faced with this contradiction, the court did the judicial equivalent of ignoring a married couple arguing in public. It stated in clear terms they could not interfere. Mr Justice Blackstone, in concluding the court had no power to release Crosby, said:

> I concur in opinion that we cannot discharge the Lord Mayor. The present case is of great importance, because the liberty of the subject is materially concerned. The House of Commons is a supreme court, and they are judges of their own privileges and contempts, more especially with respect to their own members ... and if any persons may be safely trusted with this power, they must surely be the Commons who are chosen by the people, for their privileges and powers are the privileges and powers of the people.

3.6.3 Conclusions on this area of law

It should be stressed this case is somewhat oddball, revolving as it does around the desire of Parliament to discipline one of its own. But the court's judgment can be summarised thus: Parliament is supreme; the House of Commons is elected by the general population; Parliament can make their own laws; and courts cannot intervene for fear of contradicting the will of the people. The judge in question was overstating the matter, because it is perfectly ludicrous to us today to suggest that Parliament was in some way representative of the nation. It was not. It was then a bastion of privilege and entirely the preserve of the landed minority. But the core principle of this decision remains valid: courts cannot trespass on parliamentary sovereignty. This is something subsequently stated by constitutionalists such as AV Dicey, and is a line of judicial reasoning maintained today.

The *Crosby* case mines a particular seam of law relating to Parliament and the way it handles its privileges, so we shouldn't draw too many specific conclusions from it. But it does hint at the circular nature of law creation within our legal system. Somewhere a law originates. Judges rule on that law. Parliament can then pass more law. Judges then need to interpret, or reinterpret, that law. And so on. **Figure 3.3** illustrates the process.

Figure 3.3   Relationship between legislation and case law

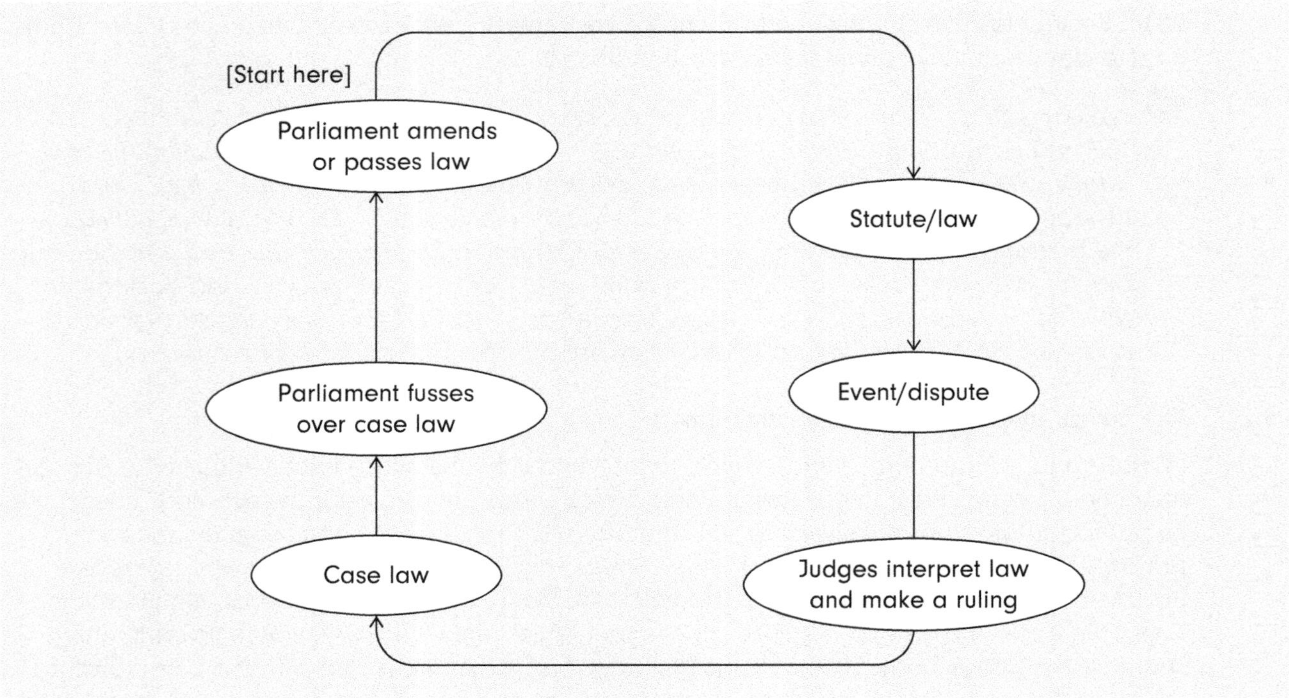

[Start here]

Parliament amends
or passes law

Statute/law

Parliament fusses
over case law

Event/dispute

Case law

Judges interpret law
and make a ruling

3.7   Matters relating to the changing nature of society

Case law contains many fascinating aspects. These include the opposing contentions of the participants; the conflicts of evidence that inevitably emerge; the ability of a persuasive advocate to make something positive of a poor case; and the involvement of the judge. The last of these concerns us here. Judges are naturally a product of their eras. As such, sometimes they appear to be cowed by the conventions of the society in which they live. Alternatively, they are capable of being forward thinking. Courts, therefore, both maintain the status quo and encourage society to change. Here, we are going to examine the subtle – some would say glacial – manner in which courts can influence society.

Let us transport ourselves back to the 1770s. Imagine you are from the state of Virginia in the American colonies. You are a slave. You and your master come to England. There, you escape. Your master wishes to sell you to someone in Jamaica. The laws of England are somewhat ambiguous as to slavery. Although the institution is wholly legal across the Atlantic, in England people are somewhat uncomfortable, although compliant, with the idea. You begin a court case to confirm your status, to avoid the nightmare of being sold abroad.

3.7.1   An important case on social change

These are the facts from Somerset v Stewart *[1772] 20 State Tr 1. The judgment of Lord Mansfield is a masterpiece of social compromise. He starts by suggesting that it would be possible for a master and a slave to agree that the slave be sold. To an observer today this is a staggering statement. How could a slave have any meaningful say in the matter? Surely, any such agreement or negotiation would be manifestly one sided.*

Lord Mansfield then goes on to make a series of relatively subdued statements, which on closer inspection have considerable significance. He states because the object of enquiry

is a slave, that makes 'a very material difference' to the debate. He says there are consequences to embracing the American principle of slavery. He thinks 'many of those consequences are absolutely contrary to the municipal law of England'. He then talks of a 'coercive power', somewhat ambiguously failing to make it clear what he means. He then says the coercive power cannot be exercised, meaning at this stage the master has no power over the slave. He makes a digression into history by talking of a decision 50 years earlier, which, he implies, relates to the freeing of 14,000–15,000 slaves. Lord Mansfield continues by saying that 'we cannot in any of these points direct the law; the law must rule us'. His judgment then tails off somewhat by suggesting the matter should be stood over 'and if we are called on for a decision proper notice shall be given'.

The reader of this case today can be forgiven for wondering at its significance. It is far from decisive, riddled with ambiguous comments and half-baked statements that suggest the court is somewhat reluctant to interfere with the slavery model. The ending is inconclusive. Throughout, Lord Mansfield appears to treat the claim as one relating to property rather than individual freedoms. But in its own way this case is a textbook example of the way in which a court can lay the foundations for future decisions. It is difficult to match cause with effect, but in 1807 Parliament prohibited the slave trade, and in 1833 it abolished slavery altogether.

Let us therefore interpret Lord Mansfield's judgment. First, he gives the impression of deferring to the established order by suggesting some sort of compromise between master and slave. This is obviously impossible on the facts, but enables him to gain support for what follows. Lord Mansfield from the outset is working the margins of what would be acceptable to the ruling classes. Sometimes it doesn't pay to go bull-headed at the establishment in a way likely to alienate it.

He then refers to 'material differences', which is again ambiguous, but which for a judge is indicating something close to disapproval. The statement about the institution of slavery being contrary to the municipal law is again a muted judicial comment with considerable significance. Essentially Lord Mansfield says slavery is unlawful, albeit in a tactful manner. His digression into speaking positively about important decisions 50 years ago implies support for the idea of freeing slaves, without actually stating as much. The passage is laudatory of the actions taken even if it is unclear as to exactly who did what, and when. Throughout, he makes it clear he is guided by the law. And indeed he was. But, under the cloak of conservative judicial principles, he managed to make statements that were ahead of their time.

3.7.2 Conclusions on the *Somerset* case

The *Somerset* case therefore has significance in the development of case law. The conclusions we can draw from it are as follows:

- Courts are frequently asked to make difficult decisions, and they should not shy away from them.

- Sometimes courts reflect the will of society and the established order, and at other times judicial decisions run ahead of legislative actions.

- Judges cannot contravene the will of Parliament. But they can still shape the law where, as was the case with Somerset's application, there is no relevant statute as a starting point, or perhaps no statute that is clear on the matter.

- Judges are usually cautious in extending the ambit of case law. This was the genius of Lord Mansfield. He gave the impression of supporting principles of property ownership. He was reluctant to state that slavery was unlawful, and indeed he could not in the face of legislation in force then. Accordingly he chose a soothing approach. But at the same time he made statements that would grow in importance over time, such as the implication that slavery was a coercive power, the 'material difference' attaching to a slave's situation, the apparent support for masters freeing their slaves, and the crucial dicta that slavery was 'contrary to municipal law' in England.

- As lawyers, we should accept campaigning in a courtroom might be an impossible task. If you are, say, Nelson Mandela in South Africa in the 1960s under the spotlight of apartheid, you can legitimately use your prosecution for sedition to challenge the state, turn the tables and put the Nationalist government on trial. But otherwise it might be better to encourage change over a period of time, and experience some success, rather than expect immediate results and be disappointed.

3.7.3 A further case on social issues

A case from the 1940s illustrates the careful tread of the courts in racial matters. Learie Constantine (1901–1977) was a famous Trinidadian sportsman. He represented the West Indies at cricket. He spent much time in England playing in Lancashire. He was one of Wisden's Cricketers of the Year in 1939 (Wisden being the most important annual cricketing reference book in the world). During the Second World War he worked for the Ministry of Labour. On 30 July 1943 he arrived at the Bedford hotel in London to fulfil a booking. The hotel refused to receive and lodge him. Constantine made a claim in the High Court.

Mr Justice Birkett presided over the case of *Constantine v Imperial London Hotels Ltd* [1944] 2 All ER 171. In every way the decision is an example of judicial restraint. The claimant himself pursued the matter in a modest manner, declining to claim either for slander or breach of contract. He simply wanted justice. But the ruling has echoed down the generations.

The court considered a number of authorities. It declined to enter the bear pit of emotion. It looked at the matter strictly from a legal point of view. In so doing it made a number of observations:

- It noted Constantine visited, and was offered a room in, a nearby hotel. The defendant owned that hotel as well as the Bedford. The court said that this made no difference to the claim. The injury remained potent despite this supposed mitigation.

- The judge in reviewing the authorities compared Constantine's situation to a number of important constitutional rights. At one stage he talked about the right to vote. Elsewhere he mentioned the freedom of the individual.

- In the face of the limited nature of Constantine's claim – where there was no claim for breach of contract or slander – the court reacted positively to the dignified nature of the complaint. In its own limited way, it interpreted the law in an expansionist manner. Today we would call this the 'purposive' approach – the idea that law should be construed in such a way as to give it effective meaning.

Matters of racial prejudice, and indeed any discrimination, are sensitive areas with which to deal. Some of us think the courts should be more assertive. Others advocate something of a graduated approach. And there are many variations in between. Judges, and their decisions, tend to be evolutionary in the thinking. This certainly seems to be the case for Mr Justice Birkett. He managed to dismiss a possible remedy of malicious prosecution whilst leaving it open as an option for the future. This is what he said:

> But although an action does not give rise to an action for malicious prosecution, inasmuch as it does not necessarily or naturally involve damage, there are legal proceedings which do necessarily and naturally involve that damage; and when proceedings of that kind have been taken falsely and maliciously, and without reasonable or probable cause, then, inasmuch as an injury has been done, the law gives a remedy. Such proceedings are indictments — I do not say every indictment, but I mean all indictments involving either scandal to reputation or the possible loss of liberty to the person, that is, all ordinary indictments for ordinary offences.

This passage contains elements vital to future decisions. It implies the behaviour of the hotel was false and malicious. When the judge says there is no 'reasonable or probable cause', he means the hotel's action was completely intolerable. The word 'indictment' implies a possible criminal element to the behaviour. And the reference to 'possible loss of liberty to the person' indicates the extremely grave nature of the allegation against the defendant.

The court gave judgment for Constantine, the judge saying as follows:

> Having given the matter the fullest consideration, I hold this action is maintainable without proof of special damage. The right, I think, is founded upon the common law. That right I find was violated in this case. The law affords a remedy and that injury imports damage.

Did you note the reference to 'common law'? In other words, the judge relied on previous decisions by other judges. This is a classic example of the use, and development, of case law. The judge awarded nominal damages by way of a remedy.

3.7.4 Conclusions on the *Constantine* case

In its own way this case is a landmark for the law on discrimination. First, it relies strictly on legal reasoning, stripping away any of the emotive issues that could arise. Second, it took a narrow cause of action and used it to discuss a wide range of remedies. Third, even if it decided those remedies were not applicable, the nature of case law allows the discussion to be continued for later generations, either in the courts or in society. Fourth, the judge interpreted the law available to him in as broad a manner as possible in the interests of justice. Fifth, as with every significant piece of case law, it hinted at future developments, in particular the criminalising of the worst discriminatory behaviour (through the word 'indictments'). As such this case remains an interesting illustration of the way in which the judiciary deals with the changing nature of society.

Learie Constantine was knighted in 1962, ennobled in 1969 as Baron Constantine of Maraval and Nelson, and died in 1971. As an international he appeared in 18 matches for the West Indies cricket team. He contributed to social change in Lancashire through his involvement in league cricket. And for our legal system he was a pathfinder in racial matters.

These cases on race illustrate a process that often, but not always, accompanies the role of case law in tracing societal developments. Society suggests something should change; courts ruminate on the matter; and eventually, or rapidly, depending on the scenario, Parliament passes a law, often as a result of judicial comment. In this way you can see the link between people, court cases and legislation.

Figure 3.4   How social attitudes run ahead of case law and legislation (generally – not always)

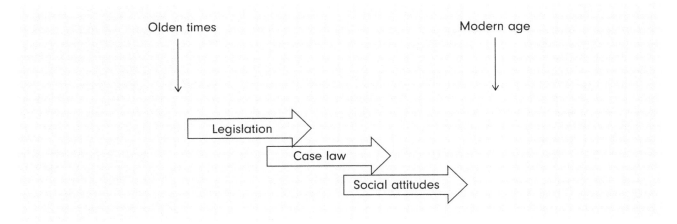

3.7.5 Case law, the legal system, cricket and the cult of the all-rounder

Certain aspects of the legal system revolve around non-lawyers. One thinks of magistrates, who are not legally qualified, and juries, who are ordinary people tasked with giving a verdict at the end of a Crown Court trial. We look at these in a subsequent chapter. They confirm British society places value on the role of the amateur, or alternatively the 'all-rounder', ie someone who has transferable skills between different disciplines. So a journalist can become prime minister (Boris Johnson); so can a general (the Duke of Wellington); an accountant can run a business; thousands read history at university and then work in areas entirely unrelated to the study of past events; literature lovers run railways; and so on.

These are not chance events: they are repeated across the decades. The comparison with Germany, say, is illustrative: there, technical skills are instilled and prioritised from an early stage, with the emphasis on excellence through specialism.

From where does this culture of the generalist stem? The answer is, at least in part, from the playing fields and sporting environment of middle England. In particular, the link between cricket, society and the law is well established. In imperial India the sport provided a means of interaction between the rulers and the ruled. Across the Commonwealth cricket represents a commonality for otherwise disparate communities.

There is a pleasing symbiosis between cricket and the law. The culture of cricket mirrors the rule of law: a set of procedures, predictable interpretations of law, impartial officials and international obligations. And of course there are hierarchies galore, from the selectors of teams downwards: captains, batsmen and, at the bottom of the ladder, the poor old bowlers who do most of the hard work.

Cricket has influenced, or perhaps tainted depending upon your viewpoint, the administration of the law for some considerable time. If you were to take a straw poll of traditional male barristers the vast majority of them would say they could advise on an extraordinarily wide range of legal matters. A majority would agree they should confine themselves to either criminal matters or civil ones but within those two spheres they would believe themselves competent to opine across a wide canvas. They are the legal world's all-rounders.

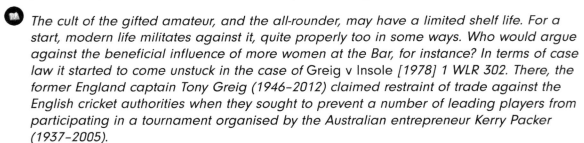 *The cult of the gifted amateur, and the all-rounder, may have a limited shelf life. For a start, modern life militates against it, quite properly too in some ways. Who would argue against the beneficial influence of more women at the Bar, for instance? In terms of case law it started to come unstuck in the case of* Greig v Insole *[1978] 1 WLR 302. There, the former England captain Tony Greig (1946–2012) claimed restraint of trade against the English cricket authorities when they sought to prevent a number of leading players from participating in a tournament organised by the Australian entrepreneur Kerry Packer (1937–2005).*

The case ended in victory for the players. The principle of participants being able to play outside the strict control of the authorities was confirmed. The idea of a patriarchal system, presided over by the few for the benefit of the many, broke down. So did the cherished concept of the all-rounder, in this instance in the form of cricketers earning low sums by playing, and then moving effortlessly into other employment at the end of their playing days. Instead, the Packer era rewarded players properly, and decently, for the job of work they did on the cricket pitch. If you would like to ponder the origins of sports people earning large sums of money, with awesome contracts to match, you might start your research with Greig v Insole.

It is a complete falsehood for people to think cricket is in some way gentlemanly and purer than the rest of society. This cult of the gentleman all-rounder took another knock, in a somewhat bruising manner, when Ian (now Lord) Botham, arguably England's greatest modern all-rounder, sued Imran Khan, his Pakistani equivalent, for defamation in a 1996 trial. There was little love lost in a contest that resulted in victory for Imran, someone who has since gone on to lead his country. You can gain a sense of the matter from a subsequent case report into costs stemming from the litigation – *Botham v Khan* [2004] EWHC 2602 (QB).

The moral of all this is as follows. The cult of the all-rounder, where you can treat sport, life and the law as a dreamy continuum, will only take you so far. Both Greig and Packer were outsiders, Greig by virtue of his South African background, and Packer through his ruthless nose for business, sharpened in the unforgiving environment of New South Wales. They were unconstrained by traditional concepts of society or law. Likewise, Botham and Imran were, and still are, non-traditionalists.

The impact of the outsider is a theme hinted at repeatedly in literature, from *Vanity Fair* by William Thackeray (1811–1863), to *The Go Between* by LP Hartley (1895–1972), and in particular *Beyond a Boundary* by the Trinidadian CLR James (1901–1989). Indeed, the last of these – an analysis of cricket in the West Indies in the mid-1900s – should be required reading for anyone seeking an insight into the relationship between the law, society and sport. It deals in crisp manner with disparities within society, and how participation in sport mirrors the world in which it takes place, including the rules that shape that world.

3.8 Cases relating to business and the creation of wealth

Court decisions on business are part of the early impulse by the courts to limit monarchical power.

 In the Case of Monopolies *(1602) Trin 44 Eliz, also known as* Darcy's Case, *the courts examined the lawfulness of a monopoly (exclusive trade rights) granted by the Crown. The facts are these. Darcy, who was based in London, claimed he had authority from the Queen to 'enjoy the whole trade traffic and merchandise of all playing cards'. This covered both the import of playing cards from abroad, and the making and selling of them by domestic manufacturers. The duration of this entitlement was for 12 years.*

Then as now, London was an international centre of trade. Merchants transacted much business there, and the city, and to an extent the rest of the country, started to grow wealthy as a result. The monopoly claimed by Darcy would have two immediate impacts: first, it would restrict consumer choice by narrowing supply. Second, it would prevent local manufacturers from making cards, selling them and earning a living. This is what you and I would refer to as 'cornering the market' – dominating it so there is little if any competition, with consumers forced to purchase from a sole supplier.

This case was a true test of the judiciary's attitude towards businesses and their relationship with the state. It would have been entirely understandable if the court had decided that a limited scope monopoly would be acceptable. It could be argued the arrangement would allow Darcy to expand his business, create employment, develop a world class business, raise wages (perhaps), and improve quality.

But the court decided the opposite. It made a ringing declaration as to the importance of free trade, ie the policy of allowing goods to cross borders in the interests of competition, customer choice and, hopefully, lower prices. The court said 'a dispensation or licence to have the sole importation and merchandising of cards is utterly against the law'. It declared the monopoly to be contrary to the will of Parliament. There are arguments for and against the notion of free trade, but in the context of the early 1600s, where the consequences for snubbing the Crown could include death, this was a brave and insightful decision.

3.8.1 Impact of case law on the business environment

This case had various consequences and they remain significant today. First, it reinforced the limits of Crown prerogative. Second, it confirmed the law should protect mercantile endeavour as much as individual liberties. That protection should be, first, against the state; second, in favour where possible of consumers; and third, against other entities that seek to abuse their powers.

Courts continue to frown on monopolies. The concept of regulated free enterprise, and controlled free trade, is part of UK democratic history and indirectly a source of law. In this, the courts take their lead from Parliament.

The MP John Bright, speaking at the Amphitheatre Liverpool on 30 August 1843 (*Liverpool Mercury*, 1 September 1843), gave the example of a fictional business person addressing a typical voter:

> He showed them how monopoly robbed them of their coffee and sugar, and of bread and butter for their children; he showed them how stonemasons, shoemakers, carpenters and every kind of artisans suffered if the trade of the country were restricted; he showed them that if their families increased, if the population increased and trade did not increase those who had no property but their labour, who must have work or must starve, suffered most; he showed them how the fierce competition for labour thus created reduced the rate of wages; he showed them that the foul fiend of monopoly ... deprived them of one third or one half of the miserable pittance of wages that they earned.

Bright spent most of his life on the back benches, ie as an ordinary MP, not involved in government. His arguments were contentious at the time. They have, however, gained currency, and his views are easy to understand, even if you disagree with his economics. He believed monopolies, and restrictions on free trade, resulted in higher prices and less choice. They also allowed businesses to dictate conditions in the labour market, with a surplus of workers chasing fewer jobs, with resulting lower wages. We could debate these policy matters indefinitely, but the courts have continued to reflect the will of Parliament in their disapproval of the monopoly principle, and this can be seen in some modern decisions.

3.8.2 Case law and business in more recent times

Let's look at one example. A well-known software and technology company develops a desirable product. The company, and the product, are very successful, with a market share of perhaps 70–80%. It decides to sell one product on the back of another. It compels consumers to purchase a media player whenever they wish to buy a personal computer operating system. The authorities take an interest in this strategy. They suspect that:

- the company in question has a stranglehold on the market;
- consumers have less choice; and
- trade is being restricted as a result.

In modern terms this is called abuse of a dominant position, and it is as close as you can get these days to an old style monopoly.

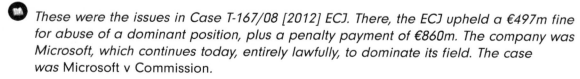 *These were the issues in Case T-167/08 [2012] ECJ. There, the ECJ upheld a €497m fine for abuse of a dominant position, plus a penalty payment of €860m. The company was Microsoft, which continues today, entirely lawfully, to dominate its field. The case was* Microsoft v Commission.

The principles discussed reflect current law within the jurisdiction of England and Wales. Our laws say it is wrong for companies to abuse a dominant position. It can thus be seen there is consistency of sorts over many centuries in the way that courts and MPs believe monopolies, whether ancient or modern, to be undesirable.

3.9 Cases where the courts got it wrong

The courts of England and Wales have always obsessed about property. This is the case for both land and possessions. From the earliest stages of history ownership of land conferred wealth, and ownership of possessions implied status. So courts as representatives, even if inadvertently, of the privileged classes placed considerable emphasis on property rights. This led to some unfortunate results.

3.9.1 Case law, and the concept of people as possessions

In the case of Osborn v Gillett *(1873) LR 8 Exch 88 Elizabeth Osborn died as a result of an accident involving a horse and wagon. The judgment makes uncomfortable reading. The court said damages could not be obtained where death was more or less instantaneous, suggesting any action ceased with death. Further, the deceased in any event had no apparent status in making any claim, and throughout the judgment Elizabeth was treated very much as a fringe player. Yet further, her father could only claim in the capacity of a master having lost a servant, rather than as a grieving parent.*

One can only imagine the distress that accompanied the process. The court in its defence held itself to be interpreting the will of Parliament, thus maintaining the doctrine of sovereignty. But courts do not always need to be restrictive. In earlier years Lord Justice Coke was prepared to make bold statements limiting the Crown's influence, and in later years Lord Denning was able to develop new reasoning in the field of administrative law. Here, the court believed itself bound. It is an example of judicial caution, laced with the unpleasant presumption that a person is akin to a possession.

3.9.2 Case law perpetuating marital injustice

We can also discuss another line of reasoning that blends somewhat obnoxious concepts of property with family relationships. Imagine you are a married woman. Your marriage is not a happy one. Your husband forces himself on you. You are obliged to participate in intimate relations against your will.

These are the outline facts of *R v R* [1992] 1 AC 599, where the House of Lords (now the Supreme Court) examined the contention that a married man could not be convicted of the rape of his wife. Their Lordships seized on *R v R* as an opportunity to review this area of law.

In the Court of Appeal the Chief Justice, Lord Lane, noted that early authorities supported the notion that a husband could control a wife. Lord Lane referred to the views of Sir Matthew Hale in his *History of the Pleas of the Crown* (1736), vol 1, ch 58, 629, where it was stated the wife through mutual consent had given herself to her husband, and consequently could not be raped by him. Ecclesiastical decisions such as *Popkin v Popkin* (1794) 1 Hag Ecc 765n embraced the notion with some enthusiasm, and, owing to the influence of such courts on society in the 18th century, this thinking became a form of received wisdom. Lord Lane noted Lord Stowell in *Popkin* had said:

> The husband has a right to the person of his wife ... but not if her health is endangered.

So by 1794 the courts appear to have accepted that wives were subservient to husbands, albeit with the implication that a wife did not need to submit in the face of danger. The concept became embedded into legal thinking from that moment on.

In summary the sequence of events is as follows.

- Sir Matthew Hale stated a concept in 1736.
- Religious courts adopted it.
- Subsequent case law embraced it.
- The notion that a husband cannot rape his wife became embedded.

It was not one of the judiciary's proudest moments.

The House of Lords in *R v R* pondered the history of marital rape and concluded a man having 'a right to the person of his wife' was a legal fiction – the closest a court can come to saying a previous ruling was not just mistaken, but horribly wrong. Accordingly *R v R* removed the presumption that a husband could not rape a wife, and this paved the way for s 1 of the Sexual Offences Act 2003, which confirmed that rape by a husband should be treated the same as rape by anyone.

3.9.3 Some conclusions

A number of conclusions can be drawn from *Osborn* and *R v R*:

- The law of England and Wales has always placed emphasis on the value of property, particularly land, and this endures to the present day.
- The law says property includes possessions.
- Historically, courts have come close to confirming possessions can include people. It must therefore be reluctantly accepted that courts have played their part in maintaining unfairness within society. Over time it could be that such unfairness dissipates, and this might be as a result of judicial wisdom, middle class pressures of the sort represented by John Bright MP, or through popular unrest and protest. Street demonstrations, incidentally, do have a part to play in the development of the legal system. They bring pressure on rulers in a direct manner, and although politicians say they will not be swayed by unlawful protests, it would be naive to suggest they have no influence.
- We should note the caveat to the 1794 *Popham* case, implying a wife has a right of self-defence in the face of danger. This anticipates important case law developments later, whereby courts extended the self-defence concept, and related discussions on premeditation, into abusive situations.

Also, an optimist could take heart from the balance of powers principle. Let's face it, judges can be a source of embarrassment occasionally. So can Parliament. But both courts and legislators have the knack of being sensible at crucial times in the democratic cycle, most notably when the other branch needs supervision or advice. So when courts allow injustice to fester, there is a fighting chance that Parliament will step in to correct the anomaly.

In general, we can see the benefits of our legal system and the development of case law. Over time it has stood the test of time. The general populus is happy with it. Otherwise, we would have had a revolution, drawn up a written constitution every decade or so, and dispensed with the rule of law. But there are many imperfections in our constitution, and one of them is the way in which powerful interests set the legal agenda. This is an ongoing dynamic. It might be illustrated diagrammatically as in **Figure 3.5**.

Figure 3.5 How case law can get things wrong

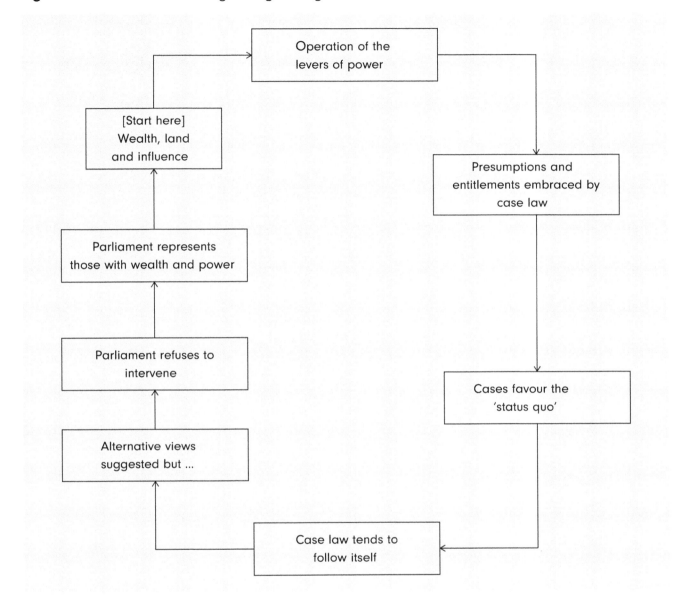

Summary

This chapter traces the development of case law. People who could be described loosely as judges have made decisions in places, and in a manner, vaguely approximate to a courtroom ever since Saxon times. But our story begins with the Tudors and the Stuarts, ie in the 1500s and 1600s.

Judgments from that period have taken root and grown over time. We have looked at cases ranging from those that protect basic freedoms to others that have failed, to put it mildly, to cover themselves with glory. There are also cases that deal with constitutionality, societal developments, personal matters such as contracts, and the operation of business.

All these areas can be studied in more detail when you progress your learning to the specific areas of law mentioned. For the moment, you can reflect on the cases and principles mentioned, and gain an insight into an important aspect of the constitution of England and Wales, its legal system and its sources of law. Case law is truly a pillar of our society.

Sample questions

Question 1

A judge is presiding over a trial of a business dispute. A statute is relevant to the outcome. The judge is aware of a recent debate in Parliament and knows a majority of MPs in the House of Commons think the law in question should change. He is also aware of a number of previous relevant cases.

Should the judge take account of the views of MPs in coming to his decision?

A   Yes, because Parliament is sovereign.

B   Yes, because the uncodified constitution places great weight on the view of MPs.

C   Yes, because a court can, in the interests of justice, anticipate future changes to legislation.

D   No, because a judge's role is to apply the rule of law.

E   No, because the judge should follow the earlier cases.

Answer

Option D is correct. All judges are principally guided by the rule of law. This means they should consider the relevant facts and the relevant law, and come to a decision in the interests of justice in the fullest sense. Lord Mansfield hinted at this when stating in the *Somerset* case [1772] that 'we cannot in any of these points direct the law; the law must rule us'.

Option A is wrong because, although Parliament is indeed sovereign, that relates to legislation rather than the views of MPs in a debate.

Option B is wrong because the constitution, which is indeed uncodified, does not allow MPs to influence judges. In fact it is an important aspect of the balance of powers within the constitution that the judiciary is independent of political influence.

Option C is wrong because, although a court can hint at possible unfairness in legislation, it cannot give a judgment that anticipates new law. It can only rule on the law as it is today.

Option E is wrong because judges are guided by previous case law but are not obliged to follow it in every circumstance.

Question 2

A judge in a criminal court is hearing an application for the detention of a man. The authorities believe the man has breached immigration law. However, they have no conclusive evidence. The man has a previous criminal record. There is some confusion within the computer systems of the authorities as to his identity. He has, however, given a name and address. The judge is aware of the views of many MPs in the House of Commons who wish to restrict immigration.

Which of the following is the best option for the judge?

A   The judge should detain the man indefinitely until the authorities can correct their computer systems.

B   The judge should rely on the evidence of the authorities alone in coming to a decision.

C   The judge should rely on the man's previous criminal record in making a ruling.

D   The judge should take note of the wish of MPs to restrict immigration.

E   The judge should consider the doctrine of habeas corpus in coming to a decision.

Answer

Option E is correct. Habeas corpus is the doctrine that says that no one can be detained without lawful reason. Here, there is an allegation of breach of the law without proof. At the moment the detention is unsubstantiated, and the administrative procedures of the authorities appear to be inadequate. The judge should therefore make a decision as to the release or detention of the man on the basis of the principle of habeas corpus. There might be other law to consider as well and habeas corpus would therefore be one of several considerations. As a result, option A is wrong – the judge cannot simply allow the man to be detained indefinitely.

Option B is wrong because a judge should always consider both sides of the argument, and so should assess the evidence on behalf of the man as well as evidence on behalf of the authorities. Option C is wrong because relying on the man's previous criminal record would not be an appropriate application of the rule of law. A consideration of that record may be appropriate but the most important requirement is an assessment of the offence alleged. Option D is wrong because no judge should be swayed by the views of MPs in Parliament. The balance of powers within the constitution require the judiciary to be independent from politicians.

Question 3

A judge is presiding over a court case on a matrimonial matter. The wife wants a divorce. The wife alleges coercive control – that her husband threatens force, and does not allow her to see friends or relatives. The advocates for the parties refer to numerous cases in support of their arguments.

Which of the following statements by previous courts would provide relevant guidance to the judge in deciding the issue of coercive control?

A   Mr Justice Birkett in *Constantine v Imperial Hotels* [1943]: 'I hold this action is maintainable without proof of special damage. The right, I think, is founded upon the common law'.

B   The judge in *R v Dudley and Stephens* [1884]: 'law and morality are not the same and many things may be immoral which are not necessarily illegal'.

C   Lord Mansfield in *Somerset v Stewart* [1772]: 'In five or six cases of this nature, I have known it to be accommodated by agreement between the parties'.

D   Lord Stowell in *Popkin v Popkin* [1794]: 'The husband has a right to the person of his wife'.

E   Lord Coke in *Darnel's Case* [1627]: 'A freeman imprisoned without cause is civilly dead'.

Answer

Option E is correct. Courts refer to previous cases to help them arrive at a just decision. *Darnel's Case* involved the principle of habeas corpus. The wife's situation here may not be a matter of imprisonment or liberty in the sense discussed by Lord Coke, but judges are entitled to draw parallels across the centuries. Here, the wife clearly feels fear in the face of the withdrawal of certain freedoms.

Option A is wrong as proof in a matter as grave as an allegation of control and abuse would be needed. Option B is wrong because a discussion of morality is not needed in this instance. It is purely a matter of law, in this instance relating to matrimonial matters and violence. Option C is wrong because here it would be inappropriate for allegations of violence in this context to be resolved privately. The parties require and deserve a decision of the court. Option D is wrong as the statement in *Popkin* is now discredited law.

4 Legislation and Acts of Parliament

SQE1 syllabus

This chapter will enable you to achieve the SQE1 assessment specification in relation to functioning legal knowledge concerning legislation and Acts of Parliament.

Note that, for SQE1, candidates are not usually required to recall specific case names or cite statutory or regulatory authorities. Cases are provided for illustrative purposes only.

Learning outcomes

By the end of this chapter you will be able to apply relevant core legal principles and rules appropriately and effectively, at the level of a competent newly qualified solicitor in practice, to realistic client-based and ethical problems and situations in the following areas:

- the interpretation of primary legislation, ie Acts of Parliament;
- the doctrine of parliamentary sovereignty;
- the format, layout and structure of a typical Act;
- different types of Act;
- why Acts are created;
- the link between Parliament and society when passing or amending Acts; and
- Acts from the devolved Welsh National Assembly.

4.1 Language and legislation

Language is often accompanied by ambiguity. This is hardly surprising when society is so dynamic. It would be unrealistic to say something that means the same to everyone. Here are two examples of everyday statements that have more than one meaning:

I could see Bob on top of the hill with my binoculars.

This could mean one of two things. First, that I was using my binoculars, and through them I could see Bob on the hill. Alternatively, it could mean I was sufficiently close to Bob to see him on the hill, and that he had my binoculars with him.

Jeremy rode the horse in a blue suit.

This could mean that Jeremy was wearing a blue suit while riding the horse, or it might mean the equine had some sort of blue livery.

You would expect the law to mirror society. And there are indeed examples of the law having a meaning that is less than clear. But we could put it another way: that there is more than one meaning to a particular piece of law, and this is not necessarily a bad thing. In some instances, it could be said that a certain fluffiness in word construction could have a beneficial effect.

For instance, imagine legislators are seeking to pass a law, but they can't agree. After much debate they reach a compromise that means the law can be passed and the business of governing can continue. The resulting sentence says, 'This section shall be reviewed each year'. This part of the law allows considerable flexibility. It doesn't say who shall do the reviewing, it declines to be specific as to when within any year the review should take place, or what the review involves, and it does not say what sort of year, ie a calendar one, a tax one or indeed any other variation on a period of 12 months.

The conclusions we draw are as follows:

* You should not expect words to be automatically understood by the recipient of them. What one person says, and what another person hears, is subject to interpretation.

* As lawyers, you should check carefully what you write, and what you receive in writing.

* Legislation is no different. It needs careful drafting, and will often be subject to interpretation. It could well mean different things to different people.

* Sometimes there will be ambiguity, which in most circumstances will be unhelpful, and in others, perhaps more limited in number, might be constructive. As an example of the latter, one thinks for instance of s 17 of the Northern Ireland Act 1998 relating to the Stormont Assembly, which allowed for the First and Deputy Ministers to act jointly in determining the functions exercisable by the holders of ministerial office. This looseness in outcome allowed room for compromises to emerge, eventually, in the practicalities of power-sharing between the various parties.

* It is a key part of a lawyer's job to be able to interpret the law and advise on it. This includes the ability to interpret legislation.

4.2 Interpreting an Act of Parliament – an example

On 9 September 2019 the European Union (Withdrawal) (No 2) Act 2019 received Royal Assent. This was part of the UK's painful legislative journey towards leaving the EU following the 23 June 2016 referendum. As we all know, the outcome of that referendum was a slim majority in favour of departure. The years following the referendum result were marked by dissent and delay in Parliament, one aspect of this being regular disagreements between the Government of the day and backbench MPs.

The Withdrawal (No 2) Act was a statute seeking to constrain the executive from conducting departure negotiations with too much of a free hand. It sought to bind the Government to avoid any withdrawal without negotiated agreement by the EU. The first section of the Act states as follows:

> 1. Duties in Connection with the Withdrawal of the UK from the European Union.
>
> ...
>
> (4) The Prime Minister must seek to obtain from the European Council an extension of the period under Article 50(3) of the Treaty on European Union ending at 11.00pm on 31 October 2019 by sending to the President of the European Council a letter in the form set out in the Schedule to this Act requesting an extension of that period ...

The schedule to the Act then stated the exact wording of the letter to be sent.

So in summary this provision required the prime minister (PM), in the absence of an agreed arrangement with the EU, to seek an extension to any departure timetable, thus avoiding a so-called hard 'Brexit' (as it is popularly known). The Act was specific as to how the extension should be requested: it should be by way of a letter, to the European Council, and the exact wording was mentioned in the relevant schedule.

One would be forgiven for thinking there was no question of interpretation here. How many nuances are there, one wonders, to a requirement that a letter in particular terms should be sent from one person to another?

Here is a list of people who thought that this provision was entirely straightforward, requiring simply the writing and sending of the necessary letter:

- the vast majority of MPs in the House of Commons;
- members of the House of Lords;
- the press;
- academics;
- most newspaper readers and television viewers;
- the media;
- EU officials;
- the man and woman on the fabled Clapham omnibus (this is a well-known phrase from *Hall v Brooklands Automobile Club* [1933] 1 KB 205, a case you can enjoy when dealing in more detail with the law of tort).

Here is a list of people who thought differently:

- the PM Boris Johnson, and some of his advisers.

When the time came to send the letter mandated by the Act, most of us thought the letter would be typed, signed and sent in the normal way. But instead the PM simply sent a photocopy of the letter, unsigned, and accompanied by another letter arguing against the idea of an extension. By doing this the PM complied with the law whilst at the same time preserving his political capital by indicating his reluctance to agree with the contents and intent of the Act.

This is a wonderful example of legislation being capable of mixed interpretations. According to the PM, the requirement of 'sending ... a letter' – something the PM was temperamentally and politically uncomfortable with – could be achieved by providing an unsigned photocopy. And there was nothing in the Act to prevent the PM accompanying that copy with another communication, this time typed and signed, countermanding and undermining the contents of the first.

In conclusion, you can see laws are capable of endless interpretation, depending on how they are drafted. Indeed, there is something of a cycle, or dynamic, to the process. First, there is an impetus for a law to be passed. Second, Parliament drafts the law, with a particular intent given to its wording, and creates an Act. Third, your average person – let's call them Joe Public – interprets that Act. Fourth, someone else – Josephine Public, perhaps – construes the same Act differently.

Fifth, lawyers get involved. Sixth, the courts give a ruling (and perhaps there are appeals on the matter if judges differ from each other). Seventh, legislators take a renewed interest in the matter, and step in to pass a law to simplify, or correct, or address the situation. And then the process could begin again. (You could say this sort of thing gives lawyers a bad name, but remember the role of the client, for without them lawyers wouldn't be instructed in the first place.)

This scenario might be illustrated as in **Figure 4.1**. We have taken as a fictional example a public groundswell for, and an Act of Parliament dealing with, measures dealing with additives in sweets (or candy, as they are called in the USA).

Figure 4.1 How to interpret an Act of Parliament

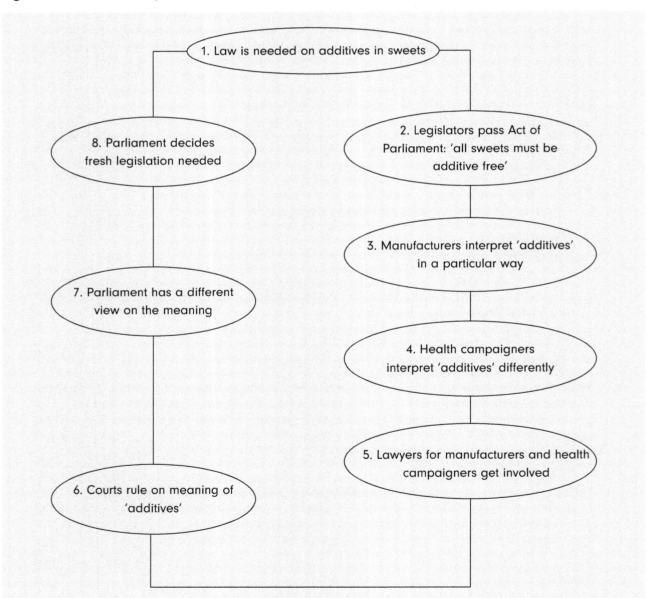

Incidentally care is needed when discussing the UK's EU departure laws. Following the referendum, the EU (Notification of Withdrawal) Act 2017 triggered the start of the departure process. The EU (Withdrawal) Act 2018 provides the substantive basis for enacting any departure into UK law, but does not actually confirm the departure itself. The EU (Withdrawal Agreement) Act 2020 takes things considerably further, providing a legislative mandate for the UK's exit.

Along the way various other Acts relating to Brexit became law, usually as a result of overnight cabals or similarly hasty meetings conducted by MPs with their own agendas. Commentators have also noted that these, essentially satellite, Acts, such as the Withdrawal (No 2) Act discussed above, represent something of a triumph for the principle that the legislature should not be browbeaten by the executive. As such they have made their own contributions to the legal system of England and Wales and its sources of law.

4.3   The doctrine of parliamentary sovereignty

Parliament is the supreme law-making body in the country. Statute can amend case law, but not vice versa. The principle that only Parliament can make or unmake a law is known as the doctrine of parliamentary sovereignty, or the legislative supremacy of Parliament.

Since the UK joined the EU, this doctrine has had a tense relationship with a competing concept, namely the idea that EU law is supreme over the national law of EU member states. This line of jurisprudence has gathered pace in the face of considerable popular, political and media opposition. Indeed, it could be considered one of the reasons why the UK voted to leave in 2016. Curiously, despite that decision, EU law will continue to have influence over our legal system for some time to come. That is something best left for greater scrutiny in another book. The important points to note for now are:

*   the doctrine of parliamentary sovereignty has renewed significance at the moment, owing to the UK vote to leave the EU; but

*   the doctrine is still subject to EU law concepts, if only for a limited time; and

*   the exact nature of the relationship between the UK and EU legal systems has an element of speculation to it.

Anyway, the doctrine, subject to the caveats mentioned above, may be explained as follows:

*   Parliament has the freedom to make laws of any kind. It does not matter if the law is unfair, unjust or practically impossible to enforce.

*   Statute cannot be overridden by a body outside Parliament. This means:

    (i)   UK courts and international courts have no power under English law to declare an Act of Parliament invalid. UK judges have powers to make declarations of incompatibility under the Human Rights Act 1998, but this is not the same as saying an Act is unlawful.

    (ii) In the event of conflict between a statute and some other kind of law, statute prevails. As we keep saying, owing to Brexit, this idea is tempered by EU law at the moment, most notably through the *Factortame* decision – see *R (Factortame Ltd) v Secretary of State for Transport (No 2)* [1991] 1 AC 603. This case, and the accompanying debate on the relationship between national and EU law, is something for you to explore further when you consider constitutional law matters elsewhere.

    (iii) Parliament cannot bind its successors. A statute cannot be protected from repeal, and a later Parliament can always change the Acts of its predecessor, whatever words the previous Act may contain to prevent its own repeal. Otherwise, if a Parliament could bind its successors, the doctrine of parliamentary supremacy would disappear.

There are a number of types of legislation, which we will discuss below.

4.4   Different types of legislation

The two principal types of legislation within the UK are Acts of Parliament and statutory instruments. Acts of Parliament as primary legislation go through a particular process culminating in the Royal Assent. We will look at primary legislation in a moment.

4.4.1   Statutory instruments

Statutory instruments (SIs) are also known as secondary, subordinate or delegated legislation, and are in effect creatures of ministers and civil servants, requiring no discussion before becoming law. They have as their starting point a reference in a given statute: a 'parent' Act. They are 'laid' in draft for a period of days in an office in the House of Commons before being 'made', or signed, by the minister, at which point they become law. SIs are a routine part of parliamentary life, and their number far exceeds Acts of Parliament. For instance, in 2018, 34 general public Acts were passed; in contrast some 3,500 statutory instruments are typically passed each year.

Here are some examples of SIs. These have no particular significance to us in this book: they are mentioned to give you a flavour of the miniscule detail that typically accompany them.

- The Polish Potatoes (Notification) Order 2004 makes it an offence to import potatoes from Poland without giving at least two days' notice to a plant health inspector.

- The Films (Definition of 'British Film') (No 2) Order 2006 modifies the cultural test relevant to the financing of films. Under a points-based system, there are four points for depiction of a British story.

- The Submarine Pipelines (Designated Owners) Order 2010 does not, I'm afraid, deal with underwater vessels. *Das Boot* (as in the 1981 German war film about a U-Boat) it is not. In a nice example of legislative ambiguity, at least in its name, it in fact confirms the commercial ownership of a submerged (hence 'submarine') petroleum pipeline in the North Sea. This pipeline reaches from the Scott drilling and process platform to the outboard flange connecting to the subsea spool piece at the Forties Unity Platform Riser.

4.4.2   Byelaws

Another sort of secondary legislation is council byelaws. These are local laws made by local councils under an enabling provision granted by an Act of Parliament. They are usually accompanied by some sort of sanction or punishment for non-observance. Typical byelaws would include measures relating to open spaces, parks, burial grounds and marketplaces. Byelaws cannot take effect until they are confirmed by the appropriate minister.

As an example of the subject matter of a byelaw, in 1988 Coventry City Council was one of the first local authorities to ban the drinking of alcohol in the street.

4.4.3   Flowchart illustrating types of legislation

Figure 4.2 contains a flowchart illustrating primary and secondary legislation. This chapter deals principally with primary legislation, but it is useful to have the overview and context so you can see the relationship with other sorts of laws generated by the legal process. You will see there is a reference to private and public statutes, and consolidating and codifying legislation, and we will explain those later.

Figure 4.2 Types of legislation

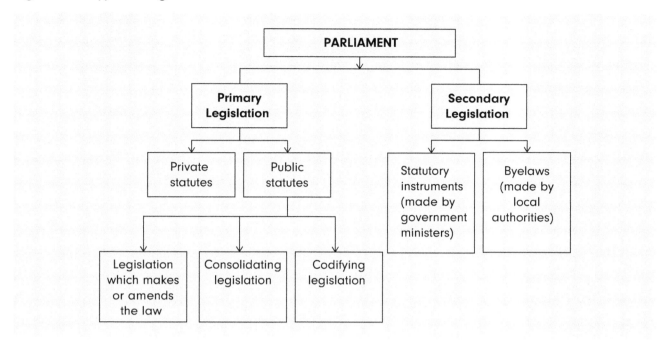

4.5 Format of Acts of Parliament

We have seen earlier the sequence of events that leads to Acts of Parliament – which as we have said are primary legislation – being passed and becoming law. Now we should consider their typical structure.

First, there is the name of the Act or what is called the short title. Taking a well-known piece of law, the Human Rights Act (HRA) 1998, as an example, the short title is the name of it. It sits underneath an intriguing image featuring a lion on one side and a unicorn on the other, with the words 'Dieu et mon droit' ('God and my right') on a banner underneath. This is the Royal coat of arms and symbolises both the nature of legislation as an ancient creation of monarchy and the involvement of the Crown when giving Royal Assent.

Next comes the year of the Act together with the chapter. The year is self-explanatory, and the chapter simply means the number of the Act within a given sequence. So '1998 Chapter 42' means the 42nd Act within the 1998 parliamentary year.

An Act also has a long title, explaining in more detail the subject matter. For the HRA 1998 this is stated as follows:

> An Act to give further effect to rights and freedoms guaranteed under the European Convention on Human Rights; to make provision with respect to holders of certain judicial offices who become judges of the European Court of Human Rights; and for connected purposes.

You will note there is a reference to the ECHR, originally ratified in 1950. Somehow this will need to be set out in the HRA 1998 and we will see in a moment how bulk amounts of information, too detailed for any given section within an Act, are handled.

A date then indicates when Royal Assent was given. Here, it is 9 November 1998.

There is then the enacting formula, indicating the Act has passed through the necessary constitutional process, namely approval by and consent of the monarch and Parliament. A typical form of wording for this would be:

> Be it enacted by the King's most Excellent Majesty, by and with the advice and consent of the Lords Spiritual and Temporal, and Commons, in this present Parliament assembled, and by the authority of the same, as follows:

In circumstances where the Lords are seeking to hold up or deny the passage of a Bill sent to it by the Commons, it is possible for an Act to be passed without the agreement of the Lords. This is as a result of the Parliament Acts 1911 and 1949. An example of this is the Hunting Act 2004, where the Lords expressed resistance to legislation banning the hunting of wild mammals with dogs. But this particular aspect of parliamentary procedure, where the Commons marginalises the Lords, and indeed elbows them aside completely, is unusual.

Some Acts routinely adopt a different form of enacting formula, for instance the annual Finance Acts, which refer to 'defraying the monarch's public expenses', and 'making an addition to the revenue'.

A typical Act is then organised into sections, with each section usually having a descriptive tagline indicating its content. Sometimes there are headings that indicate the broad subject matter of various sections. Some longer Acts are divided into parts, in order to provide further structure and organisation.

Most Acts adopt a sequence that attempts to be logical. So early sections might deal with definitions before addressing the key purpose of the law. There then might follow additional provisions and perhaps administrative requirements. Towards the end there will be interpretation sections and matters relating to commencement, application and extent. Commencement will either be on a specific date, or subject to subsequent secondary legislation dealing with the matter, by reference to a step or measures taken by a Secretary of State.

The word 'extent' refers to the geographical reach of the Act: unless it says it specifically applies to a particular country, the presumption is that it will apply to the whole of the United Kingdom. As Wales (and indeed Scotland and Northern Ireland) have devolved assemblies, consideration must be given to the ambit and reach of a statute, and care must be taken by drafters of laws to ensure that the distinction between devolved and reserved matters is observed.

Frequently there will be schedules at the end of the Act, typically where there is a significant volume of detail that would be inappropriate for a section or sections. So with the HRA 1998 this is where the ECHR would appear.

Applying this template to our example of the HRA 1998, there are 22 sections dealing with the incorporation into UK law of the ECHR together with schedules detailing the convention itself.

Thus this is an insight into the structure and layout of Acts of Parliament. There is no substitute for reading some of them yourself to understand their flavour and approach. Continuing with the HRA 1998, **Figure 4.3** presents a snapshot of it, with marginal notes explaining its various aspects.

Figure 4.3 Structure and layout of an Act of Parliament – the Human Rights Act 1998

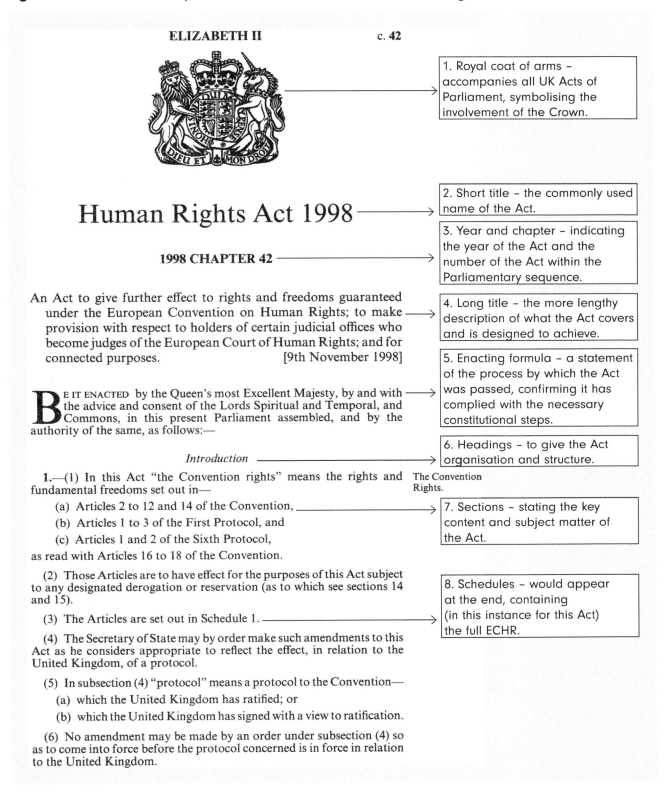

ELIZABETH II   **c. 42**

1. Royal coat of arms – accompanies all UK Acts of Parliament, symbolising the involvement of the Crown.

Human Rights Act 1998

2. Short title – the commonly used name of the Act.

1998 CHAPTER 42

3. Year and chapter – indicating the year of the Act and the number of the Act within the Parliamentary sequence.

An Act to give further effect to rights and freedoms guaranteed under the European Convention on Human Rights; to make provision with respect to holders of certain judicial offices who become judges of the European Court of Human Rights; and for connected purposes.   [9th November 1998]

4. Long title – the more lengthy description of what the Act covers and is designed to achieve.

B E IT ENACTED by the Queen's most Excellent Majesty, by and with the advice and consent of the Lords Spiritual and Temporal, and Commons, in this present Parliament assembled, and by the authority of the same, as follows:—

5. Enacting formula – a statement of the process by which the Act was passed, confirming it has complied with the necessary constitutional steps.

Introduction

6. Headings – to give the Act organisation and structure.

1.—(1) In this Act "the Convention rights" means the rights and fundamental freedoms set out in—

The Convention Rights.

   (a) Articles 2 to 12 and 14 of the Convention,

   (b) Articles 1 to 3 of the First Protocol, and

   (c) Articles 1 and 2 of the Sixth Protocol,

as read with Articles 16 to 18 of the Convention.

7. Sections – stating the key content and subject matter of the Act.

   (2) Those Articles are to have effect for the purposes of this Act subject to any designated derogation or reservation (as to which see sections 14 and 15).

   (3) The Articles are set out in Schedule 1.

8. Schedules – would appear at the end, containing (in this instance for this Act) the full ECHR.

   (4) The Secretary of State may by order make such amendments to this Act as he considers appropriate to reflect the effect, in relation to the United Kingdom, of a protocol.

   (5) In subsection (4) "protocol" means a protocol to the Convention—

   (a) which the United Kingdom has ratified; or

   (b) which the United Kingdom has signed with a view to ratification.

   (6) No amendment may be made by an order under subsection (4) so as to come into force before the protocol concerned is in force in relation to the United Kingdom.

4.6   An early Act of Parliament

The earliest known Act of Parliament still in force is the Statute of Marlborough 1267 (Distress). This is the short title. The year and chapter are 1267 Chapter 1 52 Hen 3. The preamble refers to 'manifold troubles and dissensions', and there is no mention of the Lords and Commons for the simple reason that, in those days, the king alone was able to pass laws.

The main body of the Act then goes on to discuss the alleged problem of 'many great men' taking 'revenges and distresses' on their neighbours. The Act alludes to one of the key principles of the Magna Carta 52 years earlier, stating that all persons 'shall receive justice in the King's Courts', thus confirming the concept of the rule of law.

4.7   Public and Private Bills

4.7.1   How Acts of Parliament begin their existence

All new (as opposed to routine) legislation stems from the same basic source: a groundswell of opinion that a particular law is required to deal with a specific problem or matter. This is as true today as it was in the olden days when the main influencers were the Crown, clergy, nobility and gentry. Then, powerful men would lobby for things to happen. Nowadays, there are more egalitarian pressure groups, consumer organisations, charities, businesses, local communities and other organisations all capable of making the case for a new law.

The initial step, in Parliament at least, towards the creation of a new law would be the production of something called a Green Paper. This would contain outline proposals for, and discussion of, laws that are still at a formative stage.

If a Green Paper receives a favourable response and continues to have sufficient support within Whitehall, the next stage would be a White Paper. This is a more developed and nuanced document, issued by the Government as a statement of policy, setting out proposals for legislative change. This could be accompanied by debate within Parliament.

Green and White Papers may invite comments from the general public. Note that not all Bills begin life as a Green or White Paper. A good example would be some of the laws passed in 2017–2019 relating to the various attempts to legislate on the UK's departure from the EU. The main Withdrawal Act 2018 was subject to a White Paper but other, supplementary and satellite, Bills dealing with Brexit were not. This was because those Bills were drafted in a hurry by backbench MPs without Government support.

The terminology here is important: 'Bills' are the laws as drafted, discussed, amended and progressed through Parliament; 'Acts' are the final version of the law as given the Royal Assent.

As noted above, Bills, whether Public or Private, are known as primary legislation to distinguish them from secondary or delegated legislation. It is a presumption that all primary legislation will apply throughout the UK unless the statute specifically states otherwise.

4.7.2   Public Bills

Public Bills concern matters affecting the public as a whole. Virtually all Acts of Parliament that have any relevance to the majority of the population begin life as Public Bills. Examples of these abound. For instance, in the first five months of 2020, the monarch gave Royal Assent to Public Acts across areas as diverse as the Northern Ireland budget, payments to farmers, restrictions on the early release of terrorists, supply and appropriation (financial matters generated by the Treasury), and measures relating to the coronavirus pandemic.

Public Bills fall into two broad categories. First there are Government Bills, introduced by a minister as part of the Government's legislative programme, prompted either through medium and long-term planning or short-term responses to emergency, as with the 2020 pandemic. The ones mentioned above are examples of these. Second, there are Private Members Bills, which are non-Government-sponsored Bills introduced by backbench MPs.

4.7.2.1 Government Bills

We will look at Government Bills in a moment, when considering categories of primary legislation. Government Bills are to be contrasted with Private Members Bills.

4.7.2.2 Private Members Bills

Private Members Bills are very much the scraps of the legislative process, thrown to MPs by an executive that is always keen to give the impression of inclusivity. In reality, the Government controls the legislative timetable tightly with the result that few of these find their way into law.

The process begins with a ballot for the entitlement to present a Bill. A lucky number of MPs – 20 is the current headcount – are then able to present their titles and nominate a date for a second reading. MPs can also introduce Bills by way of a 10-minute rule procedure, or what is called an ordinary presentation. These two methods only operate once the ballot Bills have taken precedence, so they have limited significance. This is not to say the alternative is particularly attractive, because Private Members Bills themselves have limited parliamentary time, typically no more than 13 Fridays in each session. Consequently very few become law. For some MPs the process is in reality a way of publicising a particular hobby horse. They have little expectation of the Bill becoming an Act. Other MPs have a genuine hope of progress, only to see their hopes dashed through lack of parliamentary exposure.

So only the fortunate minority progress onto the statute book. The subject matter for successful Private Members Bills is a varied one. They usually have a beneficial public interest flavour that attracts Government support, without which the item would be unlikely to move forward. Successful initiatives from the 2017–2019 parliamentary session include the Assaults on Emergency Workers (Offences) Bill from the Labour MP for Rhondda, Chris Bryant; the Homes (Fitness for Human Habitation and Liability for Housing Standards) Bill from the Labour MP for Westminster North, Karen Buck; and the Parental Bereavement (Leave and Pay) Bill from the Conservative MP for Thirsk and Malton, Kevin Hollinrake.

In 2019 the 20 successful MPs had no opportunity to forward their agendas because Parliament dissolved shortly after the ballot. Parliamentary rules, and the intervening election, meant they lost their chance.

The list of unsuccessful Private Members Bills for the period 2017–2019 includes measures relating to refugees' families, overseas electors, votes for younger people, licensing of taxis and the regulation of physician associates. In the past, unsuccessful topics have included initiatives relating to the breeding and sale of dogs (1997/8), the control of hedges (1998/9), organic food and farming targets (2000/1) and football spectators (2001/2) (source: House of Commons Briefing Paper Number 04055, 6 February 2020).

Some Private Members Bills appear on a repeat basis, languishing in the foothills of parliamentary business for years before becoming conventional wisdom. This happened to the Bill that sought to ban fox hunting, as presented by Michael Foster and Ken Livingstone at different times in the 1990s and 2000s. Eventually the Labour Government elected in 1997 embraced the concept, and so the Hunting Act 2004 was passed, prohibiting the hunting of wild mammals with dogs.

4.7.3 Private Bills

Private Bills affect particular people, organisations or localities. They can start in either House of Parliament. They must be publicised in a suitable manner. Any group or individual directly affected by a Bill's proposals can object to it through petitions. Examples of Private Bills from the 2017–2019 parliamentary session include the City of London Corporation (Open Spaces) Act 2018, the New Southgate Cemetery Act 2017, the Middle Level Act 2018, relating to navigation on the Peterborough fens, and the University of London Act 2018.

4.8   Hybrid Bills

Sometimes Acts of Parliament combine elements of both Public and Private Bills. These are called Hybrid Bills, reflecting the fact that they contain elements relevant to both the general public and private or commercial organisations.

Good examples of this would be the Channel Tunnel Rail Link Act 1996 and the Crossrail Act 2008. The former combines the public interest in travel between the UK and the continent with the need to recognise the rights and obligations of the Tunnel's operators. The latter combines the public interest in a new rail service crossing London from East to West with the commercial interests of the companies and organisations constructing and operating the service. Also, these Acts required consideration of the use of both public and private land, something else that orientates such legislation towards the Hybrid variety.

4.9   Categories of Acts of Parliament

One might wonder exactly what causes Bills to begin life, and then morph into Acts of Parliament. The simple answer is that society requires it. Parliament and the people collectively deem it to be the best way of enacting the national will. Broadly, there are four different triggers for the creation of primary legislation:

- party political manifesto pledges, which result in promises that a successful party, when in Government, believes it should keep. This sort of initiative has a loose relationship to vote seeking by MPs who have one eye on retaining their seats at the next election;

- administrative, technical and managerial matters necessary to the organised functioning of Government; some but not all of this is relatively mundane;

- changes in the nature of society, and the demands of the electorate, over short, medium or long-term timescales; and

- unexpected events, and even crises, that require the immediate and pressing attention of the executive.

We can now look at examples of each of these. One piece of primary legislation, going to the heart of the UK mindset, deserves initial mention. This is because it reflects all four of the categories mentioned above. The Act in question had part of its origins in a party's manifesto promise. From its inception it has dealt with a host of routine administrative and managerial matters. Over time it has changed form and shape to reflect the wish of the electorate. And finally it has also embraced the need to be flexible in times of crisis. The Act in question is the National Health Service Act 1946, an initiative resulting from a pledge by the Labour Party, and indeed many years of debate before that.

The long title of the Act says it is to 'provide for the establishment of a comprehensive health service for England and Wales'. Section 1(1) states:

it shall be the duty of the Minister of Health ... to promote the establishment in England and Wales of a comprehensive health service designed to secure improvement in the physical and mental health of the people ... and the prevention, diagnosis and treatment of illness, and for the purpose to provide or secure the effective provisions of services.

These simple and clear statements provide the foundations for a service that most of us take for granted today. It also combines the four reasons for generating new legislation mentioned above:

- It stemmed from a political promise, and politicians today still use health legislation for electoral purposes.
- It allows for the administration, management and growth of the NHS.
- It reflects changes in society, such as the demand for increased primary care, and the decrease in hospital beds, as a result of lifestyle developments in the population, for instance.
- It has also proved flexible in times of crisis, as during the 2020 pandemic.

Note there are similar NHS Acts for Scotland and Northern Ireland.

We now consider other Acts illustrating the four reasons for creating primary legislation.

4.9.1 Manifesto pledges/vote seeking

These reasons are demonstrated by Conservative party initiatives in 1979–1997 relating to the privatisation of public utilities. An example would be the Gas Act 1986, which allowed for the sale of shares in British Gas to the general public. This was in pursuit of the stated objective of greater efficiency in the provision of services, and the simultaneous growth of a shareholder democracy. The Railways Act 1993 privatised the rail network and continues to provide a framework for operational matters today. Acts privatising electricity and water utilities also continue to impact on our lives today.

4.9.2 Administrative and technical matters

A good example would be the various Finance Acts that accompany every Parliament. The Finance Act 2019 for instance contains provisions relating to income tax rates, capital allowances, reliefs and the like. These provisions, much loved by tax experts, have electoral consequences but the reason for the Acts is essentially administrative and an annual event.

4.9.3 Societal change

One thinks of Environmental Acts that have grown up recently. One recent Environmental Bill was accompanied by a statement that it would 'enshrine environmental values at the heart of government policy', something few people would overtly contest in principle.

4.9.4 Crisis management

This sort of legislation would include Acts restricting the freedom of the individual during the 1939–1945 war, for instance the Emergency Powers (Defence) Act 1939, repealed in 1959. A more recent example would be the Coronavirus Act of 2020, passed in a hurry to deal with previously unforeseen issues.

4.10 The influence of popular protest on Acts of Parliament

Legislators and the general public have an often tense relationship. Some people have a suspicion Parliamentarians lose touch with their roots once they arrive in London. Sometimes individuals do not believe an email or letter to Parliament will have any effect. They therefore resort to protest, usually within the law and sometimes outside it. The question therefore becomes whether such agitation contributes positively to the pluralism of our legal system. In particular, should popular protest be allowed to influence legislation? This is something for the reader to decide but here are two examples that make it clear mass demonstrations have their place in the creation, amendment and termination of legislation.

4.10.1   The Enclosure Acts

Three centuries and more ago, a predominantly landowning ruling class embraced a particular property-based policy. This was to create large portfolios of land at the expense of smaller plots taken from individuals. The result was a reduction in land used by the general populace, and the aggregation of economically useful resources into larger units available to big landowners.

This caused economic hardship and resulted in protest. The Inclosure Act 1773 represented an attempt to bring some sort of order to an inflammatory situation. During the 19th century a compromise of sorts arose: the rights of smaller landowners would be respected, and common land would be preserved for the use of the public, rather than being accumulated by the powerful. The current status quo, and the existence of tracts of parkland and woodland for public use around the country, would not have arisen without manifestations of popular discontent and their influence on the legislative process.

4.10.2   The Local Government Finance Act 1988

Three decades and more ago, a predominantly property-owning class embraced a particular policy relating to home ownership, tax and the provision of local services. The Community Charge, popularly known as the poll tax, replaced a levy on the ownership of property – known as 'rates' – with one on individuals living in a given household.

This was unpopular on a number of fronts, but the broad thrust of protest revolved around the perceived notion that the local fiscal burden had shifted from those who could afford it – owners of property – to those who could not. Protest turned into riots, the most serious of which was at the end of March 1990. The Conservative Government of John Major recognised the limitations of the Community Charge provisions – in particular difficulties in the registration of individuals and collection of funds – and replaced them in the Local Government Finance Act 1992.

The 1992 Act created the Council Tax, which endures today. The 1988 Act is still in force, incidentally, and contains tax regimes of a different sort in relation to non-domestic property.

4.10.3   Thoughts on these case studies

Various points arise. They indicate that the development of law, and influences on the legal system in England and Wales, are far from genteel and academic. They suggest there is a complex relationship between voters, members of the public who do not necessarily vote, parliamentarians, and laws created in London. Some points for discussion or reflection therefore include:

- how power is apportioned within society, and in particular the continuing importance of property as a driver for the creation of law. This could result in laws on behalf of property owners (such as help to buy legislation) or to assist those perceived to be excluded or disenfranchised in some way (such as measures protecting tenants, or dealing with the homeless);

- the ability of popular protest to influence law making;

- the way in which Acts of Parliament are not always popular – of course, good governance will always involve difficult decisions that may be lacking in attractiveness; and

- the continuing ability of the legislative process to compromise in order to retain a sense of equilibrium within society as a whole. Examples of this would be the abandonment of the Community Charge, and steps to decentralise power from Westminster to the regions as contained in the Local Democracy, Economic Development and Construction Act 2009.

By way of conclusion, it can be seen there are numerous reasons for the creation of legislation. These range from public protest on the part of the general population to an instinct for self-preservation on the part of legislators keen to look good in the eyes of their constituents.

Figure 4.4 sets out various factors to consider. This does not pretend to be comprehensive – you can reflect on other influences too, and add them in.

Figure 4.4   Influences on the creation of legislation

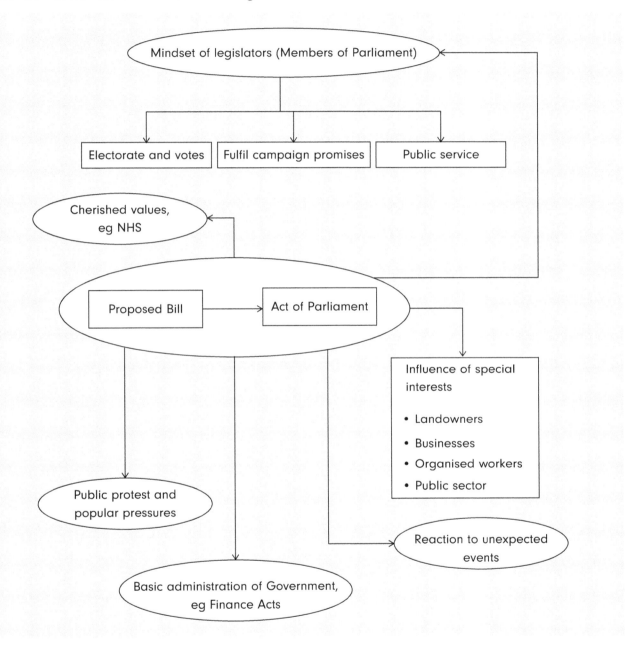

4.11   Consolidating and codifying legislation

Not all law is new. Legislation may also be consolidating or codifying, in which case it does not necessarily make or change law.

You need to be careful as to the distinction between these terms. *Consolidation* is where one statute re-enacts law that was previously contained in several different statutes (for example, the Insolvency Act 1986). There is a (rebuttable) presumption that consolidation does not materially change earlier legislation. Effectively, consolidating Acts 'tidy up' the law.

Codification is where all the law on some topic, which may previously have been covered by common law, custom and even statute(s), is brought together in one new statute. The codifying statute may, if necessary, change the pre-existing law. A good example is the Theft Act 1968.

The law relating to the sale of goods is also an interesting example. The law originated in medieval mercantile custom, much of it was then embodied in case law and then the law was then codified by the Sale of Goods Act (SGA) 1893. Over the course of nearly a century, this Act was the subject of a number of statutory amendments, which changed and repealed parts of it. These statutes were then consolidated into the SGA 1979, which makes the seller of goods in certain circumstances liable to the buyer if the goods supplied are not of satisfactory quality. That Act has since been the subject of further amendment, notably by the Sale and Supply of Goods Act 1994. Further changes to the SGA 1979 were made by the Consumer Rights Act 2015.

Consolidation and codification can be summarised in tabular form as follows:

Legislation	Can it include case law?	Can it change the old law?
Consolidating	No	Usually not
Codifying	Yes	Yes

4.12 The devolved settlement for Wales and its legislation (and a comment on Scottish matters)

In the 1960s and 1970s a renewed desire for independence developed in Wales. A referendum in 1979 rejected the concept. A further referendum in 1997 asked the Welsh people if they would like a degree of self-government through their own Parliament, a National Assembly (or Senedd). The question was answered in the affirmative, and accordingly the Government of Wales Acts 1998–2017 provide for the establishment of the National Assembly together with the necessary devolved powers.

Under the Wales settlement, as it is called, there is a trade-off between those areas of policy that remain the preserve of central government, and other areas that fall within the embrace of the National Assembly. This is called the Reserved Powers Model. Schedule 7A of the Wales Act 2017 mentions matters reserved to the UK Parliament. Schedule 7B sets out certain restrictions on the Senedd's powers.

To give an example of areas legislated on by the National Assembly, primary legislation for the period 2017–2020 deals with the abolition of certain defences relating to the punishment of children, fees relating to the renting of homes, minimum prices for the sale of alcohol, learning needs, a landfill disposals tax and certain public health measures.

Acts passed in 2022 include the Welsh Tax Acts etc (Power to Modify) Act 2022, relating to fiscal matters, and the Tertiary Education and Research (Wales) Act 2022. Both these statutes point to the increasing maturity, and confidence, of the Welsh establishment in embracing its increased responsibilities.

The format of an Act of the National Assembly essentially echoes that of Westminster primary legislation. The coat of arms at the top of an Act is unique to Wales, but otherwise there are the usual elements, eg the short title, long title, year and chapter, date, enacting formula, substantive sections and any necessary schedules.

The various stages for the passing of a National Assembly Act are as follows. After the Bill is formally introduced, stage one begins with an initial committee report. There is then consideration of correspondence, a timetable and consideration by the finance committee. A debate on general principles in plenary, followed by a financial resolution, come next. Stage two consists of a detailed committee stage where amendments are considered. Stage three involves a plenary consideration of amendments. The Bill then receives the Royal Assent.

Scotland and Northern Ireland have their own devolved settlements. This manual deals with the jurisdiction of England and Wales, primarily, and not Scotland. Therefore, it tends to skirt around Scottish issues. But recent developments around devolution have reminded us that events at Holyrood – the home of the Scottish Parliament – inevitably impact on the other home nations.

First, the Supreme Court in the *Lord Advocate's Reference* [2022] UKSC 31 ruled that the Scottish administration cannot, on its own, legislate for a second independence referendum. You may be aware that the Scottish electorate rejected independence at the first referendum in 2014. Their Lordships in 2022 held that the topic of independence, being a devolution argument, was a political event with political consequences and reserved to London as a matter of the Union and sovereignty. This decision thus reinforces the established concept of parliamentary supremacy resting with Westminster, not the regions.

Secondly, the UK Government in January 2023 made a s 35 order under the Scotland Act 1998 to refuse Royal Assent to the Gender Recognition Reform (Scotland) Bill 2022. The Scottish National Party (SNP) had made the Bill an important part of its legislative programme. Gender is devolved to Holyrood. Equality matters, however, remain reserved to Westminster. The Secretary of State for Scotland, in a statement of reasons, accepted that the Bill was within the competence of the Scottish Government but still had a significant effect on reserved law. Once again, therefore, the London Parliament has asserted its supremacy. SNP ministers have duly published a petition challenging the UK Government's decision, and court action awaits.

Summary

In this chapter you have considered the importance of Acts of Parliament and their place within the legal system of England and Wales. You have pondered the following:

- the use of language within an Act of Parliament, and how Acts can be interpreted in different ways by different people;

- the principle of supremacy of Parliament, with an acknowledgement of the role of EU law as a backdrop, which could become increasingly historical as the Brexit process continues;

- the distinction between an Act, which is primary legislation, and statutory instruments and byelaws, which are secondary legislation;

- the format and layout of a typical Act of Parliament;

- examples of some Acts of Parliament;

- what happens when Acts of Parliament are subject to protest by elements of the population;

- codifying and consolidating Acts; and

- Acts passed by the Welsh National Assembly.

Sample questions

Question 1

The Domestic Pets Act 2020 (fictitious) states in its long title that it is 'An Act to regulate the keeping and use of domestic pets; and for purposes connected therewith'. Part of its purpose is to put into law a vets' code of practice ('the code') in relation to welfare.

Which of the following statements about the Act is correct?

A   If the Act is silent on its extent, it applies just to England and Wales.

B   The code would be contained in various sections of the Act.

C   It would not be possible for the Act to come into force on the date of Royal Assent, as that would give pet owners no notice of changes to the law.

D   The code would in all likelihood appear as a schedule to the Act.

E   The code would in all likelihood appear as a subsequent statutory instrument.

Answer

Option D is correct – the code would appear as a schedule to the Act. This is because it is conventional for additional documents and extra material, which are too bulky to be contained within the sections of an Act, to appear as schedules instead.

Option A is wrong because where an Act is silent as to its extent it applies to the whole of the UK. Option B is wrong because as explained above the code would go into a schedule. Option C is wrong because any Act can stipulate that it comes into force on the date of Royal Assent (in this instance it is possible pet owners would be alerted to any changes to the law through the media and other publicity). Option E is wrong because a statutory instrument would only be required where there is significant extra detail required to supplement the original Act.

Question 2

The Government passes the Alcoholic Drinks Act (fictitious), which for public health reasons prevents anyone drinking more than one pint of beer a day. There is a section that says the provision cannot be amended for 10 years.

Which of the following statements is true?

A   Judges can declare the Act invalid.

B   It will be a consolidating Act if it deals with previous Acts and court decisions.

C   The Act must be preceded by a Green Paper.

D   Parliament can amend the Act next year despite the section to the contrary.

E   The Act would be a Hybrid Act as it combines public health matters with individual choice.

Answer

Option D is correct. Parliament, being supreme, can always amend its own laws. It would simply vote to amend the 10-year stipulation.

Option A is wrong because judges do not have the power to declare an Act of Parliament invalid – they can comment on it when judging a case, and they can make a declaration of incompatibility under the Human Rights Act 1998, but they have no power to declare it unlawful. Option B is wrong because a consolidating Act does not incorporate previous case law – that would be a codifying Act.

Option C is wrong because not all Acts require a Green Paper, which is essentially a discussion document. Option E is also incorrect – a Hybrid Act combines elements of both Public and Private Acts, and this Act is aimed at the whole population rather than any one company, group or geographical area. There is therefore no Private Act aspect to it.

Question 3

A solicitor specialising in constitutional matters is advising the Government. A minister wishes to steer an important public health Bill through Parliament. The House of Commons ('the Commons') has passed the Bill but the House of Lords ('the Lords') has twice rejected various key provisions. There appears to be a stalemate in that the Bill cannot progress. The Speaker of the Commons has not certified the Bill as meeting the necessary criteria for progressing the Bill without the say-so of the Lords.

Which of the following best explains the advice the solicitor should give the minister?

A   Consideration should be given to use of the Parliament Acts to progress the Bill without the agreement of the Lords.

B   The Bill should be amended as there is no support for it.

C   The Bill should be presented for Royal Assent now.

D   The minister should suggest the Prime Minister seeks to reform the Lords.

E   The Bill should be withdrawn and replaced by a statutory instrument.

Answer

Option A is correct. The Parliament Acts allow a Bill to progress through Parliament even without the support of the Lords. An example of this would be the Hunting Act 2004.

Option B is wrong because there is support for the Bill in the Commons, and over time the legal system and constitution have recognised the Commons as having greater importance in the legislative process than the Lords. Option C is wrong as a Bill cannot be presented for Royal Assent without progressing through the correct procedures, which here would be the Speaker of the Commons' certification that the requirements of the Parliament Acts have been met.

Option D is wrong as reform of the Lords, although a regular topic of debate within society, would take many years and wouldn't assist in the Government's immediate objective of passing the relevant Bill. Option E is wrong because a statutory instrument (SI) can only stem from an earlier Act of Parliament, so it would not be appropriate for a SI here to 'replace' the Bill.

5

Statutory Interpretation

SQE1 syllabus

This chapter will enable you to achieve the SQE1 assessment specification in relation to functioning legal knowledge concerning statutory interpretation.

Note that, for SQE1, candidates are not usually required to recall specific case names or cite statutory or regulatory authorities. Cases are provided for illustrative purposes only, with the exception of *Pepper v Hart* (see later), which is both a case name and a rule of law.

Learning outcomes

By the end of this chapter you will be able to apply relevant core legal principles and rules appropriately and effectively, at the level of a competent newly qualified solicitor in practice, to realistic client-based and ethical problems and situations in the following areas:

- ambiguity in language;
- problems in interpretation of statutes and language;
- rules of construction when interpreting statutes, and the purposive approach;
- the need to interpret statutes in the context of client problems and court cases;
- the Human Rights Act 1998 and issues of interpretation;

- rules of language;
- intrinsic and extrinsic aids to interpretation; and
- certain key presumptions of law.

5.1 Introduction

Lawyers and judges spend a great deal of time interpreting legal documents. Inevitably issues of interpretation arise. Here are some legal documents that require interpretation:

- Contracts (ie agreements between people or organisations)
- Wills (documents where individuals leave their possessions to others on death)
- Workplace notices (for instance relating to health and safety)
- Property 'deeds' (detailing ownership of homes, boundaries, and related matters)
- Consumer paperwork (ie receipts or guarantees accompanying goods purchased in stores or via the internet)
- Acts of Parliament

We will focus in this chapter on the last of these – the interpretation and application of Acts of Parliament.

We have seen from earlier chapters that some key sources of English law include case law and legislation. Others would include EU law and the ECHR, and these will be revisited later.

Case law and legislation have historically had something of a tense relationship, as legislators balk at the judiciary interpreting their laws with a free hand. One half of Parliament – the House of Commons – is elected whereas judges are not, which adds another element to the dynamic. We could have a considerable debate on how, and why, and in what manner appointed officials such as judges should be able to influence laws passed by elected representatives.

Be that as it may, the courts continue to have the key role of interpreting legislation, for the simple reason that they are best positioned to do so. However conscientious parliamentary draftspeople strive to be, the language used is not always as clear as it could be. This is not necessarily the fault of those tasked with drafting laws: it could be the result of oblique, jumbled and downright confusing statements from those instructing them.

Alternatively, changes in our society mean that statutes are being applied to issues that even the most far-sighted drafters could not have foreseen. Who could have predicted the prevalence of internet shopping when the Sale of Goods Act was passed in 1979, when the internet was unknown; or contemplated websites when defining 'publisher' for the purposes of the Defamation Act 1996, when libel was mainly something to be found in newspapers and magazines?

This chapter sets out the rules used by practitioners and the courts in seeking to resolve the hugely significant matter of how to interpret legislation. Over time, various rules and principles of statutory interpretation have arisen, and these can guide judges – and therefore us as well – when deciding the meaning of legislation. The application of these rules can affect the outcome of a case when argued in court. Accordingly, knowledge of these principles, and the ability to use them effectively, are essential tools in a lawyer's armoury.

5.2 Why is statutory interpretation necessary?

Statute is the primary source of law in England and Wales. Creators of legislation must often turn complex concepts and subtle nuances into reliable and, in an ideal world, clear language. As time passes statutes need to be applied in a world beyond the imagination of even the most forward-thinking drafter. Some statutes can become outdated, or out of context, and even lead to absurd consequences.

So, the simple answer as to why we need to interpret legislation is to ensure a fair and just result. That often involves resolving ambiguities to find a suitable meaning.

The best place to start this discussion is with ordinary language, unrelated to legislation or the law. Even straightforward sentences can have more than one meaning. Consider this example:

> He fed her dog food.

You can probably guess the problems caused by the conflicting interpretations here. We need to understand the context before deciding whether the man is feeding the woman's dog, or giving the woman the dog's meal.

Ambiguity also arises where there is an absence of punctuation. Consider this sentence:

> Those who can do those who can't teach.

Without punctuation, this sentence either means nothing at all, or perhaps something garbled, or on closer inspection perhaps that people who are enabled to achieve things will rise above, or outdo, those who have no talent for teaching. But the meaning changes if you add punctuation as follows:

> Those who can, do; those who can't, teach.

The sentence now has an altogether different sentiment. It means that dynamic people press on and do things; those who aren't capable of action and achievement instead become teachers (I'm sure you will agree this is an unfounded generalisation, and that many of us know teachers who are high achievers in every way).

Another instance of ambiguity would be a sign in a highrise building saying: 'Do not use lifts in case of fire'. This is capable of two interpretations. The first is that you should not use the lift *in case you cause a fire*. This is a somewhat literal interpretation of the sign. The true intention of the sign is that lifts should not be used *when there is a fire*. As we shall see in a moment, interpreting something in too literal a manner can have its disadvantages.

5.3 The meaning of words

Despite the best endeavours of people who draft statutes, the meaning of words is not always clear. Sometimes the drafting is at fault, using a vague or general word rather than a specific word, and sometimes a word has more than one meaning. This arises because the tradition in English legal drafting (unlike the continental system) is to be all-embracing. Traditionally in England and Wales we attempt to cover every eventuality. Therefore the statute or document must be both general and precise. You may think the solution is to choose words that have only one meaning. However, this is easier said than done.

5.4 An example of how one word within a statute can cause debate

The meaning attributed to just one word was considered in the case of Corkery v Carpenter *[1951] 1 KB 102. The issue of statutory interpretation that arose here related to the word 'carriage'.*

The facts are these. A man was in possession of a bicycle. He was behaving in a rowdy manner on the street. He was drunk. The police arrested him. The issue before the court was whether a 'carriage' as mentioned in the Licensing Act 1872 could include a bicycle. The suggestion in favour of the defendant was carriage should really mean something pulled by a horse, or alternatively someone with cattle, or a steam engine, but not a method of self-propulsion involving peddles.

The prosecution took a different tack: they argued the thrust of the law was to prevent public disorder by drunken people travelling along the highway, and this should include someone with a bike. The court found the defendant guilty. It used its powers of interpretation to update the 1872 Act to the 1940s and 1950s, and had little hesitation in declaring the word 'carriage' to include a bike. As the defendant was found to be on a highway and behaving drunkenly, the prosecution duly succeeded. This illustrates the significance of a single word in an Act, and the importance of judicial interpretation in dispensing justice.

5.5 Problems of interpretation

There is another reason why we need to interpret legislation: to decide whether it applies to a particular set of facts. We will look at this now.

Assume there is a statute that says: 'It a criminal offence to wear red socks in a public place'. Various problems could arise with this wording. Let's say Albert wears crimson socks on his way to work. There could be a debate as to the colour of his socks. Is crimson a type of red, or something different?

Other elements of the offence could give rise to issues of interpretation as follows:

- 'wear' – what if Albert on a cold day was using a red sock as a glove on his hand? Would this be considered the *wearing* of a sock?

- 'socks' – what if he was wearing one red and one blue sock? Albert could be forgiven for arguing that he is not breaking the law because he is not wearing 'red socks' (plural).

- 'public place' – what if Albert was in a shopping centre – is that a public place?

To assist in solving problems of interpretation of this sort, over time various rules of construction have arisen. Effectively, these are judicial 'tools'.

5.6 Rules of construction

The word 'construction' means the same as 'interpretation'. When we talk about the 'rules of construction' we mean a method used by lawyers and academics to assist in the interpretation, understanding and administration of legislation. And when we talk about rules we really mean principles – in other words, guidance rather than a strict and rigid formula.

As you study this area of law, you will notice different outcomes may result from the use of different rules. Indeed, how a judge arrives at the use of a particular rule of construction is a matter of choice. It could be they give grave consideration to previous cases, academic sources and the thoughts of legislators.

Alternatively, they might simply arrive at what they believe to be the correct decision, and then choose whichever rule helps them arrive at that result. Or they might not give much thought to the application of a particular rule at all, as there is no obligation on judges to state which rule they are using, and therefore it may not always be easy to work this out from the judgment. Indeed, it is entirely permissible to interpret legislation without using any particular rule of construction. Judges don't have a handbook in the same way that, say, drivers have the Highway Code or retailers have a Code of Practice.

Let's look now at some rules of construction.

5.6.1 The literal rule

This rule states words in a statute must be given their plain, ordinary and literal meaning.

If the words are clear, they must be applied, even though the intention of the legislator may have been different, or the result is harsh or undesirable.

 An explanation of the rule was given in the Sussex Peerage Case *(1844) 1 Cl & Fin 85:*

> *If the words of the statute are in themselves precise and unambiguous, then no more can be necessary than to expound those words in that natural and ordinary sense. The words themselves alone do, in such a case, best declare the intention of the law giver.*

This is the oldest of the rules, and like all the rules of construction is in common use today. It is perhaps the starting point for construction of legislation, on account of the desire of most judges to give effect to the apparently obvious meaning of an Act.

One aspect of this rule is a reliance on the ordinary natural meaning of words, something that might lead you to look up any doubtful words in a dictionary. This is perfectly logical because we start from the assumption that words in an Act have been carefully chosen in order to carry out the intention of Parliament, or that of the person on whose behalf the document has been drafted.

5.6.1.1 Problems with the rule

You will remember Parliament is sovereign, and judges cannot declare an Act of Parliament unlawful. Leading on from this is the notion – or perhaps it is in fact more of a generalised and perhaps wistful concept, given the huge significance of court decisions and the role of precedent (something discussed elsewhere in this book) – judges are not supposed to 'make' law. They are only supposed to *interpret* the law. Of course this is a fine distinction. But even so, judges are very much aware they should not thwart the will of Parliament, and for this reason the judiciary often likes to begin its process of interpretation with the literal rule.

But the irony of this rule is its very use may defeat the intention of Parliament and lead to absurd results. In other words, the practice of interpreting a statute or part of it literally could result in an outcome not intended when the Act was passed.

5.6.1.2 Some examples of the use of the literal rule

 For instance, in the case of Whiteley v Chappell *(1868) LR 4 QB 147 the defendant pretended to be someone who was on the voters list but who had died. He was charged with impersonating 'a person entitled to vote' but was found not guilty. The reluctant conclusion drawn by the court was Whiteley could not be convicted of the statutory offence because the person he impersonated was dead, and on a literal construction of the relevant statutory provision, the deceased was not 'a person entitled to vote'.*

With Whiteley *the law resulted in a declaration of innocence. The literal rule can also lead to injustice. For example, in the case of* London & North Eastern Railway Co v Berriman *[1946] AC 278, a railway worker's widow was denied compensation because her husband was killed when oiling points and this was 'maintaining' the line – not 're-laying or repairing it', as required by the relevant statute.*

It is unlikely these decisions reflected the intention of Parliament. However, the literal rule does not take into account the consequences of a literal interpretation, only whether words have a clear meaning that makes sense in that context. As Lord Esher stated in 1892:

> If the words of an Act are clear, then you must follow them even though they lead to a manifest absurdity.

The underlying concept is, if Parliament does not like the literal interpretation, it can always amend the legislation. After all, Parliament is supreme within the context of UK law making.

5.6.2 The golden rule

The golden rule is an adaptation of the literal rule. It provides, where there are two meanings to a word or words, they should be given their ordinary meaning as far as possible, but only to the extent they do not produce an absurd or totally obnoxious result.

As Lord Wensleydale stated in *Grey v Pearson* (1857) 6 HL Cas 61:

> the grammatical and ordinary sense of the words is to be adhered to, unless that would lead to some absurdity or inconsistency with the rest of the instrument, in which case the grammatical and ordinary sense of the words may be modified, so as to avoid that absurdity or inconsistency, but not farther.

5.6.2.1   An instance of the golden rule

 In Adler v George *[1964] 2 QB 7, the defendant was convicted by the magistrates of an offence under s 3 of the Official Secrets Act 1920, because he had obstructed a member of His Majesty's forces while 'in the vicinity of any prohibited place'. In this instance, the defendant was inside Royal Air Force (RAF) Marham, and he argued he could not therefore have been 'in the vicinity' of the base as he was actually inside RAF Marham itself.*

The court decided it would be an absurd result for the defendant to be found not guilty. The purpose of the Act was to protect military bases and as such it would be nonsense for a distinction to be made between someone being 'on' the base rather than 'in the vicinity'.

Comment

Incidentally, when we discuss cases of this sort we are not asking you to agree with the judicial reasoning behind them. You are free to opine that with the Act in question Parliament should have been more specific in making a distinction between someone's presence inside an area as opposed to 'in the vicinity' of an area – and the court should (or perhaps could) have found the defendant not guilty. Either way it is important you use your powers of analysis and intellectual decision-making in coming to a conclusion.

Note this rule may be used in two ways, that is:

*   a narrow sense; and
*   a wider sense.

5.6.2.2   Use of the rule – the narrow sense

The golden rule is applied most frequently in a narrow sense where there is some ambiguity or absurdity in the words themselves. As Lord Reid stated in 1962, if a word is capable of more than one meaning, you can choose between those meanings, 'but beyond this you cannot go'. This was the situation in the *Adler* case above.

Here is another example of the narrow use of the golden rule. The case of R v Allen *(1872) LR 1 CCR 367 required an interpretation of s 57 of the Offences Against the Person Act 1861. This section provided that:*

> *Whosoever being married, shall marry any other person during the lifetime of his spouse ... shall commit the offence of bigamy.*

The court said the word 'marry' can in the context of the Act mean two things. It could mean either 'to become legally married to a person' or 'to go through a marriage ceremony'. If the word 'marry' had been given the first interpretation, it would be impossible for anyone ever to commit this offence. The court therefore interpreted the word as meaning 'going through the ceremony' of marriage. It therefore chose the more appropriate of two meanings. Here, the literal interpretation would be completely inappropriate as a means of deciding the case, as on a literal reading of the Act the law would be impossible to infringe.

In *Adler v George* as we have seen the defendant argued the natural meaning of 'vicinity' was the state of being '*near* in space' rather than *in* the Air Force station. Lord Parker CJ rejected the argument as follows:

> It would be extraordinary, I venture to think it would be absurd, if an indictable offence was thereby created when the obstruction took place outside the precincts of the station, albeit in the vicinity, and no offence at all was created if the obstruction occurred on the station itself.

This is a good example of the narrow use of the golden rule. There was more than one interpretation of the word vicinity, and the court opted for the interpretation that it believed avoided an obviously absurd result.

5.6.2.3 Use of the rule – the wider sense

The second use of the golden rule is in a wider sense – to avoid a result that is obnoxious to principles of public policy, even where words have only one meaning. When we say obnoxious, we mean contrary to good governance in the broadest sense.

 In Re Sigsworth *[1935] Ch 89, the court had to consider the meaning of s 46 of the Administration of Estates Act 1925, in a case where the son had murdered his mother. Because there was no will, under the intestacy rules as set out in the Act, the son would have inherited his mother's residuary estate as her 'issue', ie child.*

There was no ambiguity in the Act, but the court held the son, as issue, could not inherit because this would produce an obnoxious result, contrary to the general principle of public policy that a murderer should not reap the fruits of his crime. As a consequence, the judges effectively wrote into the Act the 'issue' would not be entitled to inherit where he had killed the deceased.

 More recently, in Inco Europe Ltd v First Choice Distribution *[2000] 1 WLR 586, the House of Lords (now the Supreme Court) stated words could be added to a statute to resolve an obvious drafting error. In this instance, a right of appeal from the High Court to the Court of Appeal was added to s 9 of the Arbitration Act 1996, despite the absence of any relevant words in the statute.*

Part of the judgment of Lord Nicholls in the Inco Europe *case illustrates the way in which judges approach the matter of interpretation, and in particular the wider sense of the golden rule:*

Several features make it plain that something went awry in the drafting. What the section was seeking to do, but on a literal meaning of the language failed to achieve, is also abundantly plain ... I am left in no doubt that, for once, the draughtsman slipped up. Given the intended object of the section is plain, it should be read in a manner which gives effect to parliamentary intention.

The key part of this passage of the judgment comes in the last few words. Lord Nicholls is saying that the object of the section is clear and so it should be interpreted in such a way as to make sense overall, rather than focusing on the exact wording of the provision, which as he says was in all likelihood founded on an error.

5.6.3 The mischief rule

The mischief rule requires the interpreter of the statute to ascertain the legislator's intention.

'Mischief' is itself a good example of a word having more than one meaning. To many of us it means impish behaviour. But the original meaning, which is the one intended here, was 'harm or wrong', and it is this latter version of the word that is relevant to statutory interpretation. When using this rule, the court considers what 'mischief', or defect in the existing law, the statute was intended to remedy.

5.6.3.1 An example of the mischief rule

The Licensing Act 1872 stated a person found drunk in charge of a 'carriage' on the highway can be arrested without a warrant. In *Corkery v Carpenter*, mentioned above, the court took the view that the word 'carriage' could include a bicycle for the purpose of construing the Act.

5.6.3.2 Application of the rule in this instance

Here, the Act was aimed at drunken persons in charge of some form of transportation and the exact nature of that transportation was interpreted widely. As part of its decision the court decided the mischief the statute intended to remedy was injury to the public from drunken drivers in order to preserve public order. The court therefore actively considered why the Act was passed in the form it took, and drew the necessary conclusions from that, namely that the defendant's behaviour while on, or with, the bike broke the law.

5.6.3.3 Further example of the mischief rule

 In DPP v Johnson [1995] 1 WLR 728 the court was required to consider the provisions of the Road Traffic Act 1988 relating to consumption of alcohol.

Sometime before the events in question the defendant's doctor had prescribed an injection of aqueous solution of benzyl alcohol for a spinal injury. The nature of the treatment involved the slow release of medical alcohol into the defendant's system. Later, the police stopped the defendant in his vehicle. His breath specimens showed him to be over the limit.

Using the mischief rule, the court held the word 'consuming' should not be restricted to oral intake, and could include the injection of alcoholic fluid into the defendant's spine. The court decided the intention of the 1988 Act was to protect the public from the driving of vehicles by people influenced by alcohol, no matter how absorbed into the driver's body.

The flowchart in **Figure 5.1** summarises in diagrammatic form the three rules of statutory interpretation. At the start of the chart is the law requiring explanation. Around this flow the three concepts. Sometimes they stand alone, often they require consideration together. Our illustration here links them together.

Figure 5.1 Three rules of statutory interpretation

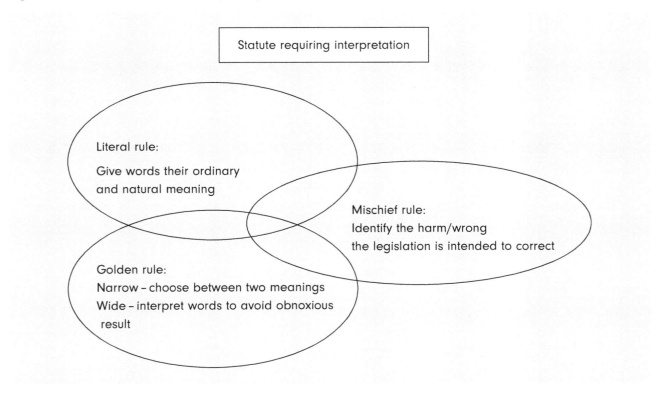

5.7 Interaction between the different rules of construction

The effect of these rules of construction is that different decisions can be reached, depending upon which is used on the given facts. For example, in *Whiteley v Chappell* (above), you will recall that the defendant was found not guilty of the offence of impersonating 'a person entitled to vote', because the person had died and therefore was not entitled to vote in the literal meaning of the words.

In this situation the court almost certainly favoured the defendant on the basis of another principle of justice, namely that a guilty verdict can only be arrived at where guilt is 'beyond reasonable doubt'. Also, where Acts of Parliament impose criminal sanctions, the wording of the offence must be extraordinarily precise. And in the event of any ambiguity judges should give the benefit of any doubt to the defendant.

Even so it is possible the court could have arrived at a different conclusion and found the defendant guilty. If this had happened, one could argue the mischief rule would support such an outcome. This would be on the basis the relevant legislation was designed to prevent people from voting unlawfully, something the individual charged had in all likelihood intended.

There will always be scope for widespread distinctions to emerge from the different rules.

🔲 *This can be demonstrated by the case of* Smith v Hughes *[1960] 2 All ER 859, which considered the meaning of s 1(1) of the Street Offences Act 1959. Under this section it is an offence for a prostitute to solicit in a 'street or public place'. Here, various women were arrested and charged. They were not actually in the street but were inside their homes, tapping on their windows and calling to attract attention.*

The literal rule would have resulted in the women being acquitted. The reason is that they were in their own homes and, using the plain, ordinary or literal meaning, 'a street or public place' does not include private residences.

But instead Lord Parker used the mischief rule and stated that the aim of the Act was 'to clean up the streets, to enable people to walk along the streets without being molested or solicited by common prostitutes'. You can see how the language of judges changes over time, and it is unlikely today a court would address the matter in quite such stark terms. But the principle of interpretation remains sound: the court considered the ambit of the Act by reference to the issue it sought to correct.

Contemporary comment

Two interesting satellite issues arise from this case. First, the maxim that an 'English person's home is their castle' – the idea that people are relatively free to do as they wish within the confines of their own home, so long as it is lawful – did not apply here. Second, one wonders if similar laws at the time curbed, say, men who caused a disturbance through drinking alcohol, partying and carousing within their homes. Looking back in time, we can see that sometimes the law is as capable of fostering discrimination as much as resolving it.

5.8   The purposive approach and the culture of EU law

The purposive approach is a more modern style of interpreting statutes, and it has overtaken, or in the views of some supplemented, the mischief rule in relevance. Here, judges look at the reasons why the statute was passed and its purpose, even if it means departing from the ordinary meaning of the words. This approach has been influenced by our membership of the EU and the provisions of the ECA 1972.

5.8.1   The EU

 Of particular significance is the ECJ decision in Case C-106/89 Marleasing SA v La Comercial Internacional de Alimentacion SA. *This involved the interpretation of an EU Directive (a form of legislation you will consider when discussing EU law in more detail elsewhere). The judgment states:*

> *It follows that, in applying national law, whether the provisions in question were adopted before or after the directive, the national court called upon to interpret it is required to do so, as far as possible, in the light of the wording and the purpose of the directive in order to achieve the result pursued by the latter and thereby comply with ... the Treaty.*

This passage states two important points. First it confirms the principle of supremacy of EU law, and in particular the Treaty of Rome 1957 as updated, over national law. This is something you would expect to reverse with Brexit. Second, and of relevance to the subject matter of this chapter, it mentions the word *purpose*, thus articulating the purposive concept.

This means in effect that judges should consider the policy behind the words of any given law. As you would expect after decades of exposure to EU law, the principle today is not confined purely to EU law. It is instead well and truly embedded in the law of our jurisdiction.

Note that as a matter of practice, the mischief rule and the purposive approach tend to be used interchangeably and it could be said that the two principles are so close as to make any distinction between them somewhat academic.

5.8.2 The impact of the purposive approach

The purposive approach is important as it strongly implies that questions of a wider economic or social nature should be considered by the courts when assessing the impact of legislation on disputes.

 This is illustrated by Litster v Forth Dry Dock and Engineering Co Ltd *[1989] 1 All ER 1134. Here, employees were dismissed one hour before a business was transferred to a new owner. The employees claimed they were unfairly dismissed. Regulation 5 of the Transfer of Undertakings (Protection of Employment) Regulations 1981 (TUPE) (SI 1981/1794) (a statutory instrument that implemented an EU Directive) provided that a transfer shall not terminate the contract of any person employed 'immediately before the transfer'.*

The House of Lords (now the Supreme Court) read in the additional words 'or would have been so employed if he had not been unfairly dismissed before the transfer' for a reason connected with the transfer. This meant that the Court took the view it was obliged to achieve the purpose of the EU Directive, which was to protect employees on the transfer of a business.

5.8.3 The purposive approach and other rules of interpretation

The decision in *Litster* indicates the proximity of the mischief rule to the purposive approach. They are first cousins – or even siblings – in the broader family of statutory interpretation.

It could also be argued that the golden rule would have protected the employees in *Litster*, as it would be 'absurd' to allow employers to evade liability under the law by dismissing their employees minutes before signing the transfer document under TUPE.

As you will see from your study of EU law elsewhere, decisions of the ECJ are stated under the ECA 1972 to be binding on our courts. The purposive approach, as a result of decades of exposure to EU influence, has thus permeated all levels of judicial decision-making in the UK and is an integral part of our legal system. We hesitate to predict the future when discussing Brexit, but one expects the principle to endure even after any departure from the EU.

5.8.4 Concluding thoughts on the purposive approach and EU law

As we have indicated elsewhere, with Brexit one would not expect courts to be bound so closely in the future to EU laws, but the principle remains clear: courts are prepared to interpret UK legislation in a broad manner to help achieve a just result, bearing in mind the intent of the legislation under consideration.

5.9 The Human Rights Act 1998 and principles of statutory interpretation

The HRA 1998 enacted the ECHR 1950 into UK law. Section 3 of the HRA 1998 states that 'so far as it is possible to do so, primary and subordinate legislation must be read and given effect in a way that is compatible with the Convention rights'. If the court cannot achieve this, it may make a declaration of incompatibility in respect of the relevant piece of legislation.

The ECHR occupies a somewhat ambivalent position in UK jurisprudence. Very few people object to the principles mentioned in the Convention. The differentiation comes between those who regard the rule of law within the UK sufficient as it is; those who believe the ECHR represents some sort of unwarranted entryism into the UK's constitutional operation, a bit like extremists taking over a political party; and those who regard the protections provided by the Convention as adding a valuable layer of support for individual freedoms.

The Brexit debate was conducted to political mood music concerning the HRA 1998. Some people believe it, and thus the Convention rights contained within it, should be repealed as part of the departure culture. Others take the view the Convention is now beneficially embedded into UK law, a concept illustrated by cases such as *Benkharbouche* [2017] UKSC 62, a case mentioned elsewhere in this book.

In the context of rules of construction it is useful to see how courts have approached s 3.

 The matter was considered by the House of Lords (now the Supreme Court) in the case of R v A (No 2) [2002] 1 AC 45.

The House of Lords had to consider whether s 41 of the Youth Justice and Criminal Evidence Act (YJCEA) 1999 was compatible with a defendant's right to a fair trial under Article 6 of the ECHR. The details of this provision, relating to restrictions on the ability of a defendant to cross examine the complainant in a rape trial, need not detain us. The ruling indicated the YJCEA 1999 did not infringe the right to a fair trial.

In so doing the judiciary used a broad, rather than a literal, approach to the contents of the YJCEA 1999 in order to give effect to s 3 of the HRA 1998. R v A thus provides an interesting illustration of three aspects of construction: first, the purposive approach; second, what some consider to be a thin line between judges interpreting the law on the one hand and creating it on the other; and third, the impact of the HRA 1998 on UK law making.

5.10 Rules of language

5.10.1 Introduction

Rules of language are similar to rules of construction in that they are general principles for judges and other lawyers to consider when interpreting legislation. We do this most obviously when considering particular scenarios and cases that confront our clients. As with rules of interpretation, judges will not always make it clear in their judgments which, if any, of the rules of language they utilise.

Incidentally these rules of language are keen on the use of Latin. The modern law does not usually encourage Latin, but we make an exception here. Note also judges can use rules of language and rules of construction alongside each other.

5.10.2 *Noscitur a sociis* (recognition by associated words)

Noscitur a sociis literally means 'known by the company it keeps'. One way of approaching this is to think of it as: a word derives meaning from surrounding words.

Here's an example. A clause in a lease agreement states:

> Only the following animals are permitted in this block of flats – dogs, cats, hamsters and gerbils.

Would this include a leopard? Common sense would suggest that leopards would not be included. However, lawyers must be able to justify this conclusion, and the rule *noscitur a sociis* helps in confirming this, because the clause contains an exhaustive list of animals, which have the common theme of domesticity. Looking at the animals in the list, they are all essentially ones that ordinary people could keep in their homes – in other words, pets. One would not expect 'cats' in this context to include a wild and feral leopard.

Noscitur a sociis was used to assist in the interpretation of the Factories Act 1961, which required that all 'floors, steps, stairs, passageways and gangways' had to be kept free from obstruction.

The question that the court had to decide in Pengelly v Bell Punch Co Ltd *[1964] 1 WLR 1055 was whether a floor used for storage came under the provisions of the Act. The court held that, as all the other words were used to indicate passage, a floor used exclusively for storage did not fall within the Act.*

5.10.3 *Eiusdem generis* (of the same kind or nature)

The rule in *eiusdem generis* is this: if a general word follows two or more specific words, that general word will only apply to items of the same type as the specific words.

The case of Wood v Commissioner of Police of the Metropolis *[1986] 1 WLR 796 illustrates the principle. The issue under discussion was the definition of an offensive weapon. This was defined by s 4 of the Vagrancy Act 1824 as being:*

> *any gun, pistol, hanger, cutlass, bludgeon or other offensive weapon.*

Mr Wood was charged under this Act for using a piece of broken glass, which had fallen out of his front door, as a weapon.

We have no way of reading the minds of the judiciary, but one way of coming to a conclusion on the matter would be as follows. First, are there general words following a list of specific words? Second, if so, what type are the specific words? Third, as a matter of interpretation under this rule, you would expect any new items to be added into the list only if they are of the same type as the specific words. So first, in Wood's case, there are general words ('or other offensive weapon') following a list of specific words. Second, the specific words are all of the same type in that they refer to objects designed and used as weapons. Because of this, they have a common feature. Third, as a matter of interpretation, broken glass is not of the same type as those weapons, because it was not created as a weapon, ie something intended to cause injury. The conclusion was that the piece of glass was not therefore a weapon.

Note: It might have been different if the relevant wording of s 4 had been '... any other offensive weapon whatsoever'. The addition of the word 'whatsoever' would indicate that the legislature had not discounted the idea that a sliver of glass, used to cause injury, could fall within the section.

Another example of the use of the rule of eiusdem generis *can be found in the case of* Powell v Kempton Park Racecourse Co *[1899] AC 143. Here, the House of Lords (now the Supreme Court) had to decide whether s 1 of the Betting Act 1853, which prohibited the keeping of a 'house, office, room or other place' for the purpose of betting, applied to Tattersall's Ring, an outdoor area at the racecourse. The court said it did not, as the specific places were all indoors, and so the Ring could not be included within the ambit of 'other place'.*

Is there an easy way of summing up the distinction between these two rules? You have to look carefully at the law in question, but one distinction is that *noscitur a sociis* tends to involve the restrictive impact of a particular list of words, whereas *eiusdem generis* deals with specific words influencing a subsequent general phrase.

Take the *Pengelly* case, concerning the use of a floor for storage, as an instance of *noscitur*, and the *Powell* case as an example of *eiusdem*. With the former, the Factories Act provided a closed list of the types of floors that had to be kept free from obstruction. With the latter, there is a non-exhaustive list of indoor spaces in the relevant section of the Betting Act. So with the first, the floor in question did not 'keep company' with the list in the Factories Act. With the second, the outdoor betting venue did not fall within the preceding specific list. Hence the distinction.

5.10.4 *Expressio unius est exclusio alterius* (expressing one thing excludes another)

Expressio unius est exclusio alterius means 'to express one is to exclude others'; therefore mention of one or more specific things may be taken to exclude others of the same type. This rule applies where there is a list of words that is not followed by general words.

For example, in R v Secretary of State for the Home Department, ex p Crew *[1982] WL 221744, the rule was used to exclude the father of an illegitimate child from rights under the immigration law of the time, because the definitions section mentioned the mother alone.*

In R v Inhabitants of Sedgley *(1831) 2 B & Ald 65, the court considered whether the poor rate levied on occupiers of 'lands, houses and coal mines' under the Poor Relief Act 1601 could be levied on owners of other types of mine. Here the court held that the poor rate could not be so levied. They said the list in the 1601 Act was definitive, or 'closed'. This makes sense, because the Act expressed the word 'coal' in front of 'mine'. We can therefore logically conclude that the framers of the Act intended the list to be restricted to that particular type of mine rather than including other sorts. At least, that was the decision of the judges in this case, and who are we to disagree?*

5.10.5 Applying the rules of language

Here are two examples for us to consider by way of case study.

First, a utility statute governing the provision of electricity required an employer to protect employees from 'danger from shock, burn or other injury'.

The question arose as to whether tripping would be covered by the words 'other injury'. The eiusdem generis *rule was applied in this case (*Lane v London Electricity Board *[1955] 1 All ER 324), to conclude that tripping could not be included. You might wonder why, but there is a logic to it: shocks and burns are both dangers from electricity, and in the context of the Act the general phrase 'or other injury' did not encompass tripping. Falling over, you see, is not of the same type as electrocution.*

Second, an Act states '"equipment" includes any plant and machinery, vehicle, aircraft, and clothing'.

The conclusion of the court in Coltman v Bibby Tankers Ltd *[1988] AC 276 was that a ship could be 'equipment'. The thinking is that the insertion of the word 'includes' means there is no expression of one concept in order to exclude another. So the list mentioned in the Act allowed some leeway for the inclusion of ships. This is therefore an example of* expressio unius.

Note: You might consider the principle of *noscitur* too, on the basis that a ship 'keeps company' with the other items mentioned there. You could have quite a debate on that point and as lawyers we should welcome that (shouldn't we?). If you conclude yes, the *noscitur* rule applies. If you conclude no, then it would have no application.

Of course, when considering rules of language, you should not ignore rules of construction. You would be correct to think that in the examples here either or both of the mischief and the golden rules could be used to arrive at a decision.

Figure 5.2   Summary of some rules of language

- *Noscitur* – a word derives meaning from surrounding words

- *Eiusdem* – specific words influence the meaning/impact of subsequent general words

- *Expressio* – a list of specific words will usually be taken to exclude words which are not in that list

5.11   Aids to interpretation

5.11.1   Introduction

In addition to using the rules of construction and language discussed above, it is open for courts to use various sources to assist in their understanding. These sources are traditionally dubbed 'aids to interpretation'. As you will see, they range from referring to other parts of the Act in question to that most basic of resources, the dictionary.

5.11.2   Intrinsic aids (the use of the statute itself)

This principle means a judge can refer to other parts of the statute in order to understand the particular section under discussion. The statute must be read as a whole, and the words read in context (note the overlap with 'rules of language'). Any words that have been debated by Parliament and are part of the statute are legitimate aids. Therefore, the long and short titles, preamble (not commonly found in modern statutes), punctuation and headings may be used.

Marginal notes are not debated in Parliament and are not normally relied on by courts.

For example, in *Chandler v DPP* [1964] AC 763, the court decided that in s 1 of the Official Secrets Act 1911, 'espionage' included sabotage. The marginal note that read 'spying' was not used as an aid.

But this is far from an absolute rule. Upjohn LJ, when delivering the reserved judgment of the court in *Stephens v Cuckfield Rural District Council* [1960] 2 QB 373, 383, stated with reference to a marginal note of an Act then under consideration:

> While the marginal note to a section cannot control the language used in the section, it is at least permissible to approach a consideration of its general purpose and the mischief at which it is aimed with the note in mind.

An interpretation section in an Act may also be used, but is subject to contrary intention in the text. Most Acts now contain a section that defines the key words used. For example, s 9 of the Road Traffic (New Drivers) Act 1995, states that in the Act 'notice' means 'notice in writing'.

5.11.3   Extrinsic aids (aids outside the statute itself)

5.11.3.1   Interpretation Acts

The Interpretation Acts give definitions of words commonly found in legislation. For instance, s 6 of the Interpretation Act 1978 states that, in all legislation, the masculine includes the feminine, and the singular includes the plural unless indicated otherwise.

5.11.3.2 Dictionaries

Dictionaries can be referred to when a word has a broader general meaning as opposed to something specifically legal. Dictionaries would most obviously have value where judges are using the literal approach, but they can be used in a variety of contexts where courts wish to justify their reasoning in terms of clear language.

5.11.3.3 Other statutes

The court may look at other statutes, whether recent or long-standing. However, just because a word has been interpreted in one Act does not mean it will be interpreted the same way in another.

5.11.3.4 Hansard

Hansard is the verbatim reporting system of proceedings in Parliament. Traditionally, parliamentary debate on a Bill, prior to it becoming an Act, was treated with caution by the courts. This was because judges generally were reluctant to focus on the sayings of legislators in Westminster in case it deflected them from reading the Act in its written form.

However, over time there was some relaxation of this strict rule, particularly in order to identify the 'mischief' which an Act is intended to remedy.

 This culminated in Pepper v Hart *[1993] 1 All ER 42, when the House of Lords (now the Supreme Court) decided that courts could refer to parliamentary material recorded in Hansard if:*

(a) the statute is ambiguous or obscure, or its literal meaning leads to an absurdity; and

(b) the material consists of clear statements by a minister or other promoter of the Bill.

This case concerned teachers at an independent school whose children could be educated for one-fifth of the school's normal fee. The question was whether reduced school fees were to be treated as a taxable benefit under s 63 of the Finance Act 1976. There was an ambiguity in the statute, and the issue arose as to whether the court could take account of statements made by the Financial Secretary to the Treasury during the report stage of the Bill. The House of Lords decided that it could.

5.11.3.5 Other sources

Courts regularly refer to academic sources such as established textbooks and commentaries by learned figures. You might find for instance, *Halsbury's Laws of England* are mentioned by a judge, or Guenter Treitel is referred to in the context of contract law, or Judah Benjamin consulted in relation to the sale of goods, and so on. These venerable figures have long since died – in Benjamin's case a while after he was a Cabinet officer in the Confederate Government during the American Civil War – but this does not diminish their continuing influence on the legal system today.

By way of just one example, in *DPP v Johnson*, referred to earlier, Schiemann J referred to a quotation from Bennion, *Statutory Interpretation,* 2nd edn (1992) 513, and to a related dictum that had been applied recently in another case.

Figure 5.3 Some aids to interpretation

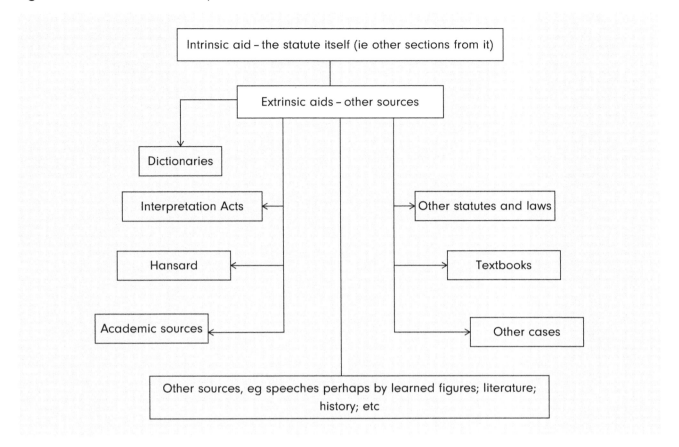

5.12 Presumptions

5.12.1 Introduction

In addition to rules and aids, courts apply certain presumptions in interpreting legislation as follows. A presumption is an understanding by judges and the legal profession a certain rule applies, with no need to prove that rule or establish its source.

5.12.2 When do presumptions apply?

A presumption applies when there is a long-standing principle at stake. It is always possible to rebut any presumption, ie to bring strong evidence to prove that Parliament had a contrary intention. Note the use of the word 'strong'. If it was only necessary to bring 'evidence', there would be no presumption at all.

Imagine an old-fashioned pair of scales. If they are evenly balanced, then it is only necessary for one party to bring *some* evidence to tilt the scales either way. However, if they are already tilted in favour of one party, the other must bring enough evidence not only to even things out, but go further and tilt them in his favour. Therefore, this evidence must be strong.

You will find presumptions in various areas of the law, but for statutory interpretation here are some examples:

- *Presumption against alteration of the common law.* Unless the statute expressly states an intention to alter the common law, the interpretation that does not alter the existing law will be preferred.

- *Presumption against the retrospective operation of statutes.* Where an Act of Parliament becomes law, a presumption arises that it will apply only to future actions. This is particularly important in relation to taxation and criminal law cases. However, some legislation is specifically stated to have retrospective effect; an example is the War Crimes Act 1991, which allows the prosecution of those suspected of committing acts of atrocity during the Second World War.

- *Presumption against criminal liability without guilty intention* (mens rea). There is a presumption in favour of ensuring a suspect has the *mens rea* or guilty mind in criminal matters. When creating new criminal offences, Parliament does not always define the *mens rea* required. In these cases, the presumption will be applied, ie there can be no conviction without the defendant having the necessary mindset. We should be aware, however, that some offences are ones of 'strict liability', where someone can be found guilty in any event. Needless to say, legislation of this sort needs to be precise and specific for this principle to apply.

In Sweet v Parsley *[1970] AC 132, a school teacher was convicted of drugs offences after her tenants were discovered growing cannabis in her rented house. She was found guilty, despite her lack of knowledge of the situation, but the decision was later overturned by the House of Lords (now the Supreme Court) using this presumption. This has a link to the next presumptions, namely:*

- *The presumption against deprivation of the liberty of the individual.* Accordingly, any ambiguity in a penal or criminal statute will be interpreted in favour of the citizen.

- *The presumption against deprivation of property or interference with private rights.* As you would expect in a jurisdiction preoccupied with the ownership of land, and its link to wealth and power, the law takes a dim view of depriving people of property.

- *The presumption against binding the Crown.* Unless there is a clear statement to the contrary, legislation is presumed not to apply to the Crown. An interesting discussion point here is income tax and its application to the royal family. At the moment both the King and the Prince of Wales pay voluntarily, thus indicating that the usual mandatory rules of the tax regime don't apply.

5.13 Applying the various rules: a scenario

In the case of *R v G* [2003] UKHL 50, the House of Lords (now the Supreme Court) was asked to consider an appeal from the Court of Appeal (Criminal Division) on the meaning of recklessness for the offence of criminal damage, under the Criminal Damage Act 1971. Criminal damage includes offences ranging from graffiti to arson. Recklessness requires the taking of an unjustified risk.

Here are some points from the case. We have mentioned the applicable rule and a brief explanation:

- A Lord Justice stated the word 'maliciously' conveys the impression that some ill-will is required against the person whose property is damaged. Rule: this is an example of the literal rule, as the court is giving the word 'maliciously' its ordinary meaning.

- The court referred to Working Paper No 23 of 1969 by the Law Commission. Rule: this is use of an external aid, namely a paper from the Law Commission.

- The court dismissed the need for 'fine and impracticable distinctions' and preferred the ordinary meaning of 'reckless'. Rule: this would again be a use of the literal rule, as the court was reinforcing the ordinary natural meaning of 'reckless'.

- The court referred to Archbold, *Pleading, Evidence and Practice in Criminal Cases* (1979). Rule: this is an example of the use of an external aid. Archbold incidentally is a well-renowned source of guidance on criminal law, and you will have the chance to explore it further when you deal with criminal matters elsewhere.

- One Lord Justice stated that 'conviction of serious crime should depend on proof not simply that the defendant caused an injurious result to another, but that his state of mind when so acting was culpable'. Rule: this is a statement conveying the presumption against criminal liability without guilty intention.

5.14 Conclusion

In some ways statutory interpretation mirrors the imperfect, but workable, nature of the legal system of England and Wales.

The process begins with a surge of support for a particular Bill. Parliament then passes an Act. The provisions of that Act require interpretation by clients and their lawyers. In the event of a dispute, the courts can provide clarification.

This sounds clinical and efficient. But it is not. At every stage there is uncertainty. What exactly does a particular section of an Act mean? You as a lawyer might have one view. Another lawyer might have a different opinion. A client might well despair of the possible variations.

However, we live in an uncertain world. It is not part of the job of a lawyer to provide certainty when none exists, unless a client specifically requests us to embark on that quest, and is aware of the pitfalls of chasing what could be an unobtainable goal. The best advice to a client is to reach an accommodation, or some form of settlement, so a precise analysis of any given section of an Act becomes unnecessary, or at least less important. And in many ways that reflects the strength of our society, legal system and constitution: the ability to resolve differences in a civil manner, without upsetting the status quo in too dramatic a fashion.

There is an intensely practical footnote to this. We should be wary of advising clients to entertain disputes about the meaning of legislation or indeed of any law. Such arguments might involve the use of lawyers. Legal advice is horrendously expensive, or at least can be. Disagreements suck up time. They ruin relationships. They turn previously equable individuals into bitter and twisted cynics. So, whether considering the law in the academic sense or the practical, we should beware rushing headlong into litigation. Clients should be advised as such.

Summary

The law is not static – it is constantly evolving to meet the needs of an ever-changing society. Its ability to adapt to new situations is a strength of our legal system. The principles of statutory interpretation are the key to this flexibility, as well as providing an essential tool in remedying obvious absurdities in statutes.

In this chapter, you have studied the way in which statutes are interpreted and the means by which this is done. You have considered the long-established literal, golden and mischief rules, and their more recent companion, the purposive approach. We have also discussed the rules of language, the aids to interpretation and certain key presumptions.

As a result, you have begun to develop your ability to interpret legislation, to understand its effect and to use this knowledge to solve legal problems. You have also looked at the role of courts in this process through case law interpretation, and have thus observed the link between legislation and the role of judges in its application.

Sample questions

Question 1

A man is being prosecuted in the magistrates' court. The court is considering the Guard Dogs Act 1975, one section of which is particularly unclear.

The following statement is made by the chair of the bench of magistrates when explaining their verdict:

'One comes to the rule that a penal statute, where there is an ambiguity, should always be construed in favour of the citizen who may find himself the subject of the penalty'.

Which rule of interpretation has the Court used here?

A   The mischief rule.

B   The purposive rule.

C   The golden rule.

D   The literal rule.

E   The presumption against alteration of the common law.

Answer

Option C is correct. This is an example of the narrow use of the golden rule. The court is choosing what it regards as the correct option between two different possibilities, in order to avoid an absurd result. In this instance, the court is alluding to the idea any statute must be clear as to its impact. It is thus also incorporating the important presumption any ambiguity in criminal legislation should favour the citizen.

Option A is wrong because there is no indication of the issue that the Act is intended to address, ie there is no apparent mischief mentioned here. Option B is wrong because the purposive rule requires a broad interpretation that goes beyond the specific meaning of an Act, and this has not happened here. Option D is wrong because a literal interpretation is not possible where, as is the case here, there is ambiguity. Option E is wrong because there is no common law point at issue here.

Question 2

A man is being tried in the magistrates for being drunk in charge of a bicycle. The prosecution say a bicycle is a carriage. He is pleading not guilty on the basis the bike is not a carriage.

The court has referred to a dictionary, which states a 'carriage' is an obsolete and archaic term, except in the case of wheeled vehicles or railway carriages.

Which of the following statements about the use of the dictionary is correct?

A   It is an internal aid.

B   It is an extrinsic aid.

C   It is illustrating the purposive rule.

D   It is being used to apply the rule of *eiusdem generis*.

E   The dictionary's use is illustrating the presumption against deprivation of liberty of the individual.

Answer

Option B is correct – dictionaries are extrinsic aids, and useful to courts in helping decide the issues.

Option A is wrong because an internal aid means that the court is referring to another part of the same Act that is being discussed as part of the court case. That is not the case here. Option C is wrong because there is no purposive approach in this instance. Option D is wrong because, although there is a reference to wheeled vehicles and railways, there is no specific list influencing a subsequent general category. Option E is wrong as there is no discussion of the applicable presumption here.

Question 3

A solicitor is advising a client who owns mobile caravans on the interpretation of a particular section of the Motor Homes Act (fictional) ('the Act'), which governs substandard facilities in certain moveable holiday accommodation. The solicitor researches the passage of the Act through Parliament. She discovers a speech from a backbench MP saying the Act is needed to regulate and control low quality hygiene facilities in vehicles used as motor homes, travelling homes and mobile caravans. Further research by the solicitor confirms this is indeed the aim of the Act, which mentions mobile caravans.

Which of the following rules is most likely to apply to the interpretation of the Act?

A   The rule in *Pepper v Hart*, because of the speech by the MP.

B   The mischief rule, because there is an indication of the wrong the Act is intended to correct.

C   The golden rule, because there is a need to choose between 'substandard' and 'low quality', ie two possible interpretations of the Act.

D   The literal rule, because the word 'substandard' needs no expansion or clarification.

E   The rule in *noscitur a sociis*, because the MP's speech mentions a list of vehicles and the client needs to know if mobile caravans are included.

Answer

Option B is correct. The mischief rule means someone interpreting an Act of Parliament can, or should, assess the reason for the Act's provisions, to assess the problem that the Act is designed to correct. The mischief rule would be relevant as there is mention of the Act's aims.

Option A is wrong because the rule in *Pepper v Hart* applies to statements made by ministers responsible for guiding legislation through Parliament, not statements by backbench MPs. Option C is wrong because there is no suggestion a choice needs to be made between two alternative interpretations of the Act or a section of it. Option D is wrong because the word 'substandard' is not clear and thus is unlikely to be subject to the literal rule. Option E is wrong because the *noscitur* rule applies to words that are not specifically stated, and here 'mobile caravans' are mentioned by the Act.

6 Judiciary and Personnel of the Court System

SQE1 syllabus

This chapter will enable you to achieve the SQE1 assessment specification in relation to functioning legal knowledge concerning the judiciary and personnel of the court system.

Note that, for SQE1, candidates are not usually required to recall specific case names or cite statutory or regulatory authorities. Cases are provided for illustrative purposes only.

Learning outcomes

By the end of this chapter you will be able to apply relevant core legal principles and rules appropriately and effectively, at the level of a competent newly qualified solicitor in practice, to realistic client-based and ethical problems and situations in the following areas:

- magistrates and their work in the criminal justice system;
- the significance of magistrates being lay people rather than legally qualified;
- some of the advantages and disadvantages of the magistrates' system;
- the role of district judges in the magistrates' courts;
- Crown Court judges and their work, and that of recorders;
- the role and significance of juries;
- the role of district judges in the civil justice system;
- how district judges are essential to the smooth functioning of the civil justice environment;
- County Court judges and their workload;
- High Court judges and their roles;
- how judges are promoted to the Court of Appeal;
- the role of the senior judiciary;
- codes of conduct and how they impact on the judiciary;
- some instances of how judges are merely human;

- the number of judges at work in the legal system currently;
- judicial diversity statistics; and
- political officers with legally significant roles.

6.1 Introduction

How are judges appointed? Some commentators from the 19th century were not convinced it was on the basis of merit. Here is one view from the operetta *The Mikado* by WS Gilbert and Sir Arthur Sullivan (1885, D'Oyly Carte Opera Company). A top official, Koko, is explaining (in song) how he got the job:

Taken from the county gaol by a set of curious chances;

liberated then on bail on my own recognisances;

wafted by a favouring gale as one sometimes is in trances;

to a height that few can scale ...

Judges still use the word 'recognisances' today. It means providing a sum of money in return for temporary freedom – an aspect of the 'bail' mentioned. Releasing someone on bail allows an arrested or charged person to go free pending their subsequent surrender to the authorities. The implication of this passage is Koko was in trouble with the police, and was sufficiently wealthy to buy his release. He then climbed the career ladder to the top job, helped no doubt by his status and contacts, whilst other less fortunate individuals made do with ordinary jobs. Although this song is satirical, there is a dose of accuracy to it. The law, then as now, carries a whiff of privilege for those who operate at its higher echelons. The difference today is there is a general acceptance it should become more inclusive.

Koko's position was Lord High Executioner – as close as you can get to a top judge in the world portrayed by the duo.

The career path has changed somewhat since the 1880s. Now, judges emerge from a process governed by the Judicial Appointments Commission, an independent body that selects candidates for judicial office. The process in its modern form stems from the provisions of the Constitutional Reform Act 2005 as amended by the Crime and Courts Act 2013. The aim of this chapter is to examine the people and personalities who emerge from that process. We shall look at their roles and culture. We are interested in getting under their skin, and peeling back the formal image to reveal the human, social and practical mechanisms underneath. In this way we can meet the SRA SQE1 specification and at the same time examine the part the judiciary plays in maintaining the legal system and contributing to its sources of law.

We have chosen to start at the bottom of the ladder and work upwards, thus examining first the workhorses of the system, who are magistrates in the criminal sphere and district judges in the civil environment. We will then progress up the respective criminal and civil chains until we reach the pinnacle of the profession with the senior judiciary.

6.2 Brief overview of judiciary and the court system

The Courts Act 2003 at Part One refers to maintaining the court system. It states there is a general duty on the Lord Chancellor – who is now the Secretary of State for Justice, a politician within the Government of the day – to ensure there is an efficient and effective system to support the carrying on of the business of the courts. In general, regardless of the detail of any legislation, the operation of the courts is one of partnership between the Lord Chancellor, Lord Chief Justice (the most senior judge), and other members of the senior judiciary.

They are supported by a host of hard-working and efficient administrators who generally operate within tight cost boundaries, making a tricky job even more difficult. Financial constraints, and their impact on the administration of justice, are for discussion elsewhere, but the bare facts are these. His Majesty's Courts and Tribunals Service (HMCTS) supervises the operation of courts and tribunals within England and Wales. It is an independent agency of the Ministry of Justice. In 2018/19, HMCTS had annual gross expenditure of £2 billion and employed 16,219 staff (full-time equivalent). In the calendar year 2018, HMCTS handled over 4.4 million criminal, civil, family and tribunal cases (source: House of Commons Library Briefing Paper Number CBP 8372, 16 December 2019).

The Ministry of Justice has, since 2019, changed its approach to the recording of court workload statistics. Of course, statistics alone should be treated with caution, but the 31 January 2023 update to CBP 8372 reads as follows:

Caseload:

- The annual criminal court caseload has been steadily declining over the last ten years. In 2020 it fell sharply as a result of the pandemic before rising in 2021 to a slightly lower level than it had been pre-pandemic.

- In 2021, magistrates' courts in England and Wales received 1.14 million cases and Crown courts received 98,000 cases.

- Both the magistrates' and Crown court have an ongoing backlog of cases, known as outstanding cases. At the end of September 2022, there were 347,820 outstanding cases in magistrates' courts, which was lower than the peak of around 422,000 cases in mid-2020.

- The Crown court had 62,766 outstanding cases at the end of September 2022, which was higher than the previous peak of around 61,000 in mid-2021.

- In 2021, civil courts received 1.6 million claims and family courts started 266,000 cases.

- Complete tribunal statistics are only available up to 2020/21, in which year 305,000 cases were started. An interim estimate of outstanding cases as of June 2022 put the number at 650,000.

In other words, we have a snapshot as of the period 2020–21, which is the latest available period of time for this data. The number of criminal cases has declined, something which does not mean criminality itself has fallen off. Rather, it indicates that there were less prosecutions. There continues to be a backlog of criminal cases. The number of civil litigation and tribunal cases remains reflective of economic and social activity within society, and at a much lower level than, for instance, the USA, which has a notoriously litigious culture.

The same CBP update states the employment headcount at HMCTS to be 16,714 as of 2021–22. HMCTS's resource expenditure limit for 2021–22 was £2,040m, and the capital expenditure limit £483m. Expenditure limits, incidentally, are the result of spending reviews by the Treasury, and are maximums rather than obligatory. So, the actual amount expended is subject to confirmation through the intricacies of central government management.

The introductory flowchart in **Figure 6.1** gives an overview of senior legal personnel and the court system. You will see it starts with us – the electorate – and mentions both political and judicial figures. It then refers to the Supreme Court, the Court of Appeal and the criminal and civil justice courts, all of which we return to shortly. There is also mention of the Ministry of Justice, which provides the administrative support (and much more) to the courts.

Figure 6.1   Overview of senior legal figures and the court system

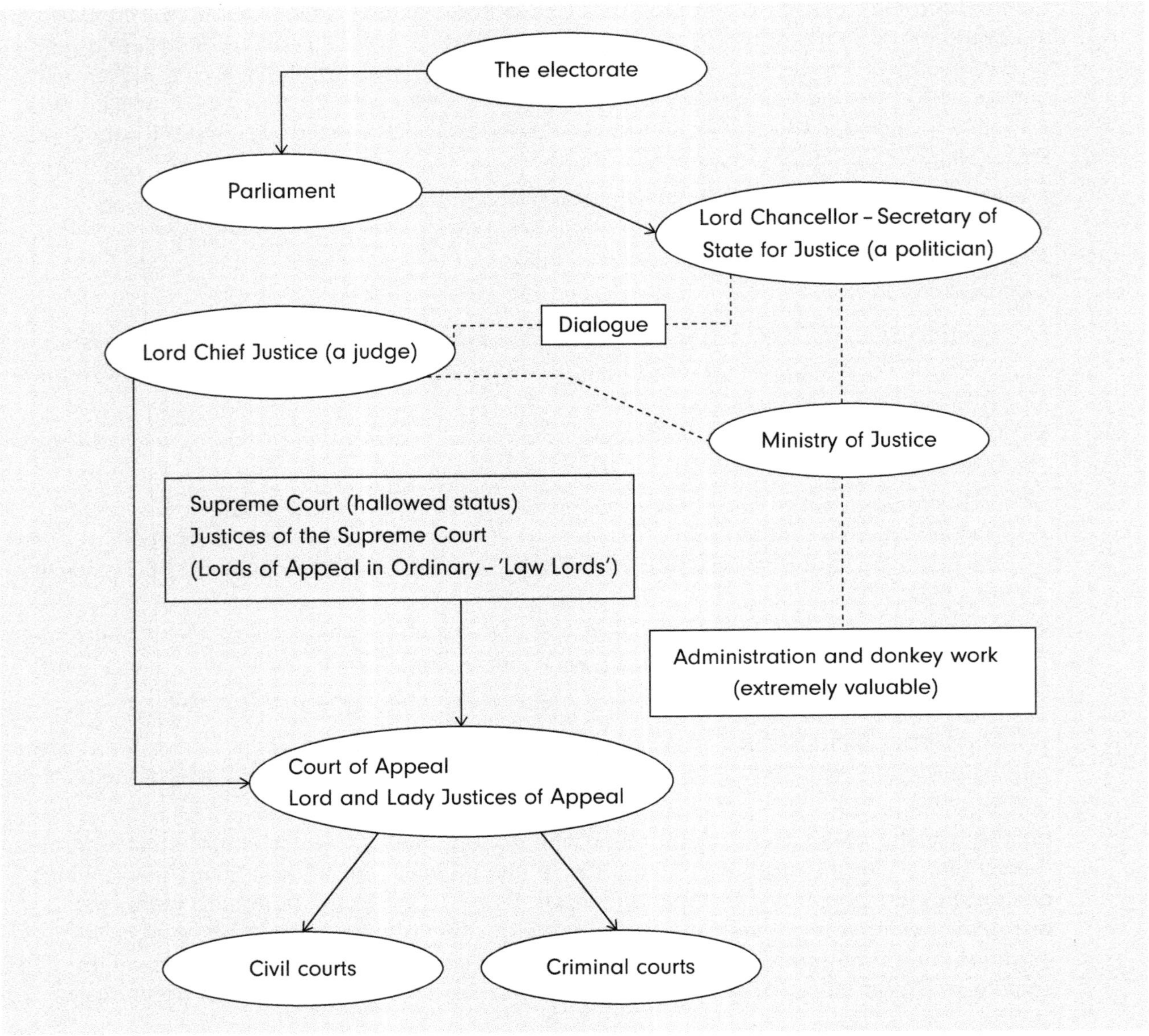

6.3   The criminal courts

Now let's look at the criminal courts starting with magistrates.

6.3.1   Magistrates

Magistrates, or justices of the peace (JPs), are the foot soldiers of criminal justice. Depending on your view of life, they represent all that is good, or alternatively bad, about handling crime. In many ways they typify the traditional affection of the ruling classes for the 'cult of the amateur' – the idea a non-specialist can learn about, manage and improve something of an essentially technical nature. This philosophy dominates UK history and is still apparent in the courts of England and Wales.

According to the House of Commons Library Constituency Data from May 2020, there were 156 magistrates' courts in England and Wales, down from 320 in 2010. As of 1 April 2019, there were 14,348 magistrates (Judicial Diversity Statistics, July 2019). The 31 January 2023 update to CBP 8372 states there to be 12,506 justices as of 2021–22, a reduction which could be the result of a basket of circumstances. The Sentencing Council website as of April 2023 says, somewhat guardedly, that 'there are over 150 magistrates' courts across England and Wales'. This global approach to the exact number reflects a recurring reluctance within central government to be overt about any possible reduction in judicial services.

We shall now look at who they are, why they exist, what they do and their role within the law and indeed wider society.

6.3.1.1 Who are magistrates?

Magistrates are not legally qualified. They are motivated by a desire to serve, and possibly by the recognition that comes with their role. They come from most walks of life, backgrounds and professions. We use that last word advisedly: relatively few magistrates come from what we would call 'blue collar' occupations. To put it bluntly they are unlikely to work on the factory floor. They are volunteers and receive expenses for their time. The expense rates do not appear to have changed since 2010. The figure for over four hours of financial loss is £116.58 for a self-employed justice, for instance. The night subsistence allowance outside London is £100, and the day subsistence allowance for over 12 hours' absence is £19.60.

This remuneration indicates magistrates are unlikely to do the work for financial gain. The job specification also implies most magistrates have other roles that allow flexibility to leave their workplace and spend time in court. This is somewhat startling to an outsider: can it really be the case that an office employee can switch off their computer at the end of one day and be sitting in judgment of alleged criminals the next? On a part-time basis? Well, yes, that is exactly what magistrates do.

6.3.1.2 Culture of magistrates

This culture also suggests those who become magistrates have an element of executive authority in their lives. It is unlikely pure 'wage slaves', to use a vulgar expression, would be able to fulfil the role. But this does not mean the magistracy is one dimensional. In fact the recruitment process is impressively open and the candidacy pool wide. There are a number of structural problems to the magistrates' system, such as cost restrictions and pressure of business, but the independence and varied nature of those sitting in judgment cannot be doubted. As with all areas of the legal system, diversity in the strict sense of the word is something of a developing concept: 56% of magistrates are women; 12% declare themselves to be black and minority ethnic; 52% are over the age of 60; and 5% are under the age of 40 (the source here is the Diversity Statistics of July 2019 mentioned above). Within these boundaries you find a range of interesting individuals who in general are open minded, fair and sensible. A number are, as the statistics suggest, retired. Some, but not many, are unemployed.

Why this system exists is an interesting question. The answer lies somewhere in a blend of history, pragmatism and culture. No doubt financial aspects have contributed too, as the 'expenses only' system represents value for money for central government.

6.3.1.3 Courts Act 2003

In historical terms magistrates were the local squires or their agents. They dealt with lesser crimes in relatively quick time, at minimal cost, while maintaining the social hierarchy in which the gentry presided over everyone else. The Courts Act 2003 puts a modern gloss on the process, adopting pretty much wholesale the idea that non-lawyers on an unpaid basis should try alleged criminals. Those who sit in judgment have changed: the job they do has not. The bench in a magistrates' court is more likely to consist of office workers, managers and business owners, and perhaps those in local government and education, rather than the landed gentry. But their core role remains the same.

The 2003 Act at s 7 states there shall be a Commission of the Peace for England and Wales issued under the Great Seal. This is a lovely example of an ancient process finessing itself into the modern world (the seal being a traditional way of confirming the authenticity of a document or piece of legislation). The 2003 Act mentions the creation of local justice areas and the appointment of lay justices. In terms of their remit, they rule on a host of minor criminal matters and therefore ensure the wheels of justice continue to turn at a local level, allowing higher courts to concentrate on more complicated matters.

The 2003 Act also has a section relating to places, dates and times of sittings. All legal systems rely on a sense of time and place, and it is interesting our lawmakers felt the need to refer specifically to these in the legislation.

6.3.1.4 Some data

Some statistics indicate the significance of JPs to our society as a whole. In 2018 magistrates' courts disposed of 1.473 million cases, a figure which had dropped somewhat by 2021 (source: House of Commons Briefing Paper 8372). 'Disposing' means they tried a matter or sentenced someone, or both. We all know that statistics on their own are meaningless, so let's examine the impact of this figure. First, we need to understand the element of compulsion when a suspect is charged with a crime. An accused cannot make some sort of private arrangement with the prosecutor, unless it is to admit guilt prior to entering the courtroom. With the exception of things like some speeding and parking offences, a defendant who protests his innocence, or a guilty person awaiting a sentence, has no option but to appear in court.

Second, this statistic means, as a consequence, JPs have a formidable workload – a combination of short hearings, applications and trials, often coming thick and fast. There is no possibility, as happens in civil courts, that a case will 'settle' and a workload theoretically diminish. They will hear from a colourful cast of characters: defendants, witnesses, medical and other experts, police officers, translators, social workers and more.

Third, this means society as a whole has significant exposure to the magistracy. Based on an anecdotal rule of thumb, each trial of a defendant pleading not guilty will involve an average of perhaps five other people – complainants, police, other witnesses, the probation service and so on. The average magistrate comes across an astonishing amount of humanity in a typical year. Or, looking at it from another perspective, taking the figure of 1.473 million cases per year, the majority of the population in England and Wales is likely, during their lifetime, to enter a magistrates' court in one capacity or another.

It could be to support an errant offspring who has had a brush with authority; to provide a character reference for a defendant; to stand surety for someone; or simply to take a group of children on a learning exercise. You might even, perish the thought, be a defendant. But one way or another, magistrates' courts tend to touch our lives.

The influence of magistrates does not end there. We all share a high likelihood of meeting a magistrate outside court, socially. Joe Public will probably not meet a County or Crown Court judge at the gym, sports club, drama group, community event, Ramadan festivity or Diwali. But JPs may well be there. They lead normal lives, generally, and it is inevitable they mix in a routine way with the rest of us. They therefore occupy a unique place in the community, pausing their normal jobs to preside over a court, and at the same time weaving themselves into the fabric of everyday society.

6.3.1.5 The job

So what do magistrates do? They deal with around 95% of all criminal cases and some non-criminal work too, such as licensing applications for pubs, bars and entertainment venues. Their main workload relates to driving offences, minor assaults, minor thefts, anti-social behaviour, bail applications, enforcement of fines and the grant of search warrants. Some magistrates can train for work in the Family Court or youth courts. Generally all magistrates are required to sit for at least 13 full days, or 26 half days, each year.

Magistrates sit on panels of three, one of them being the chair. As they are not trained in the law, they rely on healthy doses of common sense, and also the advice of the magistrate's clerk, or trained legal adviser, a fully paid and legally qualified role. More complex matters are handled by single individuals called district judges (this term appears in the civil context too but in the criminal context means a salaried lawyer capable of deciding more serious matters on their own).

The qualities required of a magistrate include an experience of life; considerable amounts of sympathy for both the police and accused who appear before them, not to mention the various witnesses; and the ability to retain their cool in the face of inefficiencies, disorganisation and delays throughout the court system. No lawyer relishes a discussion of institutional flaws but it would be artificial to ignore them. At the end of 2018 there were 293,000 magistrates' cases outstanding – in other words, still active, waiting for a decision on guilt or sentencing or both. You can imagine the human cost of these delays: uncertainty, worry, accumulated paperwork and the difficulties of attempting to remember events that are rapidly becoming distant in time. Unfortunately it is a fact of life. The number of cases outstanding may seem a lot, but it's a decrease on the backlog in 2015 of 327,000.

6.3.1.6 The essential qualities

Advisory committees undertake recruitment work for the magistracy on behalf of the Secretary of State for Justice. References are of course required, and magistrates need to demonstrate they have the six key qualities necessary for the job:

- good character;
- understanding and communication;
- social awareness;
- maturity and sound temperament;
- sound judgment; and
- commitment and reliability.

Our analysis of magistrates accentuates the positives. But not all commentators think the system is ideal and in the interests of balance we now provide the alternative view.

6.3.1.7 The non-legal aspect

As mentioned earlier, the legal system, reflective of the history of our society as a whole, has a touching belief in the concept of the gifted amateur. This is also known as the cult of the all-rounder. This phrase is taken from the sporting arena, and in particular the cricket pitch. An all-rounder is someone who can play well for the team across a range of disciplines, for instance being able to bat and bowl equally well. It implies the knack of turning your hand to a number of different areas with equal ability.

This culture is apparent within the magistrate system. Why else would you trust the outcome of a criminal process to people who are not trained as lawyers? For some analysts, this is one of the strengths of the system. It means less serious offences are decided on a community basis, by lay individuals with a rounded experience of life. They are people who have experienced success and failure, wealth and poverty, highs and lows. They treat the defendant, witnesses and the alleged offence with common sense and humanity.

6.3.1.8   A critical view

But some of those involved in the criminal justice world do not have confidence in this process. In *The Secret Barrister – Stories of the Law and How It's Broken* (Picador Macmillan, 2018) the author, who represents both prosecutors and defendants, states as follows:

> the truth is that the entire case in favour of magistrates' courts, as we currently run them, is a sham. There is little sustainable rationale for their existence in principle, and no justification whatsoever for the way in which these courts operate in practise. There is no excuse for the amateur, sausage factory paradigm of justice ... that pervades 94% of criminal cases other than that most cynical political trinity: it's cheap, it's the way we've always done it and no one who votes either knows or cares.

Figure 6.2   The mindset of a magistrate

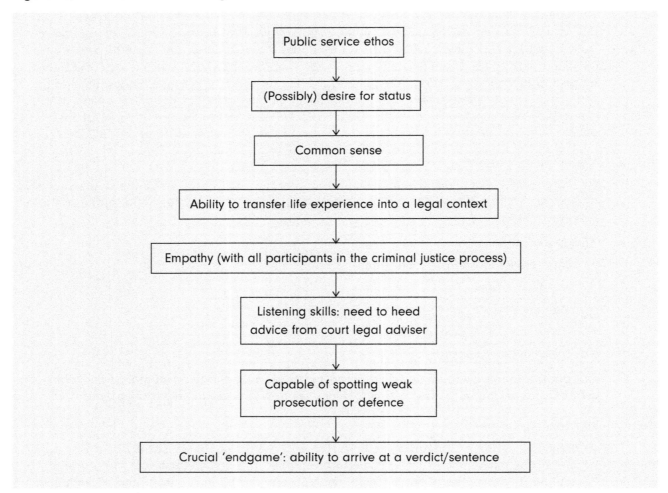

In other words, the Secret Barrister believes magistrates exist as an historical anomaly, for budgetary reasons, as part of a prefabricated process with little objective justification, unnoticed by most voters.

You now have two assessments of magistrates, and it is for you to make up your minds on the effectiveness of the system as you progress your careers.

Figure 6.2 provides a flowchart giving an insight into the mindset of a magistrate. It is somewhat informal, and indeed relatively non-legal. But that's fine – because that typifies magistrates.

6.3.2 Legal advisers in magistrates' courts

Magistrates would not be able to do their job without the involvement of trained legal advisers, who until recently were known as magistrate's clerks. These are qualified lawyers who provide skilled analysis and interpretation of the law when confronted by defendants and their crimes. Legal advisers are not able to tell magistrates whether they should find a defendant innocent or guilty, but they provide the necessary legal advice at key times. Section 28 of the Courts Act 2003 provides for the function of giving legal advice to magistrates. The Act reinforces the importance of qualifications, and s 29 asserts the independence of legal advisers in the exercise of their functions.

How does one become a court legal adviser? The Government Careers Service gives an insight. You can read more at nationalcareers.service.gov.uk. Usually you will need to be a fully qualified solicitor, which implies you have the relevant experience and knowledge. The skills needed are the ones for any effective lawyer. These would naturally include independent thought, analysis, initiative and evaluation. The most crucial role of the job is advising magistrates on law and procedure. In terms of a career path, it is possible to progress to become a district judge or a more senior legal adviser with the responsibility of running several courts.

6.3.3 District judges in the magistrates' courts

Magistrates have limited powers of sentencing. They can send the guilty to jail for a maximum of six months for a single offence, or 12 months in total, and also impose unlimited fines. Most offences are minor in nature. But others are more serious or complex or both. For instance, you might imagine an assault case with conflicting stories from the defendant and witnesses, tricky questions of admissibility of evidence from the police, perhaps unusual statements that might constitute confessions, and the involvement of medical professionals. In such circumstances the system allows the involvement of a single professional magistrate known as a district judge. The stated qualification for this is a five-year right of audience – in other words, being able to advocate in court – and they will typically have served as a deputy district judge for at least 30 days. Their career usually begins as a solicitor or barrister before graduation to the bench. Their sentencing powers remain the same as for a bench of three.

6.3.4 Crown Court judges

The Crown Court sits at something over 70 court centres across England and Wales. It deals with the more serious criminal cases. The Crown Court in London is called the Central Criminal Court and sits at the world famous Old Bailey, in the street of that name in the City. Crown Courts are presided over by High Court judges, circuit judges and recorders.

Who are these individuals? Unlike magistrates, they wear wigs and robes of a colourful nature. *High Court judges* are long-serving lawyers with an impeccable intellectual pedigree. Section 85 of the Constitutional Reform Act 2005 refers to the selection of 'puisne' judges and other office holders. 'Puisne' means an ordinary High Court judge, to the extent that any such figure could be considered ordinary (in their own eyes judges are very special and most observers would agree).

To outsiders the process of becoming a High Court judge is somewhat mysterious, but legislation nowadays requires a rigorous selection process. That process has created more openness. It is still the case, however, that the majority of High Court judges arrive from their traditional recruiting ground of the Bar. In other words they are barristers. More recently an increasing minority of High Court judges are solicitors.

Circuit judges are more junior personnel and are attached to one of the regions around England and Wales. They must have held rights of audience for at least 10 years, and generally should also have served either part time as a recorder or full time as a district judge.

What then is a *recorder*? This is the most junior level of circuit judge, mandated by s 21 of the Courts Act 1971, to preside on a part-time basis. It is usually the stepping stone to greater things.

All three of these categories of Crown Court judges are appointed on the basis of merit by the Judicial Appointments Commission.

You might wonder why there should be a distinction between the personnel of the magistrates' and Crown Court. After all, if an amateur can dispense justice in one place why not in another? The answer is rooted in a number of basic legal concepts. One concept is that a defendant should have the opportunity to be judged by a jury of their peers, something that is part and parcel of the Crown Court process. Another is that the more serious crimes should have greater resources devoted to them. Accordingly, the legal system deems it appropriate for a highly qualified judge to sit in the Crown Court, accompanied by a jury, whereas non-lawyers are deemed suitable for the magistrates'.

According to the House of Commons Library Briefing Paper CBP 8372 of 16 December 2019, the Crown Court in 2018 received 103,000 cases. The backlog at the end of that year was 33,000.

6.3.5 Juries in the Crown Court

A jury is a group of (usually 12) men and women who sit in the Crown Court during the trial of a defendant. They are ordinary citizens with no requirement for legal knowledge or understanding. In every way they represent conventional society: jurors can be rich or poor, black or white, sensible or stupid, nice or nasty.

6.3.5.1 The role of a jury

The function of a jury is to attend, listen to the advocates and witnesses – and also the defendant if they choose to give evidence – and then evaluate all they have heard. During the court process the Crown Court judge provides guidance on the law and procedure. Crucially, towards the end of proceedings, the judge will sum up what has gone before and provide directions. These are instructions on the law – guidance on the significance of what has been said, and how the law might apply.

But the jury does not need to act on these hints. At the end of the trial they will be sent to a room to deliberate. They have a monumental job: to decide on the innocence or guilt of the defendant. This decision is called a verdict. How they arrive at this endgame is a matter for them. They are free to examine merely their own consciences if they so wish, and they certainly should not be influenced by anyone, or anything, other than what they have heard in court and the thoughts of their 11 fellow jurors.

The jury system is yet another wonder of the legal system. It is only replicated in other jurisdictions that benefit, or suffer, depending on your view, from the judicial instincts of the UK. So you will find replicas or traces of the same process in the USA, Australasia, Canada and parts of the Commonwealth. But in other jurisdictions, many of which are fundamentally democratic and worthy, the jury system as we know it does not exist. A decision on innocence or guilt is considered too important to delegate to ordinary citizens. Instead there might be some sort of presiding or inquisitorial judge who drives the process. The jury system is therefore far from the norm throughout the world, and how precious it is to us depends upon your view of the judicial culture.

6.3.5.2 Some basic law

The Juries Act 1974, and subsequent legislation by way of the Criminal Justice Act 2003, provides the basis for the modern system. Jury service is considered a duty. Individuals are summoned to serve and then selected. It is obligatory to attend unless a satisfactory excuse is provided and accepted under s 9 and s 9A of the 1974 Act. You are eligible for jury service provided you are between the ages of 18 and 75, registered on the electoral roll, and have lived in the UK for the last five years.

There are exceptions for criminals and some others. A defendant can challenge the appointment of individual jurors and this guards against subsequent suggestion by the guilty that a panel was in some way biased. Under s 17 of the 1974 Act jurors are encouraged to return a unanimous verdict but if they cannot then a majority one will suffice. Jurors are entitled to receive payments by way of an allowance for travelling and subsistence, and for financial loss.

Juries are entitled, and indeed encouraged, to arrive at a common sense outcome on the basis of the evidence. The deliberations of the jury room are considered sacrosanct. A juror cannot reveal to other people the nature or detail of their ponderings. Equally, they cannot allow themselves to be swayed by any external influences, such as publicity or the media, or of course social media and the internet, in concluding their views. The verdict is announced by the jury foreman or forewoman as a simple 'guilty' or 'not guilty'. No reasons are requested or given.

6.3.5.3 The jury dynamic

The presence of the jury creates an interesting dynamic in the Crown Court. In other courts the focus is evenly split between the defence, the prosecution and the presiding official(s). The jury adds a fourth dimension to this previously tripartite arrangement. The obvious question for any advocate is: who do I need to persuade? It does not take long for the answer to emerge: if there is a choice between impressing the judge or influencing the jury, the latter wins. Advocates tailor their style to make the maximum impression on the jury. A judge has a role in ensuring inadmissible evidence is excluded, and protecting witnesses from unduly repetitive questioning or unreasonable pestering, called badgering, but they are not the ultimate decision makers when it comes to the freedom or otherwise of the accused.

Let's consider one scenario. Imagine a defendant is on trial for forgery of six cheques. He denies the charge, on the basis his wife was in fact the forger, something she has confirmed. The defendant gives evidence of a highly dubious nature in person from the witness box. Of course the rule of law allows a defendant to protest their innocence, no matter how feeble the defence.

During the trial the judge:

* interrupts the defence counsel 14 or 15 times;

- implies the defence counsel was setting up certain defences when in fact that was not the case; and

- interrupts the defence counsel's final speech to the jury, by inviting prosecuting counsel to make submissions.

What would any self-respecting advocate do in the circumstances? Clearly, they cannot allow this to happen without protest. It is incumbent on the advocate to remind the jury of the defence case, and resist interference by the judge, in order to ensure the jury have the full picture.

 These were the outline facts of R v Clewer *(1953) 37 Cr App R 37. The advocate was being restricted by the judge in their ability to connect with the jury. The advocate tried hard to rein in the judge. But despite their best efforts it was in vain. The matter was appealed to the Court of Appeal, who held the judge to have interfered with the ability of the advocate to make their case to the jury. The Court of Appeal quashed the conviction.*

6.3.5.4   Conclusion on juries

In conclusion, the jury system is another example of justice dispensed by the lay population. It has found its way into the fabric of society and most people regard it as entirely routine. But a few observers – some of them lawyers – remain dumbfounded at the nature of the process. It is costly, time-consuming and, in many instances, entirely defiant of logic and realism. Some trials are long, detailed, boring, technical or impenetrable, or a combination of all these. How, one wonders, can 12 ordinary members of the public find their way through this thicket of procedure, laced as it is with lies, grandstanding, accusations, denials and conjecture?

In recent times the suggestion has arisen juries should be used more sparingly. The Ministry of Justice has taken note of this and you will be able to study in more detail, in books dealing with criminal law and procedure, the impulse towards reviewing the jury system. Some would regard this as a dangerous path, others (but not this author) are more open to the suggestion. This is something for you to review as you progress your studies, and only you can come to a conclusion on the matter.

In summary the points to be made about the jury system are as follows:

- It is integral to Crown Court trials, and represents the legal system's faith in the deliberations of ordinary men and women.

- An advocate at a Crown Court trial needs to take account of the judge, but ultimately they must impress the jury, as it is the jury who has the decisive influence on whether the defendant walks free.

- Many jurisdictions in other parts of the world do not bother with the jury process, preferring a judge to make the decision as to innocence or guilt.

- There is a debate of sorts within the criminal justice world as to the future of the jury system.

To conclude on figures within the criminal court system, the flowchart in **Figure 6.3** gives an overview of criminal court personnel. Traditionalists like to put the Supreme Court at the top and work down. We have chosen the opposite approach, starting with the 'poor bloody infantry', ie the magistrates, and progressing from there. Note there is a reference to the Administrative Divisions of the High Court, usually a civil court, but which in criminal matters has a somewhat rarefied role in considering some appeals from lower courts.

Figure 6.3 Overview of criminal courts and personnel

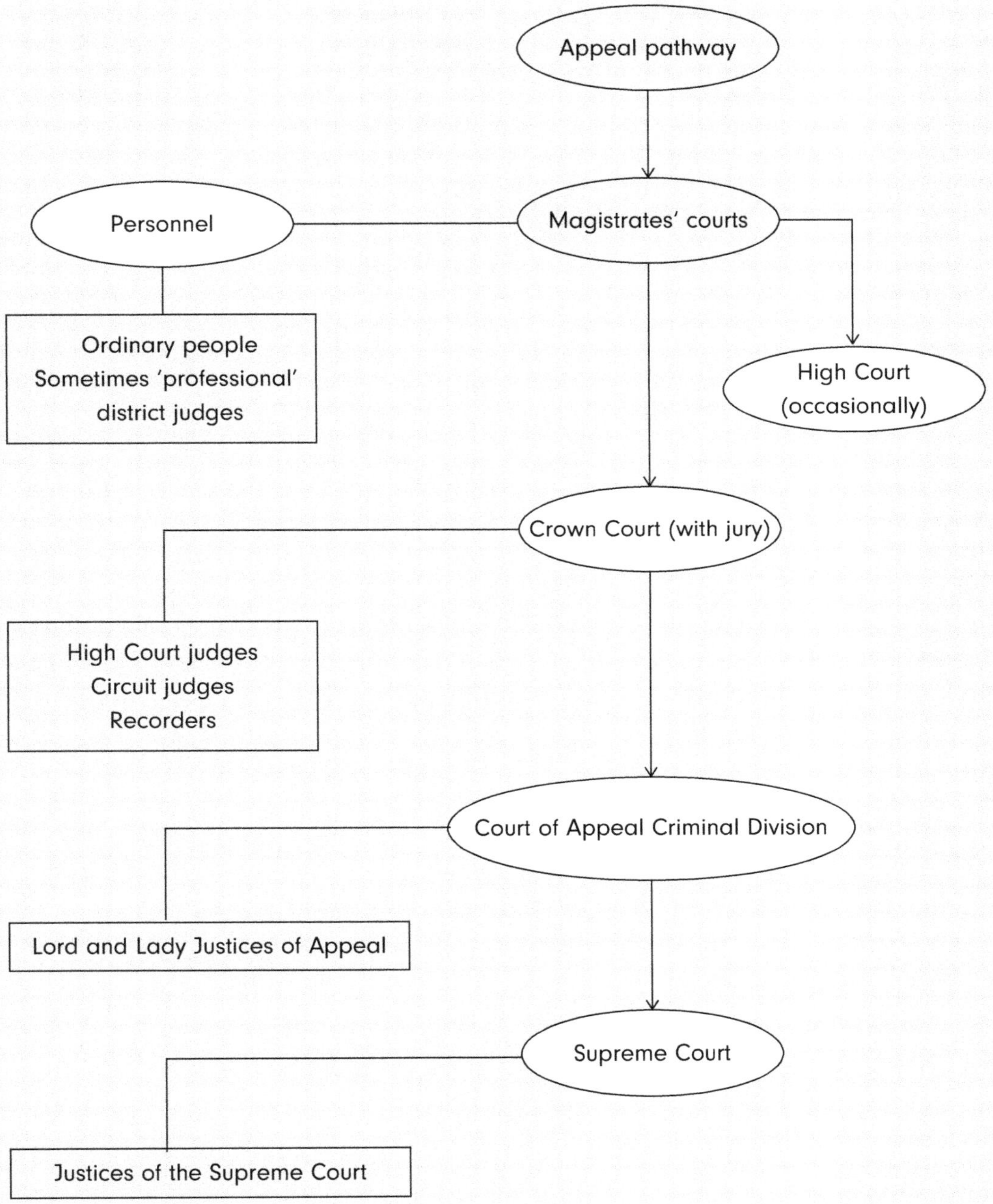

6.4   The civil courts

Let us now turn our attention to the civil courts. This is where non-criminal matters are resolved. We have mentioned in earlier chapters the distinction between civil and criminal law, so you should refresh your memory on that if necessary before continuing.

6.4.1 District judges

District judges are the most junior members of the judiciary in the civil system of England and Wales. They are the broad equivalents of magistrates in that they deal with more minor matters. But there the comparison ends. In fact, they are far from being the well-meaning amateurs of the magistracy.

District judges are very much legal insiders. They sit in District Registries – the administrative arm of local courts – up and down the country. They are solicitors or barristers by training, profession and experience, and they gravitate towards the role after years of exposure to the cut and thrust of legal practice.

They opt for the role for a variety of reasons. They wish to apply the experience they have gained, to develop their own areas of expertise and interest, and to provide effective service in the interests of justice. They usually begin on a part-time basis, combining their judicial role with a continuation of their routine work in the office or chambers before progressing to a full-time role (with an accompanying salary, which might compare favourably with their previous remuneration).

What do district judges actually do? They are effectively the junior officers of the judiciary. They do the 'heavy lifting', to use a modern expression. They deal with claims for damages by individuals and organisations against each other, property matters, matrimonial issues, personal injury, landlord and tenant matters, business disputes and a whole host of other claims. The one common denominator is that none of these are wholly criminal. You can appreciate the wide jurisdiction, and hence workload, of a district judge.

Here is a list of the typical tasks undertaken by a district judge in their average day up and down the country:

- holding case management conferences, where the progress and timetable of a case towards trial is agreed;

- holding pre-trial reviews, to ensure evidence and witnesses are ready for an imminent trial;

- hearing interim applications. These might include a request from a litigant for more time to prepare evidence; an application to dispose of a case on a summary basis, rather than having a full trial; deciding on evidential matters; and ruling on a range of procedural and administrative issues;

- undergoing training;

- reading court papers in preparation for applications and hearings;

- considering the costs implications of a piece of litigation;

- occasionally dealing with emergency applications involving children, or seizure of property by bailiffs;

- and so on.

The judiciary website provides an insight to the working day of a district judge. For a start, they do not work in a courtroom. Instead they have an office in a combined court centre. The daily diet of work is varied. A crucial aspect of the job, as you might imagine, is people management. District judges deal with a lot of litigants and witnesses, and they also interact regularly with court staff and other professionals from the legal world.

In terms of workload, in 2018 the county courts received 2.07 million claims, but only 14% of these were contested, and not all of these progressed to trial. But district judges deal with lots of pre-trial administrative and procedural matters, so there is plenty of work to do even if a matter settles before trial.

The update to CBP 8372 of 31 January 2023 states that there were 1.58m claims in 2021, of which 89% were for money, meaning that they involved the relatively simple subject of debt. Overall, just 17% of claims were defended, thus illustrating the reality of civil litigation that many disputes are initiated, with only a proportion progressed to a judicial resolution.

A district judge in the Royal Courts of Justice in the Strand in London is called a Master (and you have this title whatever your designated gender). The role of a Master is essentially the same as that of a district judge in the provinces, only the subject matter of the caseload is likely to differ to reflect the nature of surrounding society. Accordingly, the High Court in London would tend to deal with more financial matters, high value property disputes, colourful divorces, serious personal injuries, complex commercial matters and challenging mercantile cases than in the provinces. The daily regime of High Court Masters adjusts accordingly to meet this need.

6.4.2 County Court judges

County Court judges traditionally come from the ranks of barristers, and more recently solicitors. The most senior is a circuit judge, in other words someone appointed to one of the regions, or circuits, of the court system in England and Wales. There is continuity between the job of a barrister and that of a circuit judge, as the former tastes life on a circuit as part of their professional work. The transition into a judicial role is smoothed somewhat by this experience.

Circuit judges are assisted by fee paid judges and the more senior district judges. The primary role of these figures is to preside over trials and this covers an enormously wide range of topics, from breach of contract matters and negligence to financial, insolvency, property, family, trust and other matters. They also have an important role to play in the case management of litigation leading up to trial, ensuring parties are properly prepared and organised, and encouraging the use of alternative dispute resolution wherever feasible.

6.4.3 High Court judges

The High Court generally deals with more weighty, complicated and expensive civil matters. The High Court consists of the five Heads of Division. These are the Lord Chief Justice, the President of the King's Bench Division, the President of the Family Division, the Chancellor of the High Court, and the Master of the Rolls.

They are joined by the senior presiding judge and the vice-president of the King's Bench. Finally there are the High Court judges themselves. These are assigned to one of the three divisions mentioned here. We will look at the operation of these divisions in another chapter. For the moment we are concerned purely with the personnel. High Court judges are recruited in the main from the County Court. There are about 120 High Court judges in all.

6.4.3.1 Promotion of High Court judges

High Court judges can be promoted to the Court of Appeal, and in time, to the Supreme Court. The Constitutional Reform Act 2005 provides some statutory detail. Section 76 onwards refers to the Lord Chancellor – the Secretary of State for Justice – being able to recommend an appointment to fill a vacancy as a Lord Justice of Appeal. There must be consultation with the Lord Chief Justice, an interesting instance of the judiciary acting as a further, administrative, check on the executive.

The Judicial Appointments Commission then conducts the selection process from a panel including at least two non-legally qualified members. In this way some daylight filters through to a procedure that for decades if not centuries was a closely guarded secret. Then s 67 onwards of the 2005 Act provides details for selection of those at the top of the tree, ie the Lord Chief Justice and other senior judges. And that leads us nicely to the elite of the court family.

Before we get there, however, **Figure 6.4** is a flowchart of the personnel within the civil court structure. We start at the County Court and go from there to the High Court and then upwards.

Figure 6.4 Overview of civil courts and personnel

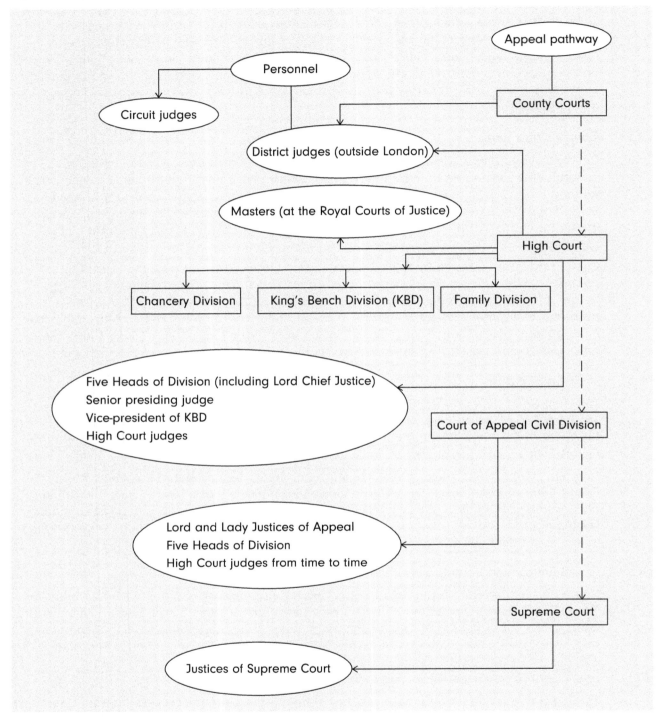

6.5 General matters

6.5.1 The senior judiciary

The senior judiciary refers mainly to Supreme Court Justices and Chief Justices of the Court of Appeal.

There are 12 *Supreme Court* justices, currently two of whom are women. They are also called Lords of Appeal in Ordinary, or the 'Law Lords'. Their head is the President of the Supreme Court. They deal with the most important cases in the land.

Section 25 of the 2005 Act says that a person is not qualified to be appointed a judge of the Supreme Court unless they have held high judicial office for a period of at least two years, having been a qualifying practitioner for a period of at least 15 years. Recommendations for office should come from the Prime Minister. There is then a selection process by a commission including at least one person who is not legally qualified. The various sections of the 2005 Act provide more guidance in the form of requirements for procedure – there is no step-by-step guide likely to fetter those participating in the process.

The *Court of Appeal* is home to the five Heads of Division mentioned previously. They are joined by the Lords and Lady Justices of Appeal. As of October 2019, there were 30 Lords and nine Lady Justices of Appeal. They are assisted in hearing cases by selected High Court judges.

All Court of Appeal justices are senior judges with lengthy judicial experience. Appointment is by the Monarch on the recommendation of a selection panel convened by the Judicial Appointments Commission. In reality, the Heads of Division are selected from the Justices of Appeal, who in turn are selected from the High Court.

6.5.2   Arbitrators, mediators and tribunal chairs

We have scrutinised the judiciary in some detail. There are, however, many other forums within the legal system, presided over by more junior and less-publicised figures. In the civil arena these include those who are involved in tribunals, arbitrations and alternative dispute resolution. The legal system could not possibly operate in any effective manner without the involvement of these supplementary processes. We will therefore mention them briefly as follows.

* *Arbitrators*: Arbitration is a time-honoured manner of resolving commercial matters without resort to the formality of the courts. The process is governed through the Arbitration Act 1996, which recognises the international nature of the forum together with its various customs and procedures. London is one of the premier centres for arbitration not least because of its much admired reliance on the rule of law, linked to its historical role in world trade. Arbitrators come from many backgrounds, but traditionally they are business people rather than lawyers.

* *Mediators*: the practise of mediating a dispute has developed steadily over the last 30 years. Imagine you are the chief executive of an international company. Your commercial department is in dispute with a supplier in another part of the world. The two organisations regularly do business together – or at least, at the moment they do. They have a network of profitable contacts throughout the globe. The dispute has a value of £20m. It is absorbing much time, energy and effort. Your stakeholders are grumbling. Customers are rattled by the high profile of the matter. Employees ridicule management for allowing things to get this far. The two companies' relationship is under threat. For you, the chief executive, it is a headache. It is something of a recurring bad dream – still vivid when you wake up each morning.

  You then hear of a mediator who comes highly recommended. The parties will meet for a few days at an independent venue in London. They will be in separate rooms on the same floor of a suitable building, with the mediator in a third room acting as an honest broker. He is prepared to charge merely £20,000 a day, this sum to be split between the parties. By the end of the third day the combatants have moved considerably closer. They may even have settled. In your view this is money well spent. From this we can deduce a number of points about mediation:

- ○ most obviously, it can be well remunerated for the mediators;
- ○ it allows litigating parties to resolve their differences out of court; and
- ○ it also allows those parties to maintain the fabric of their commercial relationships.

For this reason mediation has its supporters. Who then are mediators? Surprisingly, a number of them are not lawyers. Their attraction is their experience of and exposure to the commercial world. They come from areas as diverse as shipping, engineering, academia and a variety of business fields.

The whole point is they are meant to offer a commercial appreciation of a dispute rather than what clients see, entirely unfairly I'm sure you will agree, as a lawyer's tendency to get lost in the detail. In their own way, therefore, mediators offer yet another insight into the cult of the all-rounder. They are a further example of the legal system's faith in non-lawyers.

- *Tribunal members*: The Tribunals Courts and Enforcement Act 2007 makes provision for tribunals and enquiries. These bodies enable a host of important legal and administrative matters to be resolved without the involvement of the courts themselves, unless there is the need for judicial scrutiny as a result of an appeal by a dissatisfied participant. Tribunal members are either legally qualified tribunal judges or specialist non-legal members who have experience and expertise from the field of the tribunal subject matter. For instance in an Employment Tribunal there will typically be a legally qualified chair, a representative from an employers organisation and a representative from a trade union. A social security tribunal might involve people with experience of work-related benefits, employment and recruitment. An immigration tribunal might involve people with an understanding of asylum and nationality matters. And so on.

The work of tribunals is significant, as is their workload. In conclusion, the work of arbitrators, mediators and tribunal members is once again evidence of the legal system's faith in justice arrived at by non-lawyers.

6.5.3 Judicial Diversity House of Commons Briefing Paper CBP 8372, 16 December 2019

In 2018/19, 32% of judges were female, compared with 14% in 2000/01; 6% of judges were black, Asian and minority ethnicity (BAME) compared with 2% in 2000/01; and 42% of judges were 60 years or older, compared with 41% in 2011/12. The update to CBP 8372 of 31 January 2023 indicates that, as of 2021–22, 35% of judges were female, 8% BAME, and 37% aged 60 or older.

You can see from these statistics that progress in diversity is gradual and incremental. It is a matter of opinion as to whether the process is capable of being accelerated.

6.5.4 Codes of conduct and their influence on the judiciary

The judiciary, as with all professions, have guidelines as to their conduct and performance. Most obviously there is the Guide to Judicial Conduct last updated in March 2020 by the Courts and Tribunals Judiciary, part of the Judicial Office, which is itself part of the Ministry of Justice.

Most people, both lawyers and other members of the public, would regard it as astonishing for any organisation to seek to produce a rule book for people as obviously ethical, capable and honest as judges in England and Wales. But that is a sign of the times. Our modern world requires something akin to 'best practice', even if you are as elevated as a judge.

The more important influence on judges is their years of practice as barristers and solicitors. The most obvious source of guidance for the judiciary is therefore the codes of conduct that they followed in their previous incarnations as jobbing lawyers. The latest manifestations of these are the Solicitors Regulation Authority (SRA) Code of Conduct for solicitors, and the Bar Standards Board (BSB) Handbook from 2014, as regularly updated, for use by barristers.

The principles of the SRA code, and the core duties of the BSB code, permeate every aspect of a lawyer's, and therefore a judge's, life. The principles and core duties can be summed up as follows. We all must:

- uphold the rule of law and the proper administration of justice;

- act with integrity;

- uphold public trust and confidence in the legal profession;

- act with independence; and

- act with honesty.

These are for the whole profession, not just judges. But judges are 'perma-stamped' with the ethos of these rules. They bear them in mind when conducting judicial activities. These codes ensure judges continue to deliver justice of the highest order.

6.5.5 Disciplinary matters and termination of office

Occasionally things don't go quite as intended. The judiciary are after all only human. Here are some instances of judicial figures who received an admonition of one sort or another from their bosses. It is important when considering judicial failings to retain a sense of perspective. It could be that the individuals in question were under extreme pressure, or that there was some issue with their personal lives, or that an innocent sequence of events somehow spiralled out of control. Naturally judges should be held to an exceptionally high standard, but that doesn't mean we should abandon our compassion.

Disciplinary matters fall within the remit of the Lord Chief Justice, the Lord Chancellor, and the Judicial Conduct Investigations Office (JCIO). The following examples are anonymised in a rudimentary manner to spare the blushes of those involved. They are purely illustrative of what can occur in even the best administered organisations:

- JCIO 30/16 25 July 2016 – Recorder FE was found guilty of consuming alcohol on court premises, 'which created significant problems for the court staff assisting him'. Because of this the Lord Chancellor and Lord Chief Justice removed the recorder from office.

- In *Harb v Aziz* [2016] EWCA Civ 556 at paragraph 68 of their judgment the Court of Appeal criticised Mr Justice PS for writing a letter in somewhat intemperate terms to a senior barrister: 'It was a shocking and, we regret to say, disgraceful letter to write. It shows a deeply worrying and fundamental lack of understanding of the proper role of a judge ... We greatly regret having to criticise a judge in these strong terms but our duty requires us to do so'. The judge in question resigned in October 2017.

- In *The Science Museum Group v Jane Weiss* [2019] 5 WLUK 482 Judge Auerbach in the Employment Appeal Tribunal (EAT) found at paragraph 66 of his judgment the judge at the original hearing had fallen asleep. This was despite attempts by one of the advocates, Mr Sheppard, to rouse him by banging a cup. The judgment states:

  I find as a fact that, very unfortunately, on the afternoon of day one, 27 March 2018, during the course of the Claimant's cross-examination, the Judge fell fully asleep not once but twice, on each occasion more than just momentarily, and on the second occasion to the point where Mr Sheppard had to deliberately make a noise more than once, physically and verbally, in order to alert the Judge.

  The EAT ordered a retrial.

- JCIO 12/20 21 April 2020 – the Lord Chancellor and a representative of the Lord Chief Justice issued a magistrate, AM, with a formal warning 'after he attempted to solicit support from other members of the bench against a fellow magistrate who had made a complaint against him'.
- JCIO 29/19 16 September 2019 – a deputy district judge, one JT, received a formal warning for an impolite comment made to someone who appeared before him in court.

6.5.6 Political figures with a role in the law

Until now we have concentrated on the independent judiciary. You should note elected politicians also have a role in the administration of justice. In particular there are three parliamentary office holders and you should be careful not to confuse these with the judiciary. They are:

- *Secretary of State for Justice*: this is a member of the Cabinet, in the inner circle of Government, responsible for running the Ministry of Justice. Historically this individual was a barrister, but more recently some appointees have had no legal background at all. The Secretary of State's responsibilities include running the Court Service, the judiciary and the Prison and Probation Services. As mentioned earlier in this chapter, they also hold the title of Lord Chancellor.
- *Attorney General*: this is the chief law officer to the Government. They are responsible for the Crown Prosecution Service, the Serious Fraud Office and the Government Legal Department. They can also examine cases of contempt of court, request the Court of Appeal to review unduly lenient sentences, and occasionally deal with vexatious litigants, ie people who use up the court time in a wasteful manner.
- *Solicitor General*: this is the Attorney General's deputy and supports them in their activities.

6.5.7 Judiciary and personnel of the court system: conclusion

The judiciary play, as you would expect, a hugely significant role in running the legal system of England and Wales. It is fair to say they are a mixed bunch. At the very top of the system they are impressively intellectual, immensely practical, with something of the common touch, and very much capable of taking on the establishment in defence of the rule of law.

At the other end of the spectrum there are shopkeepers, employees and business owners who have no pretence at legal worthiness. They are skilled, however, when presiding in a magistrates' court, at detecting whether someone is a liar. Whether you approve of the judiciary as individuals, and whether you support the system that creates and sustains them, is a matter for you. But without doubt, in the main, they are the envy of the rest of the world.

Here is a summary of the numbers of judicial office holders in post as of 1 April 2019. The source is the JCIO annual report 2018/19.

- Court of Appeal justices including Heads of Division – 44
- High Court and others including Masters, Registrars and Costs Judges – 244
- Circuit bench, including judges and recorders – 1,543
- District judges from both County and magistrates' courts – 1,379
- Tribunal judges and non-legal members – 4,975
- Magistrates – 14,348
- Coroners (officials who investigate sudden and unusual deaths) – 384

The JCIO annual report of 2020–21 provides, as of April 2023, an update on these figures. There are now over 400 coroners. The number of magistrates has declined to below 13,000. The circuit bench numbers have increased to over 1,600. The 'takeaway' here is relatively simple: competing interests within HMCTS are tussling over a limited pot of money, and as with every spending exercise there are winners and losers.

Summary

In summary, a sceptic might suggest the participation of judicial figures within the legal system reflects a deep-seated inconsistency within the law's operation. On the one hand lawyers are trained, and regulated, to a considerable degree. On the other hand, mighty decisions of innocence and guilt are delegated to magistrates and juries, where legal knowledge and expertise are non-existent. In the civil sphere, likewise, disputes at a lower level are routinely resolved by non-lawyers, such as arbitrators, tribunal participants and mediators.

Higher up the chain of command courts are presided over by massively intellectual, and capable, judges, who despite (not because of) their lawyerly training tend to pride themselves on certain generalised abilities: their understanding of humanity, knowledge of business, awareness of culture, grasp of literature and so on.

We have looked at magistrates, judges, juries, tribunal participants and more. We have traversed both the criminal and civil spheres. Occasionally the system throws up anomalies where judges are found wanting, but these are extremely rare examples, mentioned as 'the exception proving the rule' when stating the judiciary in general are super-competent.

There is a mention of diversity statistics, where probably more work is needed, and codes of conduct. There are flowcharts to provide some visual explanations of a sort. You are now in a position to use this chapter as a launch pad for further study of the court system and those who preside over it.

Sample questions

Question 1

A businesswoman is community minded and wants to contribute to society. She believes she would be a good judge. She is neither a solicitor nor a barrister.

In which of the following places could the businesswoman, with the right training, be selected to sit and perform a judicial role?

A   The County Court.

B   The High Court.

C   An Employment Tribunal.

D   The magistrates' court as a district judge.

E   The Crown Court.

Answer

Option C is correct. Employment tribunals consist of three people, one of whom is usually legally qualified, the other two being lay persons. So long as the woman has the necessary attributes she could become a member of an Employment Tribunal. Option A is wrong because a judge in the County Court needs to be legally qualified. Option B is wrong for the same reason.

Option D is wrong because a district judge in the magistrates is a legally qualified person who sits alone to hear more complicated matters. The woman could become a lay magistrate sitting with two others for less serious crimes but she is not qualified to be a district judge. Option E is wrong because judges in the Crown Court must be qualified lawyers with significant experience.

Question 2

A defendant is being tried at the Crown Court for a serious offence of violence.

Which of the following will decide on guilt?

A   A jury.

B   A district judge.

C   A justice of the peace.

D   A judge.

E   A magistrates' courts legal adviser.

Answer

Option A is correct. Juries sit in the Crown Court, listen to the evidence and give a verdict at the end of the process.

Option B is wrong because a district judge sits in the magistrates' or the County Court, not the Crown Court. Option C is wrong because a justice of the peace is another term for a magistrate, and would sit in the magistrates' not the Crown Court.

Option D is wrong because a judge presides over a Crown Court trial, and controls proceedings, and gives directions and a summing up, but does not decide on the innocence or guilt of the defendant. Option E is wrong because a magistrates' court legal adviser is a legally qualified official who works in the magistrates' court not the Crown Court, and in any event advises on the law, not innocence and guilt.

Question 3

A County Court judge is hearing a difficult breach of contract case. The facts and evidence are tricky, and he is unsure which litigant is telling the truth.

Which of the following statements is correct?

A   If the judge makes a decision that is contested by one of the litigants, he could be disciplined for making a mistake.

B   The judge should be guided in his behaviour by the codes of conduct for solicitors and barristers.

C   Any appeal from the judge's decision will be heard in the Crown Court.

D   The jury will make a decision on which litigant is telling the truth.

E   The judge can ask the court legal adviser for legal advice.

Answer

Option B is correct. Judges are influenced by the codes of conduct that govern them in their earlier lives as solicitors or barrister. Option A is wrong because a litigant who believes a judge has made a mistake should appeal the decision, and there is no disciplinary consequences to a judge having a decision appealed.

Option C is wrong because the Crown Court is a criminal court and so would not hear an appeal from the County Court. Option D is wrong because there is no jury in the County Court – juries sit in the Crown Court, in criminal matters. Option E is wrong because there is no legal adviser in the County Court, and the judge would rely on his own legal experience rather than requesting assistance from somebody else.

7 Civil Court Hierarchy, Appeal System and Jurisdiction

SQE1 syllabus

This chapter will enable you to achieve the SQE1 assessment specification in relation to functioning legal knowledge concerning the civil court hierarchy, appeal system and jurisdiction.

Note that, for SQE1, candidates are not usually required to recall specific case names or cite statutory or regulatory authorities. Cases are provided for illustrative purposes only.

Learning outcomes

By the end of this chapter you will be able to apply relevant core legal principles and rules appropriately and effectively, at the level of a competent newly qualified solicitor in practice, to realistic client-based and ethical problems and situations in the following areas:

*   types of court, and their locations;
*   the jurisdiction and workload of the County Court, and appeals from it to the High Court;
*   the jurisdiction of the three divisions of the High Court, and their workload;

- appeals from the High Court to the Court of Appeal;
- appeals from the Court of Appeal to the Supreme Court, and the work of the Supreme Court;
- the overall hierarchy of the courts, and how cases progress within the court system;
- rights of audience;
- tribunals, their jurisdiction and workload; and
- the Judicial Committee of the Privy Council.

7.1 Introduction

This chapter deals with civil court hierarchy, appeals and jurisdiction. Hierarchy means seniority, and the way in which lower courts defer to superior courts. Appeals are the process by which a disappointed litigant from a hearing requests a review of their case by a more senior court. Jurisdiction means the nature and extent of a court's powers, and this broadly involves three aspects: geographical location, subject matter and financial value, ie the amounts of money at stake.

In this chapter we will start with jurisdiction. We will explain the geographical extent of courts in England and Wales. We will also review the work undertaken by them and tribunals. We will then scrutinise the links between the various courts, ie their hierarchy. We will also consider rights of audience, ie the rules on who can address a judge during a trial. Along the way we will discuss the appeal system, in other words how disputes can be referred upwards if a party is disappointed with the initial outcome.

7.2 Jurisdiction of the courts: their location

Once upon a time courthouses were a physical presence in most of our communities. Justice was essentially local. Heavyweight matters took place, then as now, in London, but judges resolved lesser issues in the provinces.

To give but one example, Dorset County Council's archives for the period 1830–1845 show an ongoing dispute over turnpike access close to the Bloxworth estate near Bere Regis and Winterborne Kingston in the heart of the countryside. A turnpike is yesterday's version of a road. Official records state one landowner 'took the case to the Queen's Bench but failed to gain satisfaction because it was stated that too much time had elapsed since the road was first closed'. A local court at Dorchester, Bere Regis or Bovington heard the case.

Courts in towns and cities up and down the land replicated this sort of community justice. Courthouses were as routine a presence in Victorian England as townhalls, manor houses and, in due course, railway stations.

No longer. Justice today is still local, but modernity has redefined the term. The Ministry of Justice suggests 97% of the population live within one hour's drive of a court. Anecdotal evidence indicates some attendees, however, have a round trip of 60, 70 or 80 miles or more. The phrase 'access to justice' is used in a variety of contexts these days. It covers the ability of individuals to instruct a lawyer, or afford one, or find one willing to act. To this we can add the proximity of courts to small towns, and the ease - or difficulty - of travel to a hearing.

So where are courts located, and how many of them are there? In London, which has dominated legal process for centuries, the Supreme Court sits in Parliament Square in Westminster SW1. The Court of Appeal and the High Court are based at the Royal Courts of Justice in the Strand WC2. These three courts – the Supreme, Appeal and High – are at the pinnacle of the centralised justice system. The Crown Court deals with family matters. Other significant satellite courts are within walking distance – for instance, the Business and Property Courts at the Rolls Building in Fetter Lane EC4.

These are the elite courts, the stars of the legal constellation. Scattered around the country we find a number of more humble participants – the County Court, magistrates' courts and the Family Court. The HMCTS website contains a list of these and other courts. Most of us are more likely to visit them than their London equivalents.

Figure 7.1 is a basic flowchart illustrating the modern court structure. It starts with the Supreme Court at the top, and progresses downwards from there.

Figure 7.1 The modern court structure

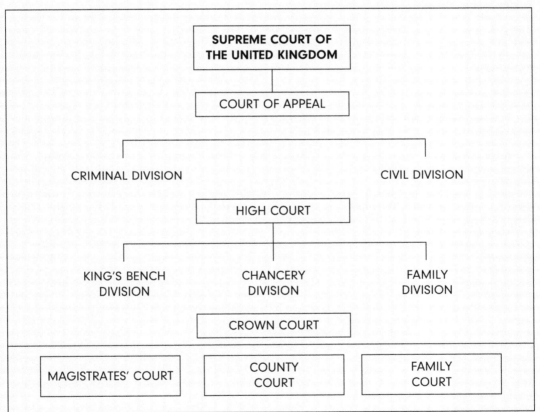

7.3   Jurisdiction: how many courts are there?

It is not immediately clear how many courts we enjoy. Interpreting the data from HMCTS is something of a puzzle. First, the list combines historic concepts with physical reality. For instance, under the letter C, it mentions the Chancery Division, which is an entity of the High Court responsible for a particular category of cases, in the same breath as the Chichester Combined Court Centre, which is a physical building in Hampshire. You can search high and low for a building called 'the Chancery Division' and you won't find it, because it is part of a greater being. It is not a physical presence, and can't be included in a headcount.

Second, there are references to a variety of courts within any one town or city. Five courts or tribunals are listed for Newcastle upon Tyne, for example. Unless you are from, or practise law, there, you are left to wonder if Newcastle Moot Hall is part of the same set up as the Newcastle Combined Court Centre, and whether the latter incorporates the Civil and Family Courts and Tribunals Centre mentioned on the website. Birmingham similarly has six courts listed. Some elementary research reveals the addresses of these bodies, but the question remains whether, being as they are within close proximity to each other, they should be seen as one institution or several entities.

Third, the list includes organisations such as collection and enforcement centres for fines for motoring offences, or maintenance in family matters. Bodies such as these have specific statutory functions and hence do not fulfil the traditional idea of a court. Fourth, the HMCTS list includes a number of miscellaneous other bodies, such as the Care Standards Tribunal (CST) in Darlington, located within other courts, as is the case with the CST, which is to be found within Darlington magistrates' court.

7.4   Court closures and 'efficiencies'

There is another barrier to grasping the geographical extent of, and numbers constituting, the court system. This is ongoing rationalisation. The House of Commons Library Debate Pack CDP 0156 of 18 June 2019 provides a summary of court closures between 2010 and 2019. The research suggests, during this period, 90 out of 240 county courts closed; 18 out of 83 dedicated tribunal buildings shut their doors for good; and 17 out of 185 family courts ceased operation. Court closures are a sensitive topic for governments. A sceptic might think an administration pondering court closures will be reluctant to make clear how many exist in the first place.

Some bare facts are apparent. Going from A to Z, so to speak, in 2011/12 courts in Aberdare, Abertillery, Acton, Alnwick, Amersham and Ashford closed. Over the same period courts at Wellingborough, West Bromwich, Whitehaven, Wimborne, Woking, Woolwich and Worksop got the chop (incidentally there are no courts beginning with X or Z, and no closures during that period of those beginning with Y). Data for 2018/19 indicates court closures occurred at Banbury, Bicester, Blackfriars, Chorley, East Berkshire, Fleetwood, Maidenhead and Wandsworth. A House of Commons Data Dashboard on magistrates' court closures, dated 13 May 2020, stated that 51% of courts closed between 2010 and 2020. A National Audit Office (NAO) report of 13 September 2019 indicates (at fig 15/p 37) that the authorities planned a further 24 site disposals in 2023–24, nine in 2024–25, and two in 2025–26. The focus of the NAO is generally on efficient use of public funds, and we can deduce from its data that there is a broad correlation here between disposals and the reduction in court buildings and thus, one presumes, court services.

For a while now courts – and by association lawyers and their culture – have been fair game for those looking to trim public expenditure. Reducing the number of courts is a natural accompaniment to cutbacks.

Politicians, and others interested in public policy, debate closures fiercely. Opponents lament the increasing distance of courts from those who appear in them. They say participants are deterred from involvement through the need to travel. Supporters of rationalisation suggest, as the Parliamentary Under-Secretary of State for Justice did in the House of Commons on 12 March 2019, many courts lie idle during the business week and so their work should be transferred to more active centres. Lucy Frazer MP, in putting the case for court closures, said 41% of courts in 2016/17 operated at just half capacity. She also mentioned an investment of £1 billion to improve service and delivery.

Courts that are decommissioned still participate in our communities. In Oldbury in the West Midlands the Court of Requests operates as a public house. The Old Courthouses in Cheltenham and Kingswinford are also pubs. Property developers are eyeing up sites. For instance, in 2019 the London Borough of Greenwich received planning application 19/1367/F, with a London-wide reference of GLA/4564/0, relating to the former magistrates' court at

Blackheath Road. The planning authority in June 2020 granted permission, with 52 conditions, for a new hotel there. The proposal mentions 293 bedrooms, a gym, swimming pool, restaurants, bars and conference facilities.

7.5 The number of courts and what they do

Whatever your views on the number of courts needed to operate our system of justice, there is no doubt their numbers have declined sharply in the last decade. Not including bodies in Scotland that have some sort of link to legal work in England and Wales, and not counting agencies that administer speeding fines, nor courts that exist in the same building as other courts, but including bodies that are linked to immigration removal centres such as that at Yarl's Wood, the number is approximately 220.

It is something of a subjective exercise arriving at a meaningful figure. But there is no guesswork to the scope of these courts, which covers every area of life imaginable. Quite apart from the everyday county and magistrates' courts, which you would expect to be listed, there are others that hint at the varied workload of the justice system: the Agricultural Land and Drainage Tribunal, the Gangmaster Licensing Appeals body, the General Regulatory Chamber, the Maintenance Enforcement Business Centre, the War Pension and Armed Forces Compensation Chamber, and the Residential Property Tribunal.

7.6 Court workloads

The work-rate of the court system remains impressive. According to CDP 0156, the caseload of civil courts has risen recently, driven by County Court activity. In 2010 there were 1.5 million County Court claims, 264,000 Family Court cases and 850,000 tribunals claims. In 2018 the equivalent figures were 2.07 million County Court claims, 262,000 Family Court claims and 484,000 tribunal cases. Anecdotally, it seems tribunal claims have declined as a result of the imposition of, or increase in, fees for making some types of application. This has deterred applicants. The surge in County Court activity has made up for this drop off. Some commentators are critical of the accuracy of Ministry of Justice figures but for our purposes they indicate that litigation remains a popular pastime. A diminishing number of courts thus needs to deal with an expanding flow of work.

The updated CBP 8372 of 31 January 2023 states that civil courts in 2021 received 1.6 million claims and family courts started 266,000 cases. Complete tribunal statistics were only available up to 2020–21, in which year 305,000 cases were started. An interim estimate of outstanding cases as of June 2022 put the number at 650,000. Collectively, this represents a decline in activity, something prompted by the Covid pandemic of 2020–21, which necessarily reduced court cases.

Let us now look at the remit of the various civil courts, starting at the bottom and working upwards. We will also look at tribunals and other methods of dispute resolution. We will also consider the role of the Judicial Committee of the Privy Council, which is a sort of glorified Supreme Court for the Commonwealth.

7.7 The role of the County Court

County courts these days usually function within combined court centres, dealing with criminal as well as civil matters. Sometimes they nestle alongside family courts, or tribunals.

We should clarify a matter of terminology. County courts do not attach to counties. They are not bucolic institutions found in sleepy lanes. In fact, they are found in provincial centres of population, both towns and cities. Confusingly, they can also be found in London, where you are no closer to a county or the countryside than to a herd of cows. This is of course a historical anomaly, reaching back to the days when London was part of Middlesex and Surrey. County courts close to the capital, or even in it, include those at Brentford, Edmonton, the Mayor's and City of London Court, Clerkenwell combined with Shoreditch and so on. The Central London County Court represents a particularly enigmatic example of something with a 'countryfied' name, yet located in the heart of the metropolis.

Large metropolitan areas outside London generally do not have standalone county courts, preferring instead to place them within combined hearing, or civil justice, centres, where they share duties with the local High Courts and District Registries. Typical locations of dedicated county courts are Gloucester, Hastings, Milton Keynes, Nuneaton, Reading, Telford and so on – in other words, middle England (and Wales). A claimant would usually commence proceedings at the venue most convenient to their home or business address. A defendant, if they would prefer a different County Court nearer them, can apply for the matter to be transferred.

County courts traditionally deal with lower value issues. The Civil Procedure Rules (CPR), a statutory instrument loaded with detail as to the management of claims, gives guidance on the financial value of cases. CPR Practice Direction (PD) 7A says any claim of £100,000 or less should commence in the County Court. Where the value is above £100,000 the claimant has a choice as to commencing in either the County or the High Court. For personal injury the relevant figure is £50,000. Practice Direction 7A says claims should start in the High Court if the financial value, complexity and importance of the outcome to the public merit it. This effectively means many claims with a value of several £100,000 or more will in fact progress through the county courts.

7.8 Example: personal injury claim

Imagine you are a 35-year-old cleaner in a National Health Service (NHS) Trust hospital in Watford, Hertfordshire. During your shift one day you slip and injure your back. You bring a claim for personal injury against the Trust. You will have restricted movement for the rest of your life, and your earnings potential is considerably reduced. You will need a certain amount of medical treatment on a long-term basis. Your claim – for loss of earnings for the rest of your working life, reduced pension entitlements, pain and suffering, and future medical care – is in the region of £200,000. Your lawyers might ponder whether to begin the claim in the High Court or the County Court, but the chances are they will opt for the latter. Your claim will therefore commence in the County Court Money Claims Centre, and be heard, in all likelihood, in the Watford County Court.

This scenario illustrates the three important aspects of jurisdiction. First, it confirms the geographic logic in commencing the claim in the court most convenient for the injured party. Second, it confirms the sort of claim a County Court will hear, namely a typical negligence claim. Third, it confirms the financial reach of the County Court as being something well over the stated benchmark of £50,000 or £100,000 mentioned earlier.

7.9 The range of County Court work

County courts deal with a wide range of work. Debt recovery and money claims are the simplest. Well, we say 'simple', but in fact these can become complicated because the defendant might turn the tables on the claimant by alleging, say, breach of contract in failing to perform work adequately (thus giving a reason not to pay). The workload otherwise reflects the nature and activity of surrounding society: personal injury and medical negligence matters, disputes over business relationships, arguments over wills, situations involving insolvency, property disputes, mortgage repossessions, claims under the Consumer Credit Act 1974, and enforcement of court orders previously made.

The CPR divides County Court cases into three financial categories. Claims of not more than £10,000 are dealt with on an expedited basis called the Small Claims track. A track, incidentally, is the pathway to trial. Cases within the £10,000–25,000 value go to the Fast Track, typically taking no more than nine months from the first hearing to trial. Claims with a value above £25,000 are allocated to the Multi Track and take longer to resolve, with a corresponding increase in costs and resources.

7.10 Typical progress of a case – CPR

The typical progress of a piece of civil litigation is as follows, whether in the County or (see later) the High Court:

- Pre-action stage. The litigant who initiates matters is called the claimant, and they make initial investigations. They write a formal letter to their opponent, the defendant, outlining the claim.

- Commencement. In the event there is no compromise between the parties, the claimant will issue and serve proceedings, with something called a Claim Form.

- Defending the claim. The defendant if they contest the claim will oppose it.

- Allocation. The County Court will then allocate the claim to the Small Claims, Fast or Multi Track, depending on its value. Higher value claims with greater complexity etc are heard in the High Court.

- Directions. The court will set a timetable of steps to trial.

- Hearing. In the event there is no settlement between the parties the trial will go ahead in front of a judge.

- Judgment. At the end of the trial the judge will make a decision. Either then or later the judge will confirm the sum of money payable by the loser to the winner. A winning claimant will expect to receive damages *and* costs. A winning defendant will seek *just* costs. This follows the standard principle that the loser pays the winner. Incidentally legal costs can be sizable.

- Enforcement. Sometimes the loser can, or will, not pay up. The next step for the winner, therefore, will be enforcement of the judgment, to recover the sums ordered.

There are regular updates to the CPR. These occur at least every couple of months, and sometimes more often. At the time of writing (May 2023) we are at the 155th update.

7.11 Appeals from the County Court

Sometimes litigants disagree with the decision of a judge. An appeal is then possible. An appeal from a district judge, ie a more junior figure than a fully fledged judge, and dealing with lesser matters, goes to a circuit judge of the County Court. Any appeal from a circuit judge is made to the High Court. The forum is usually a 'divisional' court, meaning a panel of two judges. Sometimes a single judge will sit. Insolvency matters, whether decided by a district or circuit judge, are appealed to the High Court.

An appeal can only take place by permission. Usually, this would be granted by the court being appealed. An unsuccessful party would normally request permission as soon as the judgment is handed down. Alternatively, you can apply for permission from the court where you wish the appeal to be heard. Generally, you have 21 days to file notice, although certain types of case, and hearings, have variations on this time scale. You must pay a fee when applying.

There are some well-worn traditions governing appeals. The first is that new evidence should not be introduced, the rationale for this being that any appeal should focus on the nature of the decision rather than the information and facts in dispute. This stems from the broad presumption within British justice that the original forum is best placed to decide matters such as facts, the believability of witnesses and significance of documents. Another convention is you should only appeal if you have a real chance of success, or some other strong reason for an appeal to be heard. The CPR reinforces these doctrines, requiring cases to comply with the overriding objective, a concept that includes proportionality and efficiency in the conduct of litigation. In addition, CPR 52.21 states an appeal will only be allowed if the decision of the lower court was wrong, or unjust because of a serious procedural or other irregularity in the proceedings.

The location of the appeal court depends on geography. It will be handled within the relevant circuit, ie the North East, North West, Midlands, Wales, South East and London, or South West.

Figure 7.2 presents a flowchart covering the civil appeal system, starting at the bottom with the County Court. There are references to appeals from higher courts, and we deal with those later in this chapter.

Figure 7.2 Civil appeals system

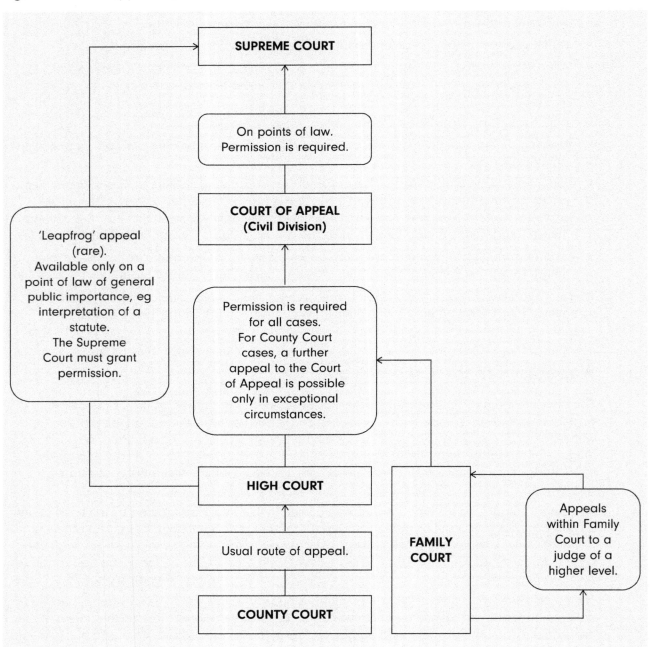

7.12 The High Court

The High Court has three divisions: The King's Bench Division (KBD), Chancery Division and Family Division. High Court cases are high value and as such equivalent to the Multi Track.

Each Division has a President, who is a senior judge. The three divisions are headquartered at the Royal Courts of Justice. Circuit judges hear cases outside London at District Registries in key centres such as Birmingham, Bristol, Cardiff, Leeds and the like.

7.12.1 King's Bench Division (KBD)

The KBD is the traditional common law arm of the High Court. It deals with contractual and tort matters. It hears breach of contract matters from businesses or individuals, landlord and tenant disputes, personal injury and clinical negligence claims and much more.

There is a number of specialist courts within the KBD. Sometimes they change their names and responsibilities, but for now they include the following:

- One of the best known is the Commercial Court, dealing with heavyweight business, finance, insurance, banking, arbitration and mercantile cases.

- Its close relative is the Admiralty Court, dealing with marine cargo disputes, collisions at sea, salvage, and claims by passengers injured on vessels. The Commercial Court, incidentally, deals with more generalised shipping matters such as contractual wrangles over shipping delays (which can be hugely expensive and a regular source of dispute).

- The Administrative Court of the KBD carries out a basket of important roles, mostly in an appeal role, such as: judicial reviews of decisions by public bodies, challenges to decisions made by ministers, planning matters, applications for habeas corpus, decisions on vexatious litigants, ie people who consistently and deliberately waste court time with hopeless applications, matters relating to coroners, proceedings for contempt of court, and appeals for extradition. It also has a criminal function in hearing appeals by way of case stated from the magistrates' or Crown Courts.

- The KBD also administers the Technology and Construction Court, which as its name implies deals with computer, software, building and engineering disputes. Within this focus it handles related matters to do with the environment, public procurement and insurance.

Observers have commented on the occasionally rigid distinctions between the different divisions, and indeed within them. The Ministry of Justice responded in 2017 by creating the Business and Property Court (BPC). It is something of an umbrella entity, bringing together different courts in the way that only administrators can. Its workload includes disputes relating to shipping, insurance, admiralty, technology, construction, insolvency, competition, intellectual property, real property and trusts. It operates in London and at regional centres traditionally key to enterprise and the generation of wealth: Birmingham, Manchester, Bristol, Liverpool and so on. There is a cross-over with court centres housing District Registries. Its jurisdiction flows across both the KBD and Chancery Division. The Circuit Commercial, or Mercantile, Court also sits within this group.

7.12.2 The Chancery Division

The Chancery Division has its origins as a counterpoint to the inflexibility, many years ago, of the common law. The name 'Chancery' stems from the role of the Lord Chancellor, then the King's chief adviser, in the 1400s. They started issuing decrees to provide a fairer resolution for previously rigid outcomes. The concept of fairness translated itself into the word 'equity', and the business of the Division today orientates itself around equitable concepts. When we talk about an equitable remedy, we mean something essentially fair in a rounded sense, and the Chancery Division today remains the guardian of this approach.

So what does the Chancery Division embrace? Its workload covers intellectual property matters, disputes over wills and trusts, certain matters relating to property loans and mortgages, partnership and business disputes, revenue and tax cases and some professional negligence claims. It also has an appeal function.

Within the Chancery Division there are specialist courts relating to:

- insolvency – when individuals suffer financial problems and become bankrupt;

- company work – dealing with insolvencies of businesses;

- patents – the protection of inventions; and

- the Intellectual Property Enterprise Court (IPEC), handling other intellectual property matters such as registered designs and trademarks. It also hears patent claims.

The Patents Court and the IPEC have similar functions to each other, with the latter usually handling lower value claims, ie those under £500,000 (yes, in the intellectual property world, half a million is a relatively small sum). The usual remedies for breach of intellectual property rights are damages, delivery up/destruction of counterfeits, an injunction, and an account of profits, ie the infringer being made to share income received. These specialist courts are currently part of the BPC.

7.12.2.1 Example of an ancient Chancery case

 The case of Mylward v Weldon (1596) Tothill 102 gives an ancient insight into the nature of Chancery cases. This was an intellectual property dispute from the late Tudor period. The Court held that Mylward was responsible for a 'replication', or copy, of 120 sheets of paper, of which 16 were 'pertinent', ie the main subject matter of the dispute. The remedy was to render useless the copies by cutting holes in them. An example of the damaged replica was then ordered to 'hang about the shoulders' of the transgressor.

Humiliatingly, he was also transported around the Fleet Street area of London 'bareheaded', on show. He had to pay a fine and costs. Today the losing party in a Chancery dispute would not be punished in this manner, but the steps taken to deliver up, destroy or confiscate counterfeit property remain a relevant remedy today.

7.12.3 Family Division and the Family Court

The Crime and Courts Act 2013 and the Children and Families Act 2014 transferred much family litigation out of the mainstream civil courts and magistrates' courts to a dedicated Family Court. The Family Division therefore has something of a lower profile as a result.

The Family Court deals with the protection of children, including local authority intervention, divorce petitions, violence remedies and adoption. A range of courts operate here: the High Court, County Court and magistrates' courts. The judiciary have special training to deal with the particular and sensitive nature of this sort of work.

Family Court proceedings have a dual focus: public law and private law.

- Public law business consists of litigation in the public interest, generated by public authorities or the National Society for the Prevention of Cruelty to Children. The thrust of this work is to intervene where necessary to protect children. This includes care orders, supervision orders and emergency protection orders.

- Private law involves applications by individuals, usually parents, relating to parental responsibility, financial issues, welfare arrangements for children such as guardianship, and the occasional application to prevent children being moved abroad.

7.12.4 Appeals from the High Court

Appeals from the High Court are to the Court of Appeal Civil Division. Decisions are by a majority, and so there will be an odd number of judges hearing the matter, usually three, but sometimes five or even seven, Lords or Lady Justices of Appeal.

CPR, Part 52 provides information on appeals. It states that permission to appeal may be given only where the court considers the appeal would have a real prospect of success, or there is some other compelling reason for the appeal to be heard. An order giving permission to appeal may limit the issues to be heard and impose conditions.

Occasionally there is an appeal of something appealed. The rules are stricter here. Permission will not be given unless the Court of Appeal believes the appeal would have a real prospect of success, and raises an important point of principle or practice, or there is some other compelling reason for the matter to be heard.

The procedure for appealing from the High Court is as follows. The party wishing to appeal, called the appellant, should initially apply for permission from the court making the original decision. Alternatively, application can be made to the Court of Appeal itself. This should be done within the time frame stated by the original court, or alternatively within 21 days after the date of the original decision. The notice should be served on the other party to the litigation, called the respondent, not later than seven days after filing. The respondent can file and serve their own notice, putting their case, within 14 days after they receive the appellant's notice. The Court will need to see the appellant's grounds for appeal and a skeleton argument, as a bare minimum. A skeleton argument, incidentally, is the outline of a party's reasons for making or defending a claim, and will be expanded on by advocates in court at the hearing itself.

There are particular provisions relating to appeals of judicial review and tribunal matters. The majority of appeals relating to decisions of the Family Court are to other judges of higher seniority within that court.

7.12.5 An example of a case that is appealed

The case of *Regeneron Pharmaceuticals Inc v Kymab Ltd* [2020] UKSC 27 illustrates the ups and downs of the appeal process. You might think it extraordinary that someone could claim intellectual property in a living being, but that is exactly what happened in this case. Regeneron filed patents for a new type of genetically modified mouse (that is, the rodent, not the electronic accessory). They sued Kymab Limited for infringement. Kymab responded by arguing the patents were invalid on the basis of insufficient detail.

The case began in the Patents Court of the Chancery Division. There, the judge declared the patents invalid, dismissing Regeneron's infringement claim. Regeneron, the appellant, appealed to the Court of Appeal, where Lord Justice Kitchin, unanimously on behalf of a panel of three, upheld the appeal. It was then Kymab's turn to appeal. They therefore became the appellant to the Supreme Court. A panel of five heard the matter.

You might wonder at the need for a patent involving a rodent. The Supreme Court explained the importance of the underlying facts to this case:

> Since the development of antibodies is a natural process shared by mammals generally, and since ethical constraints prevented the use of fellow humans as platforms for antibody development, mice had been identified as suitable platforms for the development of antibodies suitable for use in treatment of humans ...

In other words, scientists have experimented on mice for some time, for medical reasons, in particular for the purposes of developing antibodies to combat disease and illness. You can of course debate the ethical dimension here, but for practical purposes we should note the medical imperative for such research, allied to the financial benefits resulting. The clinical, reputational and financial stakes are high. Medics can save lives and progress to professorships; scientists can advance careers; and businesses make profits.

Lord Briggs gave the majority judgment (4-1) allowing Kymab's appeal. The Supreme Court said the Court of Appeal's analysis could not be held as a 'legitimate development of the law'. Lady Black gave the dissenting judgment.

The chronology of events is therefore this. The High Court judge found against the claimant Regeneron, and in favour of the defendant Kymab. All three justices of the Court of Appeal allowed Regeneron's appeal. At this stage Regeneron would naturally be happy. But in this life it does not pay to get either too excited or downcast. The highest court of the land, the Supreme Court, reversed the Court of Appeal. The defendant Kymab therefore emerged the victor. It was held the claimant Regeneron's patent was indeed insufficient, and accordingly there had been no infringement.

Figure 7.3 illustrates the ups and downs of the appeal process. As a lawyer, it is important you remain level headed throughout. Be calm with your clients. Things are rarely as optimal as they appear. Likewise, they are rarely as bad as might seem at first.

This flowchart illustrates the cut and thrust of this litigation, which was one of high value intellectual property. Big companies have deep pockets and here it was worth taking the matter to the highest court of the land. At the end of the process someone has to pay the legal fees. They would have been hefty, of course. Incidentally there is a 'tongue in cheek' tone to one aspect of this chart.

Figure 7.3   The ups and downs of the appeal process: Regeneron Pharmaceuticals

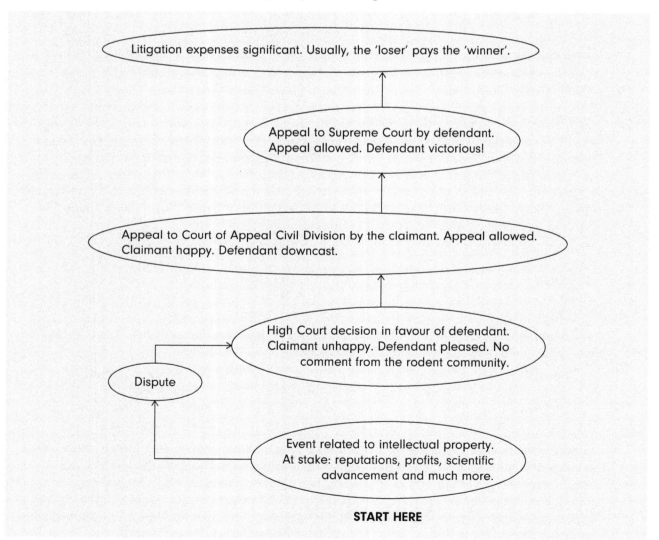

7.13   Rights of audience

It is all very well having a claim worth bringing before the courts. But there is no point spending time and effort on the matter without having an entitlement to speak in court. You could adduce evidence by way of certain documentation. You can also speak out as a witness, providing first-hand recollection of certain key facts. But none of these are as effective as standing on your own two feet and making submissions, verbally and with the necessary force, to the judiciary in person. Indeed, some would say this entitlement is an essential element of a properly functioning democracy.

The legal system gives considerable thought as to who can make submissions in court. There are a number of basic presumptions, which have grown over time, and which influence current rules on the subject. First, everyone should be allowed to have their case presented orally by an advocate. Second, professional advocates must be suitably qualified and regulated.

Third, if you wish to save money, or have no resources, or simply have a disdain for the authorities, and you therefore choose not to employ a qualified and regulated lawyer, you can ask to address the court yourself, and that request will be received in a relatively favourable light. Fourth, if you choose to go it alone, the court will be sceptical as to the involvement of someone else, however well intentioned, seeking to advocate on your behalf, particularly if they are charging a fee. You might be attracted to this last option because any fee would be vastly less, in all likelihood, than that charged by a fully fledged lawyer. But courts would be reluctant to allow it.

Courts have developed these rules to ensure the advocacy process has integrity, by controlling those who make submissions. Courts need to receive respect, to hear the truth and to prioritise the proper administration of justice. They believe this can only be achieved by allowing either properly qualified lawyers or, at a pinch, individual parties themselves. One of the wonders of our legal system is the endless patience of our courts with bumbling, inefficient, chaotic and bitter amateur litigants managing their own claims. Anyone not within these two categories is seen as something of a loose cannon, capable of misleading the court or the litigant or both.

The entitlement to make submissions in court is called a right of audience. What, then, are the rules? Thomas More (1478–1535), a Lord Chancellor from the time of King Henry VIII, wrote *Utopia* (1516) as an analysis of the supposedly optimal society. In it he suggested good governance allowed individuals to operate without lawyers:

> They have no lawyers among them, for they consider them as a sort of people whose profession it is to disguise matters, and to wrest the laws; and therefore they think it is much better that every man should plead his own cause, and trust it to the judge …

The last part of this extract suggests individuals are better off pleading their own case rather than relying on advocates. Perhaps this is one source of judicial sympathy for individuals wishing to advocate for themselves. Today, we call this 'a litigant in person', and owing to the cost of court work there are quite a few of them about, acting on their own account to save money.

We shouldn't overstate the issue of a layperson addressing the Court. Appearances in chambers – more akin to an office than a formal courtroom – are considered less severe than a full trial, and the rules are relaxed. A 'do it yourself' litigant can speak out in a small claims case, for instance. The real issue relates to 'open' court, with a set piece trial, where there is an expectation that rules should be followed to ensure the sanctity of the overall process.

The Legal Services Act 2007 provides the statutory basis for the current position. Section 1 states, as regulatory objectives, the need to protect and promote the public interest, support the constitutional principle of the rule of law, and improve access to justice. A key professional principle then states authorised persons should maintain proper standards of work.

Section 12 states the exercise of a right of audience is a reserved legal activity. Section 13(2) says a person is entitled to carry on a reserved legal activity if authorised or exempt. Section 18 says an authorised person means a person authorised to carry on the relevant activity by a relevant approved regulator. There are a number of such regulators, the main ones for our purposes being the Solicitors Regulation Authority (for solicitors) and the Bar Standards Board (for barristers). If you comply with the requirements of your regulator you will benefit from a right of audience.

The Act then deals with the amateur advocate by saying you can have rights of audience by virtue of being an exempt person. The Act's third schedule expands on this. The most relevant provision says you can be exempt if the right of audience is granted by a court on a one-off basis relating to a particular set of proceedings.

So, to summarise, statute confirms you have a right of audience in open court if you are a properly regulated individual such as, typically, a barrister or solicitor. Alternatively, Joe Public can ask the court for rights to be granted on a temporary basis for a particular case.

 Receiving permission in such a scenario is a jealously guarded entitlement. The leading case on the matter is D v S (Rights of Audience) [1997] 1 FLR 724. Here, the court confirmed the entitlement was to be granted on a case-by-case basis. The court expressed opposition to unqualified people who presented themselves as being freelance advocates, whether for remuneration or not. R v Conaghan [2017] EWCA Crim 597 noted the increasing tendency these days for individuals to negotiate the court process themselves. The Court said, speaking of the criminal process, but in tones that suggest relevance to the civil arena too, they would only allow a non-qualified third party to address the court in 'exceptional circumstances'. It also added that permission for a third party to act in a litigation role (perhaps preparing documents and advising the litigant) did not automatically extend to a right of audience in front of a judge.

You can see here the grave doubts judges harbour as to the involvement of unofficial third party advocates. Courts fear they will ignore procedure, or play fast and loose with the truth, or take advantage of the lay litigant. And as they are not regulated by a profession, judges would not be able to command a regulator to investigate improper conduct.

In conclusion, the current position appears to be this. Litigants should engage qualified advocates if at all possible. Litigants in person who wish to advocate their own cases, or who are reduced to so doing through circumstances, can apply to the court for permission, and in the general scheme of things would expect their application to be received sympathetically. Unqualified third parties seeking to advocate on behalf of a litigant in person will be discouraged.

You may read about the court process and wish to qualify as a solicitor, barrister or other legal professional in the advocacy field. This is entirely possible provided you submit to the regulatory process through the SRA or BSB or equivalent, undergo the necessary training, maintain the appropriate standards and evidence the proper qualities. It is a thrilling and rewarding job, although as with many walks of life you should not expect the career path to be easy. Note that a solicitor does not usually have rights of audience in the Crown Court unless they have obtained a higher rights of audience qualification (Solicitors' Higher Rights of Audience Regulations 2010). An exception to this rule allows a solicitor to appear before the Crown Court on an appeal from the magistrates' court. However, this exception applies only if the solicitor (or their firm) represented the individual who is making the appeal in the original trial before the magistrates' court (Practice Direction (Solicitors: Rights of Audience) (No 2) [1972]).

To end this section, here's a flowchart that summarises some issues relating to rights of audience. The starting point is the need for those rights to be exercised. It must then be accepted this is a reserved legal activity. You must then be either authorised or exempt. A litigant in person is a good example of the latter. You will see **Figure 7.4** mentions some reasons for a litigant in person to perform as their own advocate.

Figure 7.4 Considerations as to rights of audience

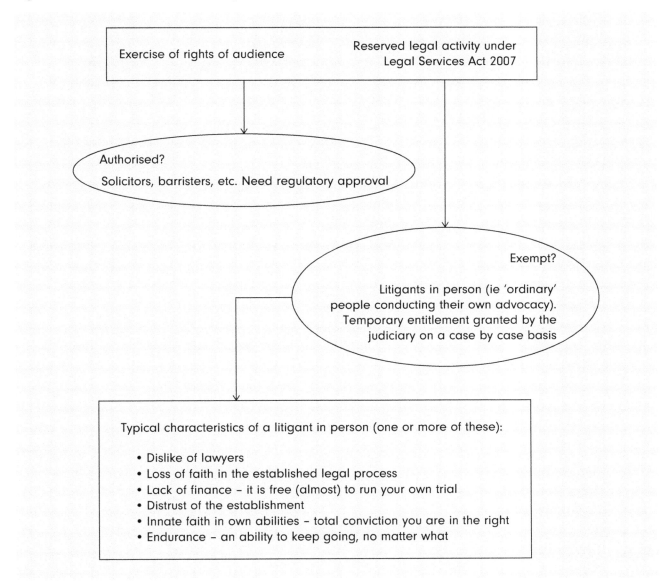

7.14 Tribunals

Modern society generates too much litigation for courts to manage on their own. For many years a system of tribunals has assisted in dealing with disputes and providing remedies. These tribunals represent the continuing culture within the legal system of streamlined justice handed down by people who are not necessarily qualified lawyers. When we say 'not necessarily', the idea is that a panel of three people will be chaired by someone with legal qualifications. The other two will be lay people. There are variations on this theme but that is the original model that endures today. Common sense exercised by non-lawyers plays a large part in arriving at a result.

The Tribunals Courts and Enforcement Act 2007 provides a structure for today's system. There are, broadly, three sorts of tribunals. First there are those administered through local authorities, for instance school exclusion panels dealing with children. Second, government departments run some, an example being the Valuation Tribunal (VT), which deals with council tax matters and non-domestic rates. The VT comes under the jurisdiction of the Ministry of Housing, Communities and Local Government. Third, there are tribunals administered by HMCTS, and we shall focus on these.

HMCTS administers a two-tier tribunal system: a First Tier, and an Upper Tribunal, both of which are split into chambers. Each chamber sub-divides into different bodies. Some chambers have jurisdiction for the whole of the United Kingdom, others for just England and Wales, and some for just Scotland.

The First Tier hears appeals against decisions by government departments or agencies.

The most important chambers are those relating to:

- social entitlement, ie social security and child support;
- health education and social care, dealing with special educational needs and care standards;
- general regulatory matters, covering information rights, claims management, gambling, and the environment;
- tax, including the expenses of MPs;
- immigration and asylum;
- property, which includes a tribunal dealing with the vexed matter of leasehold reform, something which once again reinforces the crucial role of property within our legal system; and,
- as one of the flagships of the tribunal system, employment matters.

The Upper Tribunal generally, but not exclusively, reviews and decides appeals from the First Tier. The Upper Tribunal consists of the following chambers: administrative appeals, tax and Chancery, immigration and asylum, lands and employment. A disappointed applicant can make a further appeal, from the Upper Tribunal to the Court of Appeal. CPR 52 contains the details. The appellant must generally file notice within 28 days of the decision. Judicial review and employment matters have a shorter timescale.

Figure 7.5 briefly illustrates the structure of tribunals in our jurisdiction.

It is worth dwelling on the activities of these tribunals. Let us consider employment matters. These are generally chaired by a judge, who provides legal guidance to other members of the panel, and who writes the resulting judgment.

In its own way the process is a microcosm of the operation of the legal system. First, it touches on a crucial aspect of society, namely relations between employer and employee. Today, we take it for granted the balance is broadly equal between the two, but this is only as a result of decades of struggle. Safety at work, fair wages, representation through trade unions and the right not to be dismissed unfairly only emerged after years of confrontation.

Second, society recognises the importance of employment matters within the democratic model. Everyone – not just those in employment – benefits from fairness. Employment issues impact on families, communities and the wider economy. If people lose jobs, individuals elsewhere suffer. There is a corresponding impact on growth and output. Third, the legal system accepts the best way of dealing with disputes of this nature is through the common sense of non-lawyers, albeit with the opportunity to appeal upwards if necessary.

The case of Curless v Shell *[2019] EWCA Civ 1710 provides an insight into three areas of interest when considering tribunals. First, it shows how employment tribunals operate, together with the subject matter of some disputes. Second, it provides an instance of how*

Figure 7.5 Overview of the tribunal system

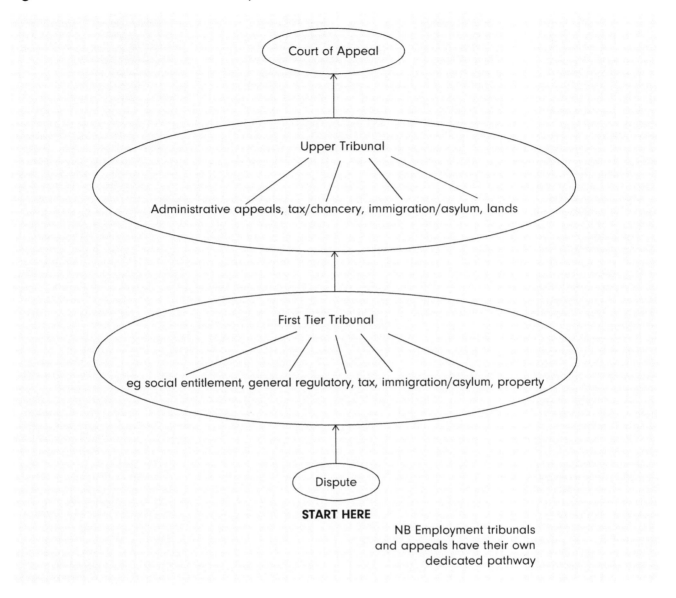

appeals progress. Third, it touches on one aspect vital to the operation of an effective legal system, namely the role of the lawyer.

The facts are these. The applicant alleged disability discrimination within a redundancy process. Part of the case revolved around an email sent by one of the respondent's in-house lawyers. The applicant suggested the email evidenced the redundancy process was a sham designed to militate against him. A central part of the dispute was whether that email benefited from privilege, ie the concept that advice provided should be for the eyes of the client only, and kept private from the other party and indeed the tribunal.

The tribunal at first instance held the email was privileged, and rejected the applicant's claim. He appealed to the Employment Appeal Tribunal (EAT). It upheld his appeal. Shell then appealed to the Court of Appeal, where a panel of three, including the Master of the Rolls, who is one of the most senior judges in the land, reversed the decision of the EAT, and declared Shell to be correct.

We can see from this case certain key aspects of the tribunal system. It starts from the point of view matters can be resolved by a panel that includes non-lawyers. It relies, however, on a proper application of the rule of law, and if there is a dispute over the law an appeal is possible. The subject matter of the appeal was very specific in this instance, relating to disability and redundancy, but the ethos remains consistent with the philosophy that has emerged since Victorian times. Tribunals are at pains to treat employer and employee equally, and to ensure the one who typically has less of a negotiating advantage, ie the employee, has an opportunity to state their case in full.

The role of lawyers in providing legal advice remains central to the process. In this instance, advice to the respondent proved contentious. Even so, the Court of Appeal held it had something of a sacrosanct status, and should be treated as highly confidential, thus protecting solicitor-client relations. The privacy of legal advice remains an important element of the legal system, and indeed could be considered one of the satellite aspects of the operation of the constitution. Without it, one party could cramp the ability of the other participant to receive full and proper advice and this could be damaging in the extreme, particularly to weaker and poorer members of society.

7.15 The Court of Appeal and the Supreme Court

The Court of Appeal has a Civil and a Criminal Division. The Civil Division hears appeals from the High Court, the Family Court and tribunals. Since November 2018 selected hearings are streamed live via YouTube.

The Supreme Court hears appeals from the Court of Appeal, the Court of Session in Scotland and the Court of Appeal in Northern Ireland. There are 12 justices in all. Usually five sit on a panel, although the number can be as low as three or as high as nine. There are criteria for deciding whether there should be a higher number. These include the following:

- if the court is being asked to depart, or they may decide to depart, from a previous decision;
- where the case has high constitutional importance, such as the decision on the lawfulness of prorogation of Parliament by the prime minister in 2019;
- if the case has great public importance;
- where there is conflict between previous decisions, and/or those decisions need to be reconciled; and
- cases involving an important point in relation to the ECHR.

The right of civil appeal is governed by a variety of statutes from the Administration of Justice Appeals Act 1934 to the Access to Justice Act 1999. There are also considerations under the Human Rights Act 1998.

Certain limited cases are allowed to jump from the High Court or Divisional Courts to the Supreme Court. As these miss out the Court of Appeal, they are referred to as 'leapfrog' appeals.

The Supreme Court caseload involves pretty much everything litigated in the courts below. But it follows its own practice directions and declines to hear various claims, such as those relating to certain rules of court, or by vexatious litigants, or from the County Court on probate matters, or certain issues relating to the Representation of the People Act 1983. It also will not hear appeals against a refusal by the Court of Appeal to hear an appeal from, say, the High

Court. This reflects the entirely sensible concern to limit the dystopian possibility of endlessly circular litigation – appeals about appeals, and that sort of thing.

Otherwise, it has a particular role in hearing civil contempt of court matters, where for instance someone has commented in an irresponsible manner on active court proceedings in such a way as to prejudice the outcome. It also decides certain devolution matters from Scotland, Wales and Northern Ireland.

A dissatisfied party from a matter tried in the Court of Appeal can only appeal to the Supreme Court with permission. Application should first be made at the Court of Appeal. If unsuccessful you can apply to the Supreme Court itself. This must be done within 28 days of the date of the Court of Appeal order. The appeal process does not suspend the decision of the court below.

The test for allowing an appeal to be heard is a strict one. Their Lords and Ladyships will only grant permission if, in their opinion, the matter raises an arguable point of law of general public importance that ought to be considered by them at that time, bearing in mind that the matter will already have been the subject of judicial decision, and may have already been reviewed on appeal.

Major decisions by the Supreme Court involve the full Court, but some procedural decisions may be taken by a single justice and the Court Registrar. These include matters relating to time limits, non-compliance with rules, withdrawal of an appeal and certain costs matters. The Registrar will normally make a decision without an oral hearing but may direct one to take place if deemed necessary.

7.16 Judicial Committee of the Privy Council (JCPC)

The United Kingdom's love–hate relationship with the Commonwealth continues through the Judicial Committee of the Privy Council. Historically, this body presided over appeals and other legal matters referred from the colonies. It represented the good and the bad of imperial rule: good in the sense it provided a benevolent application of fairness as an antidote to the behaviour of local officials; bad in the sense that the system required people to play by rules that were essentially imposed on them from London.

Today, 27 Commonwealth countries, overseas territories and Crown dependencies use the Committee as their final chance of justice when there is disagreement over decisions by local courts.

To understand the Committee we need to know a bit about the Privy Council itself. The Privy Council consists of three categories of individuals: government ministers, senior opposition politicians and judges. The title of Privy Counsellor (PC) (note, traditionally, not 'councillor') means someone who gives advice to the monarch rather than someone on a 'council'. Gradually PCs were supplanted by Ministers. A tiny minority of PCs are judicial, alongside vast numbers of MPs and Lords from Parliament. Once appointed, on the recommendation of the Government of the day, you are there forever, unless you do something horribly wrong.

The generalised Privy Council has something of an honorific role, rubberstamping legislation, supposedly shadowing government departments and committees, taking an interest in Royal Charters, and pretending to advise the Monarch. The Judicial Committee, however, has a genuinely useful legal role. The membership is the same as the Supreme Court, with a few supplementary members. Sometimes Commonwealth judges also sit.

The Committee hears a range of matters: appeals from the disciplinary committee of the body regulating vets; a ragbag of other unusual domestic matters such as disputes relating to disqualification from the House of Commons; appeals from Crown dependencies such as Jersey; Commonwealth appeals, from places such as Antigua and Barbuda, the Bahamas, Saint Lucia, Mauritius and so on; and appeals from overseas territories and sovereign bases such as Gibraltar, the Falkland Islands, St Helena, the British Virgin Islands and more. If you wanted to give it a label, in the vernacular of travel and planes, you could almost call it the Long Haul Court.

The test for bringing a matter before the Committee is suitably rigorous. In civil matters, the Court granting leave to appeal must be satisfied that the case raises a point of general public importance. In criminal matters, the case must raise questions of great and general importance, or there must have been some grave violation of principles of natural justice.

The Committee follows procedure from the Judicial Committee (Appellate Jurisdiction) Rules 2009. These cover the 'small print' of the relevant process, such as applying for permission to appeal, commencement and preparation, the hearing and decision, and of course costs. At least three, and usually five, justices sit on the panel. They read documents, hear oral submissions, and at the end of the process give advice to the monarch rather than a judgment as such. Dissenting opinions are allowed. Hearings are in open court at the venue shared with the Supreme Court in Parliament Square. It is possible to watch in person, or if you prefer home comforts you can view by video link.

The Committee workload is considerable. It heard 54 appeals in 2019, for instance. The bulk of cases relate to criminal matters but a significant minority deal with civil issues. In the first half of 2020 the Committee ruled on matters as diverse as company liquidation law in the Cayman Islands, unfair dismissal in the Caribbean, and police investigatory matters in Jamaica. Other decisions in recent years relate to a challenge on environmental grounds to the construction of a dam in Belize, and a ruling on pollution in Trinidad and Tobago.

Decisions of the Committee are persuasive, in other words influential, rather than binding. This means other courts will refer to such decisions, and place weight on them, without following them in a dogmatic manner.

Regardless of the exact legal weight given to a Committee decision, it fulfils a vital constitutional role. It represents continuity with the past, and a reassuring reminder of fairness within the law. Most importantly, it remains a court of last resort for overseas citizens who harbour doubts, however unreasonable or unlikely, as to the motives of officialdom closer to home.

Summary

We have discussed the jurisdiction of the county courts, their locations, their reducing number and how appeals operate from them to the High Court. We have seen how the High Court's three divisions – the King's Bench, Chancery and Family – cover a lot of ground. They occasionally regroup as a result of administrative developments, but fundamentally their role and workload remain consistent.

We have also noted how the Family Division has coalesced with the Family Court. We have explored appeals to the Court of Appeal and the Supreme Court. We have assessed the work of tribunals. We have explained rights of audience, and the wish of many individual litigants to represent themselves. Finally, we have assessed the role of the Judicial Committee of the Privy Council.

Sample questions

Question 1

A woman suffers an injury at work. Her employer is a company whose sole shareholder is her uncle. She wishes to claim compensation for personal injury. The likely value of the claim is £80,000. Neither the injuries nor the facts relating to the claim are particularly complex.

In which of the following courts should the woman commence the claim against the uncle?

A The King's Bench Division (KBD) of the High Court.

B The Chancery Division of the High Court.

C The Employment Tribunal.

D The County Court.

E The Family Court.

Answer

Option D is correct. Practice Direction (PD) 7A of the Civil Procedure Rules (CPR) states that, where a personal injury claim has a value of more than £50,000, a choice can be made as to commencement in either the County Court or the High Court. The PD goes on to provide that cases should only be started in the High Court if that is desirable by reason of:

(1) the financial value of the claim and the amount in dispute, and/or

(2) the complexity of the facts, legal issues, remedies or procedures involved, and/or

(3) the importance of the outcome of the claim to the public in general.

Here, because the claim is relatively straightforward, a correct interpretation of CPR PD 7A means the appropriate court would be the County Court.

Option A is wrong because the matter is not sufficiently complex, or of sufficiently considerable value, to start in the High Court (although if the value was much higher the KBD would indeed have the relevant jurisdiction). Option B is wrong because a personal injury claim would not be appropriate for the Chancery Division, which in the main deals with claims relating to mortgages, wills, trusts and so on. Option C is wrong because an Employment Tribunal deals with matters such as dismissals rather than personal injury. Option E is wrong because, although the uncle is a relative, and might be described as 'family', the Family Court deals with matrimonial and children matters not personal injury.

Question 2

A veterinary scientist has invented a device for testing the temperature of dogs to provide an early warning of canine illness. She has a patent for the device. She believes the patent could yield profits of £1m in the next two years. A manufacturer appears to have infringed the patent by manufacturing 200,000 counterfeit replicas of the device. The veterinary scientist believes her losses could be £600,000. She would like to commence court action against the manufacturer.

Which is the correct court for the veterinary scientist to commence a claim, and the appropriate remedy?

A The King's Bench Division (KBD) of the High Court, with a remedy solely of damages.

B The County Court, with damages as one possible remedy, the other being delivery up/destruction of the counterfeits.

C   The Court of Appeal, with damages as one possible remedy, the other being delivery up/destruction.

D   The Business and Property Court (BPC), with a remedy solely of damages.

E   The Patents Court within the Chancery Division of the High Court, with damages as one possible remedy, the other being delivery up/destruction.

Answer

Option E is correct. The Patents Court, which is part of the Chancery Division of the High Court, has jurisdiction for claims of this sort where the value is over £500,000. There would be remedies in both damages and delivery up / destruction of the counterfeits.

Option A is wrong because the KBD does not have jurisdiction for hearing patent matters. Option B is wrong because the value of the veterinary scientist's claim is far above the financial scope of the County Court, and the matter would also be too complex for it. Option C is wrong because no claims commence in the Court of Appeal. They always begin in a lower court such as the County or High Courts. Option D is wrong because, although the BPC would be a suitable starting point on account of the fact that it embraces the Patents Court, the remedy solely of damages would be insufficient.

Question 3

A man is defending a breach of contract claim in a County Court relating to his business selling furniture. During trial, the judge continuously interrupts the man's advocate and does not allow him to develop his defence. The man loses and wishes to appeal.

To which court should the man appeal, and what is the relevant ground?

A   The Court of Appeal, on the ground that there is a possibility of success.

B   The Chancery Division of the High Court, on the ground that the County Court had given insufficient weight to certain evidence.

C   The Technology and Construction Court within the King's Bench Division of the High Court, on the ground that the County Court's decision was unjust.

D   The King's Bench Division, to an appropriate judge, on the ground of serious procedural irregularity.

E   Another County Court, on the ground that there is an arguable point of law of general public importance.

Answer

Option D is correct. The appropriate court is the King's Bench Division of the High Court, on the ground of serious procedural irregularity by the judge who did not allow the man's advocate to develop his case.

Option A is wrong as there is no appeal to the Court of Appeal from the decision of a circuit judge, and in any event the correct ground is a 'real prospect of success', not a 'possibility'. Option B is wrong because the Chancery Division of the High Court, although it hears appeals, would not deal with a breach of contract matter relating to furniture. Also, an appeal court would not usually scrutinise a lower court's handling of the evidence.

Option C is wrong because the Technology and Construction Court, likewise, would not deal with a breach of contract matter relating to furniture. The ground of appeal – unjustness – could be correct in a different court. Option E is wrong as the decision of a circuit judge in the County Court cannot be appealed in the County Court. Also, the ground of 'an arguable point of law of general public importance' is the test for an appeal to the Supreme Court, not the High Court.

8 Criminal Court Hierarchy, Appeal System and Jurisdiction

SQE1 syllabus

This chapter will enable you to achieve the SQE1 assessment specification in relation to functioning legal knowledge concerning the criminal court hierarchy, the appeal system and jurisdiction.

Note that, for SQE1, candidates are not usually required to recall specific case names or cite statutory or regulatory authorities. Cases are provided for illustrative purposes only.

Learning outcomes

By the end of this chapter you will be able to apply relevant core legal principles and rules appropriately and effectively, at the level of a competent newly qualified solicitor in practice, to realistic client-based and ethical problems and situations in the following areas:

*   the role of the police, and their link to the court system;
*   the operation of the magistrates' courts, and the Crown Court, and their jurisdiction, including how prosecutions commence;

- issues relating to the effective operation of the court system, and in particular the need to avoid late abandonment of trials, and late adjournments;

- some of the main points of the Criminal Procedure Rules, which impact on the operation of the court system;

- thoughts on funding a criminal defence;

- the way in which courts within the hierarchy link together, and a case study illustrating the operation of hierarchy, appeals and jurisdiction, together with some drawbacks of the criminal justice system; and

- appeals from the magistrates', the Crown Court and the Court of Appeal.

8.1   Introduction

In earlier chapters we examine global principles such as the rule of law and the importance of individual freedoms. In this chapter we focus on some of the detail of the criminal justice system, such as the police role, the Crown Prosecution Service (CPS), the operation of the various courts, and some of the rules that govern the court process. As will always be the case in a mature pluralistic democracy, some aspects of the system are imperfect, and we will examine one incident that reminds us of the constant quest for self-improvement. Lastly, we will look at appeals, and how they generally allow defendants a second chance, within reason.

8.2   The police

Any discussion of the criminal court hierarchy and its jurisdiction must involve the police. They prevent crime, monitor the activities of criminals, oversee the peaceful continuity of everyday life, maintain public order and enforce the laws of the land. They arrest suspects, interview them at the police station, and coordinate with the CPS in bringing charges. Crucially, they then appear as prosecution witnesses at trials.

In addition they perform a whole host of other roles that embed them into society: checking suspects on bail behave themselves; helping local groups set up speed-watch activities; engaging with the homeless; visiting schools to reinforce the safeguarding message; working with agencies on crime prevention, drug treatment and mental health programmes; calming tempers between irate neighbours; and much more.

Home Office statistics as at 30 September 2019 indicate there were then 124,784 police officers in the 43 territorial police forces of England and Wales. The total workforce, comprising officers, staff, police community support officers (PCSOs), and so on was the full-time equivalent of 204,815 employees.

8.2.1   Assaults on the police

The job has its risks. The Office for National Statistics (ONS) assets publishing service document 'Crime in England and Wales' for the financial year 2018/19 (ie April to April) states there were 10,399 assaults with injury on a constable. There were over 20,000 assaults without injury. In December 2017 the Metropolitan Police – the largest force in the country – responded to a Freedom of Information (FoI) request relating to injuries received by officers on duty in the first six months of 2017. There were 2,596 reported incidents. These ranged from physical assault (1,108) to being hit by a moving vehicle (201). Injuries suffered make unpleasant reading. Although 625 involved bruising, and as such could be considered relatively minor, others were quite chilling. For example, 313 involved a cut or laceration. There were a number of burns, concussions, 'foreign bodies' in the eye and inhalation of smoke or toxic substances. There were six stabbings. Also, 108 were whiplash injuries, thus indicating the link between crime, the need for a speedy police response, and the use of vehicles.

You can only imagine the unpleasant nature of these incidents, not to mention the fear and anticipation accompanying the events, even if there was just a minor injury, or indeed no injury at all. The FoI response also mentioned 428 reports of an apparently more routine nature, such as injury while handling, lifting or carrying. But we suspect to the personnel involved they were anything but commonplace.

A 2020 FoI response by the Metropolitan Police, created on 17 April 2020 with a review date of exactly one year later, provides another insight into violence against officers. The response stated that, in the first three months of 2020, within the London area, there were 104 incidents of wounding of constables amounting to grievous bodily harm. In the same period, there were 401 assaults occasioning actual bodily harm on a constable.

8.2.2 Complaints against the police

Lawyers and society are quick to chastise officers who transgress. The Independent Office for Police Conduct (IOPC) oversees allegations against the police. IOPC statistics for 2018/19 show police forces recorded 30,097 complaints against them. Complaints often include multiple allegations, and many do not progress, a source of some concern for those involved in police–community relations. It is an axiom of businesspeople that a complaint can be converted into goodwill, if properly handled. That culture has yet to permeate the criminal justice process. Some sections of the population find it difficult to engage with a uniformed presence. Equally, some officers are defensive in dealing with adverse feedback.

The 2018/19 IOPC figures show police forces investigated 21,764 allegations, of which 2,262 appeared to the investigating officer to have a criminal element. In data terms these are hard to track as the court process, or at least the early stages of it, swallows them up. It is not easy, therefore, to find data on police officers convicted of crimes during service. Statistically, the number is impossibly small. Sky News in July 2020 reported it had served FoI requests on 45 forces and an incomplete set of responses indicated 211 currently serving officers and PCSOs have criminal convictions. Common sense analysis suggests these are likely to fall into three types of conviction: first, those prior to employment; second, those during employment but unrelated to service matters; and third, and of most concern, those related to wrongdoing as an officer while on duty. We do not know the seriousness and category of convictions. Naturally we should note every criminal is entitled to reform and rehabilitation. Equally, rotten apples should not be allowed to spoil the barrel, as the saying goes.

Of the 19,502 allegations not overtly indicating criminality, and investigated by local forces as part of a complaints process, 2,360 were upheld. The complaints covered oppressive behaviour, malpractice, breach of police rules relating to interviews and so on, impoliteness (or 'incivility'), operational inefficiencies and discriminatory behaviour.

Complaints that are not upheld can be appealed to the IOPC. In 2018/19 it upheld 997 appeals out of 2,677 fully investigated.

The IOPC annual report for 2020–21, the latest available as of April 2023, states that it received 764 appeals against police force investigations and local resolutions. There was also a number of appeals against a force decision not to record a complaint. The annual report shows the IOPC upheld 33% of appeals.

IOPC statistics for November 2021 – a different publication to the annual report – show that police forces and local policing bodies logged over 67,000 complaints in 2020–21. There is a distinction between 'logging' a complaint and 'recording' it, in that a considerable number benefit from the former but not the latter. In other words, the police decline to progress it. This itself then becomes a source of dissatisfaction for the complainant. The November 2021 statistics, somewhat confusingly, refer to reviews of investigations rather than appeals. Be that as it may, these statistics state that local policing bodies undertook 4,346 reviews of complaints. The IOPC undertook 969 reviews, of which 32% were upheld, ie it was decided that the handling of the original complaint was not reasonable and proportionate.

Police forces have received a certain amount of unfavourable publicity over recent years. The message therefore remains: can do better, must try harder, and changes in culture should be remorselessly pursued.

8.3   Overview of criminal court administration

It is helpful to understand the bureaucracy of the criminal justice system. The Ministry of Justice (MoJ) is the relevant government department. It has responsibility for the courts, prisons, probation service and attendance centres. One of its stated priorities is to deliver a modern court and justice system. Another is to promote the rule of law.

8.3.1   Ministry of Justice agencies

The MoJ works with 33 agencies and public bodies, the main ones relevant to the criminal justice process being:

- His Majesty's (HM) Courts and Tribunal Service (HMCTS) – its activities are discussed below;
- HM Prison and Probation Service – responsible for the prison population, jails, and rehabilitation;
- Legal Aid Agency – oversees public funding for defendants. Funding is hard to obtain for anyone other than those on the lowest ladder economically;
- Criminal Cases Review Commission – the body that reviews alleged miscarriages of justice;
- Judicial Appointments Commission – responsible for ensuring the right people sit in judgment on the rest of us;
- Legal Services Board – oversees the legal world, such as solicitors, barristers, and others, and their regulators;
- Parole Board – assesses whether serving criminals should be allowed to leave jail and be released into the community;
- Youth Justice Board – monitors the system for trying and rehabilitating young offenders (ages 10–17). One of its mottos is 'child first, offender second'. The youth courts operate through the magistrates;
- Criminal Procedure Rule Committee – a group of worthy individuals that advises on, and drafts, the rules of procedure relevant to criminal trials and their preparation;
- Sentencing Council – aims to offer guidance and rules with a view to establishing consistency in sentencing; and
- Various inspectorates and ombudspeople (officialdom still refers formally to 'ombudsman') whose role is to ensure fairness and oversight of the regime as a whole.

8.3.2   HMCTS

Let us concentrate for the moment on HMCTS. It is responsible for courts and tribunals in England and Wales. It administers the courts. Considering its importance to the democratic behaviours of England and Wales, you might think HMCTS has a slimline staffing profile. Statistics from 2017/18 show there were 15,003 magistrates, 2,978 judges, and 15,875 other staff. CBP 8372 of 31 January 2023 indicates a decline on these figures.

Discounting magistrates, therefore, who are part-time volunteers, there are something under 18,000 paid individuals with a leading role in promoting the rule of law. So that is just over twice as many bods in 2020 as Google had in Kings Cross, or 8,000 less than Transport for

London employed in 2020 to keep the capital moving, or half as many as HSBC devoted to banking in the UK, or 5,000 more than Disneyland Paris in that year. The world economy has changed somewhat since 2020, and the organisations mentioned here have altered their staffing numbers accordingly, but the message remains the same: administering the justice system continues to be a challenge.

8.3.3   Administration of the Supreme Court

HMCTS's reach does not extend to the very top, however, as the Constitutional Reform Act 2005 gives special mention to the Supreme Court, which has an independent administrative status. The Supreme Court has a senior justice as President, and a civil servant as Chief Executive. The 2005 Act mentions the Lord Chancellor – ie the Secretary of State for Justice, a member of the Government – in the context of setting the President's salary, being consulted on some rules, and having a role in the medical retirement of justices, should they lose capacity, one imagines. But generally, and quite correctly, the 2005 Act restricts the Lord Chancellor's role.

It is entirely desirable politicians should be kept at arm's length from the effective functioning of the Supreme Court. That is not to say our elected representatives have a free hand with the other courts. Far from it. They know they cannot interfere. But our top court is sufficiently important to have its own rule book.

Figure 8.1   Overview reminder of criminal court hierarchy and appeal pathways

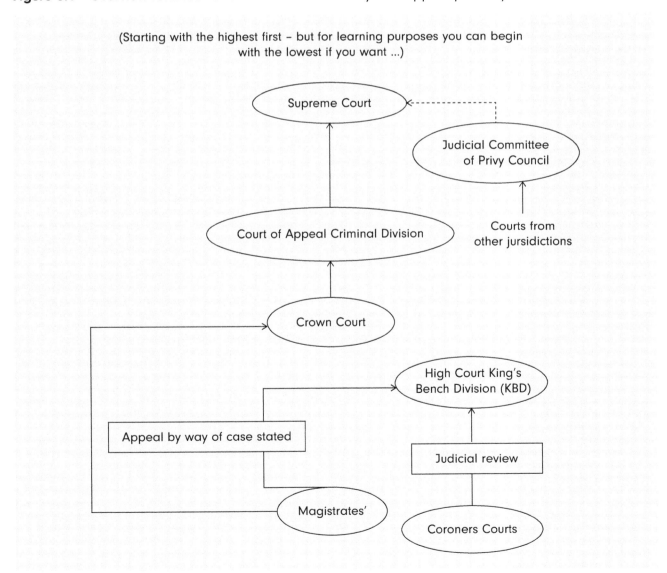

(Starting with the highest first – but for learning purposes you can begin with the lowest if you want ...)

8.4   The criminal court hierarchy

There are magistrates' courts up and down the country. They are like castles of medieval times, which were scattered around the country, guarding rivers and towns. But instead of providing military protection, magistrates guard the constitutionally vital need for swift local justice.

Well, that is the theory. The number of magistrates' courts reduced considerably between 2010 and 2019, per CBP 8372 mentioned earlier in this manual. The number of courts is subject to further reduction as administrative measures and government economies continue to bite.

CBP 8372 also states that eight Crown Court sites, out of 92, closed during the period 2010–2019. Others have been shuttered since. We know this since HMCTS says on its website (July 2020) that there are currently 77 courts dealing with Crown Court business. The tendency towards combined court centres – which allow a multiplicity of business to take place, not just that involving felons – means that this number, we suspect, has remained stable.

Prosecutions always begin in the magistrates' court. Less significant matters remain there, with the Crown Court handling more serious trials. Depending on the nature of the matter, and the Court being appealed, there is an upward ladder to the Administrative (Divisional) Court of the King's Bench Division of the High Court, and the Court of Appeal Criminal Division, and then the Supreme Court. Defendants under 18 progress through the youth courts. The Judicial Committee of the Privy Council, composed of the Law Lords, is the court of last resort for Commonwealth appeals.

Where there is a violent and unnatural death it may be investigated at an inquest under the Coroners and Justice Act 2009. Coroners Courts are linked to local authorities rather than HMCTS. They do not apportion blame or guilt but can operate in parallel to criminal courts. Inquests end with a verdict from either a jury or the coroner themselves. An interested participant, a disappointed relative for example, who disagrees with the conduct of an inquest can request judicial review at the High Court, at the Administrative Court of the KBD.

8.5   How prosecutions commence

Prosecutions commence in one of two ways. A defendant can be summonsed to court on receipt of the relevant written communication. This is the typical method for prosecuting motoring offences, for instance. Alternatively, the CPS will charge a defendant. This is the process following arrest of a suspect and questioning at the police station. The charge sheet will detail the arrest date, the offence, the relevant legislation and the details of the officers involved.

The defendant will then appear at the magistrates' at the first available opportunity. In terms of jurisdiction and geography, the appearance will be in the court local to the police and the defendant. There are three categories of offence as follows:

- Offences triable only summarily: these are minor matters and must be tried by the magistrates. Typical summary offences include minor assaults and motoring infringements.

- Offences triable either way: these are more serious, and can be tried either by a bench of magistrates or at the Crown Court in front of a judge and jury. Examples of either way offences are possession of drugs, theft, assault occasioning actual bodily harm, and burglary.

- Offences triable only on indictment: these are the most serious offences, and must be tried in the Crown Court. These include robbery, rape and murder. In terms of geography, the venue will usually be local to the defendant, but, if the crime has generated publicity and community hostility, a trial venue outside the immediate locality might be chosen. This allows the selection of a more objective pool of jurors, and a calmer overall environment for the trial.

8.6   The need for prompt justice, the CPS and prosecuting crime

The MoJ statistics for trials in 2018 show average waits as follows: 29 days between charge and the first court appearance; 108 days between the recording of an offence and someone being charged; and 157 days between reporting an offence and completion of the case.

As with all statistics these figures require interpretation. We should remember the prompt dispensation of justice is a key aspect of the rule of law. Taking the last figure first, delay in getting to a finalised trial (ie completion) is a constant source of frustration. A large number of cases at the magistrates' progress quickly, but a considerable minority experience delay. This can be damaging for all concerned, as victims grow restless and disillusioned, witnesses forget things or move away from the area, lawyers change jobs and paperwork becomes stale.

The wait between recording an offence and charge also requires context. An average of 108 days is indeed considerable. But the pressure of work on the prosecuting authorities means they must inevitably prioritise their investigations. Suspects can therefore expect a period in limbo.

MoJ data, taken from the Criminal Justice System Statistics Quarterly, and published at the end of March 2023, provides a snapshot of progress over the three months from October to December 2022. The statistics show that 29% of outstanding Crown Court cases have been open for a year or more. The MoJ describes this as a 'series high'. This phrase is revealing. It indicates that there are two issues to be addressed. The first is that a number of cases remain open, when ideally they should be concluded. The second is that a large proportion of these are dragging on for a depressingly long time. The same data shows the average time from offence to completion in the Crown Court was 371 days. The average time from offence to completion in magistrates' courts was 177 days.

Prior to prosecution, prosecutors must ask themselves:

> First, is there sufficient evidence to provide a realistic prospect of conviction? And second, is it in the public interest to prosecute?

They therefore, quite legitimately, need a fair amount of time to exhaust their enquiries. Looking on the bright side, this is preferable to a hasty and incorrect decision to charge without proper evaluation of the evidence. But most people find the period of suspense, when they are awaiting a decision from the authorities, to be uncomfortable.

The CPS is not the only body allowed to commence prosecutions. You or I can do it privately, assuming we have cause and the finances. Legislation also grants some organisations the ability to pursue criminal matters. For instance, the Health and Safety at Work Acts allow the Health and Safety Executive (HSE) to prosecute for workplace incidents. The Animal Welfare Act 2006 empowers the Royal Society for the Prevention of Cruelty to Animals (RSPCA) to prosecute in the interests of prevention of harm to, and promotion of welfare of, animals.

8.7   The Criminal Procedure Rules ('the Rules')

The Rules govern the administrative and court process of criminal prosecutions. They are important, naturally, but should not detract in any way from the key conduct obligations of lawyers acting in their client's best interests, upholding the proper administration of justice, and of course maintaining the rule of law. As a practising lawyer, you cannot avoid your ethical duties by saying: 'Oh, but the Rules say this or that'.

The Rules start with the overriding objective and the duty of participants in a criminal case. They refer to case management, case progression, preparation, directions and readiness for trial. There are details on service of documents, forms and court records, reporting restrictions, allocation of cases and much more.

Statutory instruments provide regular updates to the Rules. You can also find guides to what is new for each update. For instance, there might be a rearrangement of the case management regime, and confirmation of the ground rules for hearings. You might find a passage on low-level shoplifting, an insight into the essentially unpremeditated nature of much minor crime. You can also gain a sense of the miniscule detail, and loving care, invested in the Rules' integrity. Recently the Rule Committee explained its approach to 'connectives' within the Rules. A connective is a word such as 'and', 'but' and 'or'. The Committee received feedback these words were not correctly deployed. Indeed a court case had pressed on the matter. So the Committee amended a total of 378 rules on this basis.

8.8   Prosecutions in the magistrates'

According to CBP 8372, over 1 million cases appearing before magistrates in 2018 were summary offences, and were thus automatically tried there. Approximately 374,000 cases were triable either way, meaning there was a choice between magistrates and the Crown Court. Just 27,000 cases were triable only on indictment, and thus obliged to be sent for trial, without further ado, in the Crown Court on account of their seriousness.

The 2021 update to these figures, the latest available from CBP 8372, indicates a lowering of these numbers in all three areas of summary, either way and indictable matters.

8.8.1   Organising trials in the magistrates'

Scheduling trials remains a challenging process. According to CBP 8372, at the end of 2018 magistrates had a backlog of 293,000 cases waiting either to start, or to conclude having commenced. This figure masks a more alarming picture, namely the difficulties in cajoling a case into the court room in the first place. In 2018 over 40% of magistrates trials were effective in that they took place on the proposed day. That means something over 50% did not.

The reasons are varied. They might be classed as ineffective in that they needed to be rescheduled for a later day; or they are deemed to have 'cracked', or been abandoned at the last minute, on the basis that a trial was no longer required; or they were vacated, ie removed from the court lists, with only a possibility of reinstatement at a later date.

In contrast to some data showing a decrease in prosecutions in 2021, the update to CBP 8372 highlights a tendency towards an increase in the backlog of cases waiting to be resolved by magistrates. As of March 2022 the figure was 355,000.

8.8.2   Abandoned, or 'cracked', trials

Should the public be concerned at this data, particularly relating to 'cracked' trials? You might think it is a good result to cancel a trial at short notice with no intention of rescheduling it. Doesn't that mean the matter has gone away, reducing cost and freeing up resources? In fact, no, it is the opposite. Cracked trials are undesirable.

First, it makes one wonder why it was listed in the first place. If it was listed, shouldn't it have gone ahead? Or to put it another way, if it was doomed to be abandoned, why didn't this happen days or even weeks earlier? Second, it creates uncertainty in terms of listing other cases. Other trials will need to be rearranged, which may or may not be done with ease. Third, there is a financial cost to the state, with resources being channelled towards something that is then abandoned. That is hugely wasteful. Fourth, the toll on witnesses and victims is considerable, as they gear themselves up for a day in court, only to be let down in an inconvenient, and sometimes catastrophic, way.

Various questions arise when a trial cracks. Was the prosecution misplaced? Was the preparation inadequate? Sometimes a crack happens because a defendant enters a last-minute guilty plea. This could be beyond anyone's control, but on closer inspection even the capricious nature of some suspects does not explain the process. Who in their right minds would want to string along the entire apparatus of the state until the last minute? If you were charged with an offence, would you sit on your hands and deliberately delay the process, out of sheer bloody-mindedness perhaps?

No, the more likely reason for a late guilty plea is the absence of prosecution evidence until a late stage, or difficulties in obtaining appropriate representation, or administrative and bureaucratic issues over the timing of a trial.

The other common reason for a cracked trial is logistical challenges for the prosecution, whether they be a vital police witness being absent on more pressing operational duties, or other witnesses having trouble appearing. It is all the more concerning that these issues often present themselves only on the day of trial, exacerbating the human and financial cost of the cancellation. An assault victim, for instance, could be considerably distressed at a trial evaporating after months of expectation and worry.

8.8.3   Adjournments in the magistrates'

Those administering justice have wrestled gamely with the issue of trials that do not go ahead. There has been a renewed focus within the Rules on the adjournment culture. There is reinforced guidance on proceeding with a trial where the defendant absents themselves voluntarily. The Rules encourage identification of the issues, particularly by the prosecutor, as a means of simplifying the overall process.

They also, with the similar aim of limiting inconvenience, emphasise effectiveness of communication between prosecution and defence concerning the issues as trial approaches. So that means a rigorous focus on the crime, and the surrounding minutes, or even seconds. How many people are needed to confirm the defendant's supposed presence at the scene of a crime? To what extent is forensic evidence required, and is the expert available to explain it?

If it becomes apparent a trial will not be needed, early notification to victims, witnesses and defendants becomes crucial. Additionally, where there is a likelihood of failure to comply with key directions leading to trial, this should be notified to the other party and the court immediately.

You can therefore appreciate the thrust of the Rules is that trials should start on time with all case management issues dealt with in advance. Adjournments, particularly those requested on the day of trial, are unwelcome. Various philosophies underpin criminal justice and these are reflected in the Rules: the duty to deal justly with the case; the need for an appropriate time frame, on the basis that delay is inimical to the interests of justice; and the need to consider what is best not just for the prosecution and defendant but also witnesses. There is also the wider public interest in progressing, and disposing of, the case.

The Rules highlight the importance of efficient case management by prosecution and defence. If an adjournment is requested, the implication is the Court will want to know why, and whether there is some underlying omission or error at the root of the request. Legitimate grounds for adjournment would include the absence of the defendant or a witness; a failure to serve evidence on time; and neglecting to comply with disclosure obligations. Just because there is a 'legitimate' reason doesn't mean the request will be granted. Throughout the rules there is the continuing refrain that the hearing should go ahead if at all possible. This is clearly a desirable objective. Whether the system is suitably structured, managed and, most of all, funded to achieve this ambition is another matter.

8.9   Funding defence lawyers in criminal matters

The Legal Aid, Sentencing and Punishment of Offenders (LASPO) Act 2012 provides the latest framework for legal funding. The crucial point is how a defendant, who of course has absolutely no say in whether they are charged with an offence or not, and is thus an involuntary participant, can fund their defence.

To obtain financial assistance from the state a suspect will need to navigate through a thicket of requirements presided over by the Criminal Defence Service and its fellow traveller the Legal Aid Agency. First the applicant must show it is in the interests of justice to receive public funding to help mount their defence to the charges. You could argue this is not a difficult test to meet, involving matters such as the likelihood of losing their liberty, and the need to debate a substantial question of law. Many prosecutions encompass these.

Greater problems arise with the second limb of any application. This is the means test, the word 'means' referring to the defendant's finances. If a defendant's gross annual income, together with that of any partner, is above a certain figure, the defendant will not meet the means test and will be required to fund proceedings privately.

The relevant figure in May 2023 for the magistrates' was £22,325. There is a weighting calculation for children of the relationship, which can bring the relevant figure down considerably to allow funding to take place. Even with the child weighting, or if you have just one or no children, you can appreciate this translates into averagely salaried people paying for their own defence lawyers. Legal advice and court proceedings are both hugely expensive. Self-funding a criminal defence is therefore a crushing financial worry.

If successful in your defence, ie obtaining a not guilty verdict, you would hope to recover your costs. But this is by no means a given. In the Crown Court the figures are higher and so, of course, are the stakes, the point being proceedings there are even costlier and the penalties (if found guilty) harsher.

There is a certain amount of concern at the LASPO financial rules. The Government would say there is no magic money tree; criminals and those charged are not deserving of public largesse; and financial restrictions will encourage the guilty to plead accordingly and expedite the trial process. Critics would say these are one-sided arguments. You can therefore have a vigorous debate as to the pros and cons of the legal aid system in the criminal court environment.

8.10 Typical progress of a summary case in the magistrates'

At the initial hearing, shortly after charge, the defence will expect to receive an insight into the prosecution case. You might wonder why this is significant. Surely, as a defendant, you know whether you have done something wrong or not, and accordingly you should be able to decide for yourself whether to plead guilty or not guilty.

But the criminal law is a wondrous thing. The presumption is you are innocent until proven guilty in line with the House of Lords case of *Woolmington v DPP* [1935] AC 462. The prosecution is obliged to make their case. Canny defence lawyers, therefore, always advise their clients to wait for some prosecution details before assessing the options. Indeed the law, not to mention basic principles of fairness, requires the prosecution to show their hand before the first appearance at court.

These details are called 'disclosure' – the initial reveal of prosecution evidence and reasons for pursuing a suspect. These days the process is intensely digital, incidentally, with documents flying through the ether and magically arriving on laptops and devices. How organised those documents are once they pop into your inbox, and how much time you have to absorb them, depends on various human factors behind the scenes, of course.

At the first hearing the defendant will be invited to enter a plea. The defendant can plead guilty, not guilty, or enter no plea (perhaps by hurling abuse at someone or nobody in particular, depending on the mindset of the individual). A guilty plea will prompt sentencing, and so the defendant then enters the curious, not to say confusing, world of punishment, reform and rehabilitation. A not guilty plea will lead to a trial, in most instances at a later date.

On the day of trial there is the expectation the matter will be disposed of in one day. For this to happen a number of events must coincide. The defendant needs to arrive at court promptly, with a properly briefed legal representative. The court list must be running efficiently. Witnesses should be present. The police must be there to give evidence, rather than in some distant part of the region dealing with emergencies. The prosecutor should have received the correct information from those instructing them. The documents must be in order, rather than lost in transit or misplaced electronically.

You might think these are routine matters, easily achievable. But in the real world, where people are overworked, and witnesses confused, and courts subject to administrative stresses, these things are by no means a given.

Once in court a number of possibilities emerge. The defendant can change their plea to guilty, in which case the magistrates will proceed to sentence, with the assistance, if necessary, of the probation service who will provide reports on the defendant's qualities in an attempt to ensure the appropriate sentence is arrived at. Alternatively, the defendant will confirm their not guilty plea and the trial will go ahead. There should be no reason why the matter cannot be fully heard during the day – perhaps half a day. The magistrates will then give the verdict. If not guilty, the defendant can leave court without a stain on their character. If guilty, the sentencing process will follow.

8.11 Typical progress of an offence triable either way

At the first hearing of an either way matter the defendant will be invited to enter a plea. If the plea is guilty the next step will be sentencing. If the plea is not guilty, the justices will consider whether the trial should take place in front of them or at the Crown Court. If heard in the latter, it will be before a judge, with a verdict from a jury of 12 ordinary people.

For most defendants the choice of courts is crucial. Magistrates will hear a case quicker, and will impose a lesser sentence if finding you guilty. But the Crown Court, although capable of imposing a stiffer sentence, returns a far greater proportion of not guilty verdicts. There is an ancient, and out of date, joke as to the choice available to a defendant: would you prefer a trial by three shopkeepers or 12 shoplifters? There is therefore a decision to be made. Do you go for the swifter justice and lighter sentence of the magistrates, or do you roll the dice, opt for the Crown Court, and hope for a favourable verdict from the jury?

As part of the decision-making process, the defendant can request an indication of sentence from the magistrates. If, on hearing, for instance, the sentence would be non-custodial, the defendant can void their not guilty plea, change their mind about going to the Crown Court, admit their guilt, and receive their 'medicine' from the magistrates, secure in the knowledge that any punishment will not involve time behind bars. A defendant can also, having received the indication, decide to stay with the magistrates' and plead not guilty, but if they do the indication becomes void.

If magistrates are to hear the case, they will set a date for trial. If the trial is to be in the Crown Court, the process is more involved, with allocation and several preliminary hearings.

8.12 Case study of an either way trial in the magistrates'

Here is an insight into an either way case where the defendant consented to trial by the magistrates'. Molly is accused of assaulting two police officers. They were trying to move her on, believing she was soliciting, ie seeking customers on the street so that she could sell them sexual services. The police allege she spat at them and pulled a blade. Molly says the blade was simply her little scissors from a makeup bag, not being used as a weapon. Molly agrees to trial in the magistrates' because she wants to get it over and done with so she can move on with her life.

At Highbury Corner magistrates' court on the Holloway Road in London the solicitor for Molly seeks out the CPS prosecutor for a chat. Two of them are sitting in a room the size of a broom cupboard. If the one further into the room wishes to get up and leave, the other one has to stand up and make way (yes, their office is that small. This story is from a while ago, but it is symbolic of the court system's lack of funding).

As one prosecutor says to Molly's lawyer, exchange of bodily fluids (spitting) is a serious matter. And the defendant used a blade. Is Molly prepared to plead guilty? If so, one of the charges can be dropped, meaning a lighter sentence. The solicitor takes instructions, ie asks Molly what she thinks. The answer is no.

The case proceeds in front of three magistrates. The charges are read out. Molly confirms her not guilty plea. The two officers give evidence. They receive permission to coordinate the notes from their notebooks and hence are consistent in what they say. In a different scenario the defence might challenge this procedure, but for now they are stuck with it.

The defence lawyer cross examines the officers. This involves challenging and testing them, suggesting they are mistaken or are exaggerating. In some circumstances the defence might say they are lying, but that doesn't happen here, as the defence advocate quite understandably, with the agreement of Molly, realises the magistrates will take a dim view of such a suggestion. You don't want to alienate the justices. The police adhere to their version of events.

Molly then gives evidence. She holds to her story. This is what we call 'a conflict of evidence', where the prosecution and defence, quite predictably, have a different recollection of the facts. Molly's mobile phone goes off in the middle of her testimony. Strictly speaking this is contempt of court and is absolutely not allowed, but occasionally the bench overlooks such transgressions. Here, the chair of the bench allows Molly to answer it to explain she is busy in court. Molly apologises. She continues giving evidence. The phone rings again. She apologises once more. The chair of the bench smiles in a somewhat forced manner. Eventually Molly completes her evidence. The prosecutor briefly cross examines her. She is resolute in her evidence.

At the end the magistrates confer. They find Molly guilty of an assault on an emergency worker. Sentencing takes place. The police have long since departed to continue their duties. The magistrates move on to their next case.

In **Figure 8.2** we have a flowchart reflecting on some considerations relating to prosecutions in the magistrates'. There are a few concerns dedicated to either prosecutors or defence, and a great number more common to both sides. We have placed the warring parties – and they are most definitely opposed to each other in a highly contentious manner – at the centre of the graphic. There is a line joining them, but don't be misled. This indicates they need to communicate with each other, but apart from that there is virtually no commonality of interest between them.

Figure 8.2   Prosecutions in the magistrates: some considerations

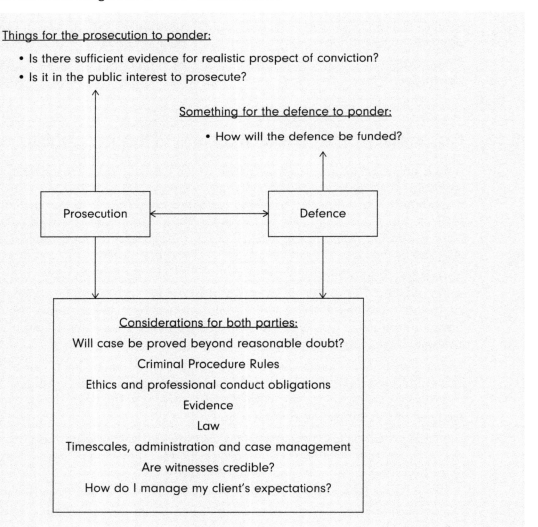

8.13 Prosecutions in the Crown Court

According to CBP 8372, in 2018 the Crown Court received 103,000 cases, of which 36% were rotated up from the magistrates' as being triable either way; 23% were indictable only offences; 33% were remitted from the magistrates' for sentencing; and 8% were appeals. The trial backlog in the Crown Court for 2018 was 33,000.

In the Crown Court in 2018, something just above 50% of trials were effective. Reasons given for ineffective trials in the Crown Court include court administration (24%), defendants absent or unfit to stand (27%), defence not ready (13%), prosecution witness absent (14%), and prosecution not ready (13%).

The update to CBP 8372 shows that, in 2021, which is the latest year for which we have information, Crown Courts received 98,000 cases and disposed of 96,000. Nearly two thirds (61%) of cases received were for trials, 32% were cases sent from the magistrates' court for sentencing, and 5% were cases of appeals against decisions in the magistrates' court. In the same year, 48% of Crown Court trials were effective.

The Criminal Procedure Rules, via the practice directions, deal with trial adjournment in the Crown Court. They reinforce the Court's discretion on the matter. The Court can consider if the trial should continue, having due regard to the interests of justice. Circumstances to be taken into account include the conduct of the defendant, the disadvantage to the defendant, the public interest, the effect of any delay, and the likely outcome if the defendant is found guilty.

Either way offences, as we have seen, are subject to the allocation process. Assuming magistrates have allocated upwards, the Crown Court will issue standard directions for case management. These typically cover the use of documents, witnesses, disputed evidence and other important matters. There will be one or more hearings before trial, orientated around effective trial preparation and admissibility of evidence.

Indictable only offences, which are so serious that they can only be tried at the Crown Court, are, at the first opportunity, sent by the magistrates for trial to the Crown Court. There is no consideration of the evidence. The preparation and timeline leading to trial is, naturally, more involved than that for other trials.

8.14 Case study: Stephen Lawrence

Events in Eltham in 1993 illustrate the operation of the Crown Court, the court hierarchy, their jurisdiction, and appeals. They also offer an insight into the fallible nature of the criminal justice process.

A group of white youths murdered Stephen Lawrence at approximately 10.30pm on 22 April 1993. Stephen and his friend Duwayne Brooks were on their way home when Stephen was fatally knifed near a bus stop in Well Hall Road. Seconds before the incident the youths addressed Stephen with a racial epithet (source: Report of an Inquiry by Sir William Macpherson, Cm 4262-I, 15 February 1999). There were two horrible lacerations, and an awful lot of blood, but little of it at the scene – because it had soaked into Stephen's five layers of clothing.

8.14.1 Stephen Lawrence: events after his death

There were numerous stages to the police and judicial processes that followed.

- *The Metropolitan Police ('the Met') detective work.* This failed to result in the trial of any suspects. At an early stage the Met treated Mr Brooks as if he had done something wrong.

- *Private prosecution of three individuals.* In April 1996, concerned at the lack of official progress, the parents of Stephen Lawrence commenced a private prosecution against Luke Knight, Gary Dobson and Neil Acourt at the Central Criminal Court in London, more popularly known as the Old Bailey. The judge ruled purported identification evidence inadmissible. Duwayne could not identify the defendants, and other evidence was not strong enough. The judge directed the jury to acquit. The jury entered not guilty verdicts (source: Court of Appeal case report, *R v Dobson* [2011] EWCA Crim 1255).

- *The inquest into Stephen's death.* On 13 February 1997 an inquest found five white youths had unlawfully killed Stephen in an unprovoked racist attack for no other reason than his colour being black (source: BBC News report, 13 February 1997). Inquests are limited to statements of fact as to who died, and how, when and where they came by their death. They cannot apportion blame or guilt. Hence the jury used the phrase 'unlawful killing' rather than murder.

- *Complaint into the handling of the murder investigation by the Met.* On 15 December 1997 Lord Williams of Mostyn stated in the House of Lords the Home Secretary would lay before Parliament a report submitted by the Police Complaints Authority (PCA), the predecessor to the IOPC (source: *Hansard, HL Deb,* 15 December 1997, vol 584 cc69-70 WA). This report, resulting from a complaint, detailed the Kent Police investigation into the work of the Met surrounding the murder. Lord Williams said the PCA report:

  > concludes that the Metropolitan Police Service has committed substantial resources over several years to the investigation of this appalling crime, and that there is no doubt that a considerable amount of hard work has been undertaken. The report also concludes that the police operation undertaken immediately after the assault was well organised and effective and that there was no evidence of racist conduct by police officers.

  We have to take the work of Kent Police and the PCA, and the statement of Lord Williams, as being in good faith. But with the benefit of hindsight the idea the police operation 'was well organised and effective' was a ludicrously superficial conclusion.

- *Public inquiry into the Stephen Lawrence case.* On 31 July 1997 the Government asked Sir William Macpherson to chair an inquiry 'to identify the lessons to be learned' from Stephen's death. On 15 February 1999 Sir William presented his 389-page report. The opening statement of the report's conclusion and summary is as follows:

  > The conclusions to be drawn from all the evidence in connection with the investigation of Stephen Lawrence's racist murder are clear. There is no doubt but that there were fundamental errors. The investigation was marred by a combination of professional incompetence, institutional racism and a failure of leadership by senior officers. A flawed Metropolitan Police Service review failed to expose these inadequacies. The second investigation could not salvage the faults of the first investigation.

  Macpherson Report

- *Change in the law to allow serious crimes to be retried.* Part 10 of the Criminal Justice Act 2003, which received Royal Assent on 20 November 2003, reversed the ancient rule that someone should not be tried twice for the same crime. Instead, it provides for a retrial if there is new and compelling evidence against the individual, and it would also be in the interests of justice to proceed (source: legislation.gov.uk).

- *Claim for compensation by Duwayne Brooks.* In 2001 Brooks attempted to make the Commissioner of the Met liable in negligence for failing in a duty of care. Brooks suggested the police had a duty to assess whether someone was a victim, and to provide support to an eye witness of violent crime. The House of Lords, now the Supreme Court, in 2005 held there was no such duty (source: *Brooks v Commissioner of Police of the Metropolis and Others* [2005] UKHL 24). Brooks continued his claim for compensation on other grounds and reached a financial settlement with the Met some years later.

- *Quashing of the not guilty verdict of Gary Dobson.* On 18 May 2011 the Court of Appeal allowed an application by the Director of Public Prosecutions to quash, ie negate, the 1996 not guilty verdict against Gary Dobson. This meant he could be tried again for the murder of Stephen (source: *R v Dobson*, mentioned above). The new and compelling evidence required by the 2003 Act revolved around forensic evidence found on clothing.

- *Murder trial of two suspects.* On 3 January 2012 David Norris and Gary Dobson were unanimously convicted of murder by a jury at the Old Bailey. Both men were refused leave to appeal by Mr Justice Treacy who presided. Their application to the Court of Appeal for permission to appeal was also refused (source: *R v Norris* [2013] EWCA Crim 712). The Court of Appeal in rejecting the application explained there was no evidence of unfairness in the prosecution or the decision of the jury, and hence no basis for overturning the verdict. The Court of Appeal emphasised the core significance of the facts as considered by the Crown Court. Lord Justice Leveson in giving the unanimous Court of Appeal judgment noted the following:

    ◦ the presumption of innocence, correctly applied;
    ◦ the trial judge devoting over 100 pages to summing up the forensic evidence;
    ◦ the handling of the facts;
    ◦ the approach of the prosecution; and
    ◦ the fact that the jury deliberated and provided a verdict.

None of that could be second guessed, and replaced, by justices in the somewhat sterile environment of the Court of Appeal.

- *A new twist on the 2005 House of Lords decision on Brooks.* On 13 March 2017 the Supreme Court gave judgment in the case of *D v Commissioner of Police*. It decided the Human Rights Act 1998, which enacted into UK law the European Convention on Human Rights 1950 ('the Convention'), imposed a duty on the state to enforce laws that prohibited conduct breaching the Convention. The Court held serious failures that were purely operational would suffice to establish a claim. The case discussed prohibition of torture, which has only a fleeting parallel with the Brooks situation, but even so the case is significant for suggesting there is a direct link between police failings in a criminal investigation and compensation payable to a wronged party (source: court report of *D v Commissioner of Police of the Metropolis* [2018] UKSC 11).

We can make various observations from this series of events. These fall into two categories. First, there are points relating to procedure and the courts. Second, there are comments as to the wider operation of the legal system.

8.14.2   Stephen Lawrence: points on procedure and the courts

- We can observe the functioning of the Crown Court. In the aftermath of Stephen's murder, the CPS did not believe they had a realistic prospect of conviction. Hence there was no prosecution.

- Stephen's parents therefore commenced a private prosecution. Murder is an indictable offence. The trial must take place in the Crown Court. There, at the Old Bailey, the judge was obliged to direct the jury to acquit the defendants as, on the basis of the evidence available at the time, there was no arguable case for the trial to proceed.

- The inquest process played a somewhat ambiguous, some would say unconvincing, role in the sequence of events. On the positive side it allowed a scrutiny of the facts. Less constructively, it did not arrive at any conclusion as to who committed the murder. It therefore confirmed the limited scope – as defined by statute – of the coronial process.

- A change in legislation allowed the not guilty verdict of 1996 to be revisited in the 2012 public prosecution. The 2003 Act allowed a retrial because there was new and compelling evidence, in this instance the forensic material. It was also, somewhat obviously, in the interests of justice for a retrial to take place.

- The guilty defendants then requested leave to appeal to the Court of Appeal Criminal Division. That request was refused as there was no indication the verdict was unsafe. We deal with appeals later.

8.14.3 Stephen Lawrence: the wider operation of the legal system

- The various components of the legal system failed the Lawrence family and Mr Brooks. The police muddled the investigation; the CPS could not construct a prosecution case; the inquest process could only deal in facts; the courts were unable to rectify earlier failings until very late in the day; an attempt at compensation through civil litigation channels proved heavy going.

- Without the determination of the family and supporters the legal process would have stalled long ago.

- The timeline does, however, show how events can prompt the law to evolve. The inquest encouraged continuing debate over the value of the coronial process; the Macpherson report placed a focus on the role of police within the criminal justice system; the 2003 Act now allows not guilty verdicts for serious crimes to be revisited in certain circumstances; and the 2017 Supreme Court decision in *D* reinforced the entitlement of victims and witnesses to compensation where the state fails to comply with the human rights aspect of investigating crime.

- There are many continuing areas of discussion resulting from Stephen's murder. One conclusion is we should resist complacency in believing our society, and system of justice, treats everyone fairly. A key question is therefore how we as lawyers can nurture fairness across our legal system.

Figure 8.3 Stephen Lawrence

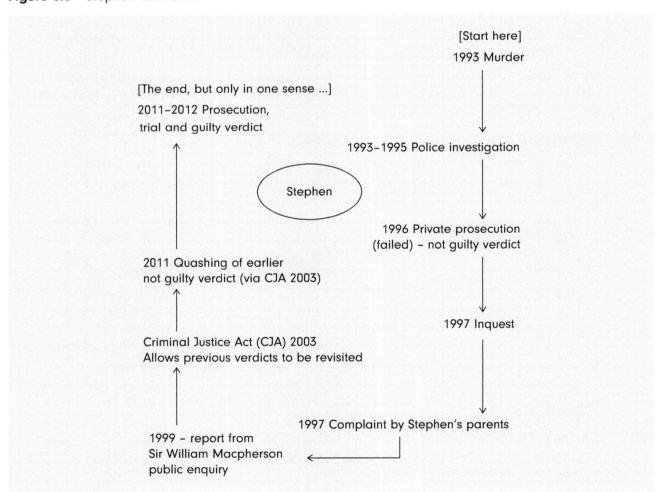

Figure 8.3 presents a flowchart summarising the various events stemming from Stephen's murder. You can see the different judicial procedures and legal interventions. You will see we have a starting point and an end – but whether the last item really is an 'end' to the wider process, and continuing issues, is a matter for debate.

8.15 Criminal appeals generally

Criminal appeals differ from civil ones in at least two respects. First, the freedom of the individual is at stake, so there is a presumption there should be greater opportunity for the defendant to have a second chance to establish their innocence. Second, the entitlement of the prosecution to appeal is restricted. There would be something undignified in the prosecutor appealing against an innocent verdict so as a general rule it is not allowed. The prosecution can, however, appeal from the lower courts on a point of law. Let's look at the details now.

8.15.1 Appeals from magistrates'

A convicted defendant can appeal against conviction or sentence or both. The appeal is to the Crown Court. If appealing against conviction there will be a full rehearing in front of a judge and at least two magistrates. The judge provides legal analysis, which magistrates are obliged to follow. The decision on guilt or innocence, however, is of course a joint one. Witnesses give evidence again. At the end of the process the appeal will either be allowed or refused.

It is extremely unusual, if not impossible, for a summary matter to be appealed further. The main reason for this is public policy. There is a consensus shared by policymakers, the judiciary and the population at large that relatively minor criminal matters should not suck up time and resources. There is also the common sense point that two trials, surely, should be enough. Thus any request to appeal a summary matter beyond the Crown Court will be refused.

A similar bench of a judge and two magistrates also hears appeals against sentencing. There is less argument over the facts in this situation, and more attention to the law and practice of the sentencing regime.

The defendant does not need leave to appeal. It is an automatic right. Appellants should file a notice of appeal within 21 days of the verdict. The Crown Court may conduct a case management hearing to ensure the efficient progress of the appeal.

Both prosecution and defence can appeal on a point of law. This is known as an appeal by way of case stated, on the basis of an error of law, a ruling in excess of jurisdiction (*R v Wilson* [2019] EWCA Crim 2410), or insufficient evidence. Confusingly, this appeal is not to the Crown Court but to the Administrative (Divisional) Court of the KBD of the High Court, a forum more usually associated with civil matters.

The governing law for this process is the Magistrates' Courts Act 1980. An application to the magistrates must be made within 21 days. Magistrates can refuse a request on the basis of frivolity. If so, the applicant in this situation – the defendant in most cases – can apply to the High Court for a mandatory order requiring the case to be stated.

In a case stated two judges will review the matter. They will take the facts as decided by the lower court. If successful, the decision of the court below will be set aside.

8.15.2 An example of an appeal by way of case stated

The case of *Richardson v Director of Public Prosecutions* [2014] UKSC 8 offers an illustration of an appeal by way of case stated that travelled up the ladder to the Supreme Court. In

October 2010, two individuals mounted a non-violent protest in a shop in London's Covent Garden. The protesters objected to the sale of items connected with an Israeli-owned business in the Occupied Palestinian Territory. A district judge at Highbury Corner magistrates' court convicted the two of aggravated trespass under the Criminal Justice and Public Order Act 1994, concluding they had interfered with a 'lawful activity' as stated in the Act.

The two then appealed by way of case stated. The Administrative Court rejected that appeal. It, however, certified, as a point of law of general public importance the need to clarify the phrase 'lawful activity', and allowed a further appeal to the Supreme Court. The Law Lords therefore considered the matter. They concluded the phrase referred to acts or events integral to the activities at the premises in question. The protesters' appeal was therefore dismissed.

8.15.3 Appeals from the Crown Court

The Criminal Appeal Acts 1968 and 1995 deal with appeals from the Crown Court to the Court of Appeal Criminal Division. Leave to appeal is required, unless the trial judge has already certified the matter is fit for appeal, in which case an appellant should serve notice within 28 days of conviction or sentence.

A convicted defendant can appeal to the Court of Appeal, with permission either from the trial judge or the Court of Appeal itself. There is no guarantee a request will be granted. The appellant should show solid grounds, in essence to establish the conviction was unsafe, as stated by s 2(1) of the 1995 Act. This explains why Dobson and Norris failed in their application to appeal conviction in 2012. Typical examples of reasons to appeal would include:

* an error of law (in the summing up of the judge before the jury retires to give its verdict, for instance); or

* material irregularity (such as inappropriate behaviour by jurors, for instance sharing jury room discussions with the outside world via social media); or

* obtaining fresh evidence that was not available, or not relied on, at trial.

The defendant can also appeal against sentence if the sentence is manifestly excessive, or if the court imposed a sentence it has no power to make. There is no full rehearing. However, the court may hear new evidence if it provides a basis for allowing an appeal.

Under the Criminal Justice Act 1972 the Attorney General, a Government minister, may refer a point of law to the Court of Appeal on behalf of the prosecution following acquittal. This does not change the original verdict, purely serving to clarify the law for future reference.

Under the Criminal Justice Act 1988 it is also possible for the Attorney General to request the Court of Appeal to review an unduly lenient sentence. Politicians can perhaps be forgiven for using both these options as a form of showboating to capture the popular imagination. There are of course votes in being seen to favour stiffer sentences.

Both the prosecution and the defence can appeal by way of case stated to the KBD Administrative Court. The rules and procedure are broadly the same as for the magistrates'.

8.15.4 Appeals to the Supreme Court

Appeals to the Supreme Court can be made from either the Court of Appeal or the Administrative Court. You should request permission from the court in question, or failing that, the Supreme Court itself. The appellant has 28 days within which to apply for leave. Either the defendant or the prosecutor can appeal. For a party to obtain a right to appeal there must be an exceptional case of general public importance.

The Court of Appeal is somewhat miserly in granting this possibility, and it is common for leave to be refused by the Court of Appeal initially. There will then be an application to the Supreme Court. It will be heard on the papers by at least three justices.

For the Supreme Court to hear a matter, the court below must certify there is a point of law of general public importance, and it must appear to either that court or the Supreme Court the point is one that ought to be considered for appeal. A select few appeals do not require such a certificate: for instance, an application for habeas corpus, appeals relating to declarations of incompatibility under the Human Rights Act 1998, and certain instances governing contempt of court.

There are also strict time limits to be followed. For instance, if permission is granted, notice of appeal should then be lodged within 14 days.

By way of summarising one aspect of the appeal process, **Figure 8.4** presents a flowchart indicating, in very much an overview manner, some appeal options for the prosecution. Note there are only limited rights of appeal for prosecutors from the magistrates', eg against the refusal to make a football banning order. There are more options from the Crown Court but even there the entitlement is closely controlled.

Figure 8.4   Appeal routes for prosecution

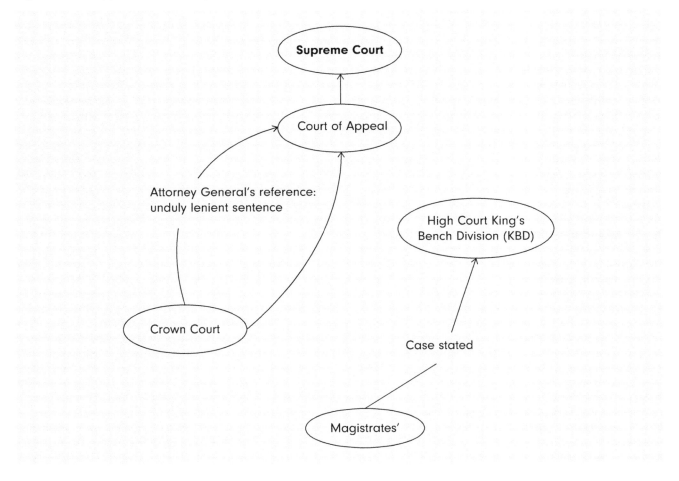

8.15.5   Appeals to the Judicial Committee of the Privy Council (JCPC)

The JCPC is the court of last resort for criminal appeals from Commonwealth countries. It is unusual for the lower court to have the power to grant leave unless the case raises questions of great and general importance, or there has been some grave violation of the principles of natural justice. If permission is refused by the lower court, you can apply to the Privy Council itself for permission providing this is done within 56 days.

8.16 Conclusion

This chapter explains the process of commencing a prosecution in the magistrates' and Crown courts, the jurisdiction of those and higher courts, and the appeal process. The presumption is the defendant is innocent until proven guilty, something that played to the advantage of the killers of Stephen Lawrence. But that should not diminish the principle. In addition, the prosecution must prove its case beyond reasonable doubt.

A guilty verdict at the magistrates' court can be appealed by the defence as of right to the Crown Court. A guilty verdict in the Crown Court can only be appealed by the defendant to the Court of Appeal if it can be shown the verdict was unsafe, or by way of case stated to the KBD of the High Court.

The entire system of criminal justice is underpinned by the professional conduct obligations of lawyers. Conduct matters pervade court work. At all stages solicitors, barristers and other legal professionals must prioritise the rule of law, the proper administration of justice, independence, honesty, integrity and the duty to each client. Without these, the criminal justice system would be woefully inadequate.

Summary

We have studied the role of the police. They are important players in the drama of the criminal court process. Generally they are saints, and sometimes sinners. We have considered prosecutions in the magistrates and the Crown Court, and assessed their different jurisdictions. We have pondered their place in the hierarchy of justice. We have studied the appeal ladder. There is mention of the Judicial Committee of the Privy Council. We have ended with a brief reminder of the conduct obligations of criminal justice lawyers, something that pervades our work, whether acting for the prosecution or the defence.

Sample questions

Question 1

A prosecutor with the Crown Prosecution Service (CPS) prosecutes a defendant in the magistrates' court for the summary offence of threatening behaviour. The magistrates find the defendant not guilty. The prosecutor believes the magistrates have erred in law in their interpretation of the relevant law, and this is an important point of law of general public importance. The prosecutor wishes to appeal.

Which of the following statements correctly describes the right of appeal for the CPS?

A The CPS can appeal direct to the Court of Appeal.

B The CPS can appeal by way of case stated to the Crown Court, and if the appeal is refused can appeal to the Supreme Court.

C The CPS can appeal by way of case stated to the Administrative (Divisional) Court of the King's Bench Division of the High Court, and if the appeal is allowed the defendant can appeal against that decision to the Court of Appeal.

D The CPS can appeal by way of case stated to the Administrative (Divisional) Court of the King's Bench Division of the High Court, and if the appeal is granted the defendant will be retried at the Crown Court.

E   The CPS can appeal by way of case stated to the Administrative (Divisional) Court of the King's Bench Division of the High Court, and if the appeal is refused can appeal to the Supreme Court.

Answer

Option E is correct. An appeal by way of case stated is possible where the magistrates err in law or act in excess of jurisdiction. If the case is refused it is then possible to appeal from the High Court to the Supreme Court, providing it is an exceptional case of general public importance.

Option A is wrong because it is not possible to appeal direct from the magistrates' to the Court of Appeal. Option B is wrong because an appeal by way of case stated is to the Administrative (Divisional) Court of the King's Bench Division (KBD) not the Crown Court. Option C is wrong because a further appeal from the KBD, when it has heard a case stated, is to the Supreme Court not the Court of Appeal. Option D is wrong because, where the prosecution is successful in a case stated, the High Court can sentence the defendant, or quash the acquittal and return it to the magistrates' for sentencing. The Crown Court is not involved.

Question 2

A man has been found guilty by a Crown Court jury of burglary. There were no contentious points of law to consider. The evidence was also relatively straightforward. The man is sentenced to five years' imprisonment. The defence believes the sentence is too harsh. The man believes the trial judge was not concentrating throughout the trial, but the man's lawyers do not share this view as the summing up was entirely fair. The prosecutor is surprised at the verdict, and has indicated he believes the sentence is too lenient.

Which of the following appeal options would be most appropriate?

A   The prosecutor can appeal to the Court of Appeal on the basis the sentence is too lenient.

B   The defence can appeal against conviction to the Court of Appeal on the basis the verdict is unsafe as a result of the trial judge's conduct.

C   The defence can appeal against sentence to the Court of Appeal if the sentence is manifestly excessive.

D   The prosecution can appeal by way of case stated to the King's Bench Division of the High Court.

E   The prosecution could ask for a retrial on the basis the verdict is unsafe.

Answer

Option C is correct. The defence can appeal from the Crown Court to the Court of Appeal where the sentence is manifestly excessive.

Option A is wrong because the prosecutor cannot appeal a sentence in the Crown Court. Instead, the Attorney General may refer a sentence to the Court of Appeal if they consider there is undue leniency. Option B is not the best answer as there is no evidence the verdict is unsafe, although, if there were, the Court of Appeal would be the correct venue. Option D is wrong because the prosecution cannot appeal by way of case stated from the Crown Court unless the case originally commences in the magistrates', which is not what has happened here. In any event, on the facts, there is no evidence the court erred in law, and hence there is no basis for the case to be stated.

Option E is wrong because the prosecution can only ask the Court of Appeal to quash an acquittal if new and compelling evidence comes to light, and the facts suggest this is not the case as the evidence is uncontroversial. In fact, out of interest, the right to order a new trial where such evidence becomes available is not applicable to burglary. Also, it is not possible for the prosecution to object to an acquittal on the basis of it being unsafe.

Question 3

Police in the north of England have arrested and interviewed a woman, and charged her with the murder of her brother. She denies it and indicates she will plead not guilty on the basis of self-defence. She has asked for an explanation of the relevant court procedure.

Which of the following represents the best advice for the woman on appropriate court procedure?

A   The local magistrates will consider the evidence, and then send the case to the Crown Court for trial.

B   The prosecution will provide initial disclosure at the magistrates, and a decision will then be made as to trial by either the magistrates or the Crown Court.

C   The case will be sent for trial to the Crown Court, where a judge and two magistrates will hear the case.

D   The case will be sent for trial to the Old Bailey, where the woman will be invited to give a plea, and there will be a trial by jury at the first appearance there.

E   The case will be sent for trial to a suitable Crown Court venue either in Manchester or nearby, and the woman will be tried in front of a jury after the necessary number of preliminary hearings.

Answer

Option E is correct. The woman is being tried for an offence triable only on indictment, and will be sent for trial at the Crown Court at the first available opportunity. The trial will be in front of a judge and jury.

Option A is wrong because, where there is an offence triable only on indictment, the magistrates do not consider the evidence. The matter is sent for trial at the Crown Court. Option B is wrong because, with an offence triable on indictment, there is no decision to be made as to trial by magistrates. An either way offence requires a choice to be made between the magistrates and the Crown Court, but an offence triable on indictment, such as this one, *must* be tried in the Crown Court.

Option C is wrong because Crown Court trials are heard by a jury, who decide on innocence or guilt. They are presided over by a single judge, with no involvement of magistrates. Option D is wrong because, on the facts, there is no reason for the trial to be heard in the Old Bailey, which is in London, and which is thus geographically inconvenient for both prosecution and defence. In any event a Crown Court trial is always sufficiently important and complex to justify some preliminary hearings.

9 Civil Case Law and Precedent

SQE1 syllabus

This chapter will enable you to achieve the SQE1 assessment specification in relation to functioning legal knowledge concerning civil (as opposed to criminal) case law and precedent.

Note that, for SQE1, candidates are not usually required to recall specific case names or cite statutory or regulatory authorities. Cases are provided for illustrative purposes only.

Learning outcomes

By the end of this chapter you will be able to apply relevant core legal principles and rules appropriately and effectively, at the level of a competent newly qualified solicitor in practice, to realistic client-based and ethical problems and situations in the following areas:

- the role of judges as interpreters of law, and creators of it;
- the development of precedent;
- the role and hierarchy of the courts concerning precedent, starting with the Supreme Court, and moving downwards from there;
- how to find, and decipher, a precedent;
- whether the Supreme Court and the Court of Appeal are bound by their own previous decisions;
- the meaning of *ratio decidendi*, and its application;

- narrow and wide *ratios*, with examples;
- obiter statements, what they are, how they are made, and their significance;
- techniques used by judges to interpret and adapt precedent;
- terminology used by courts when making decisions;
- the structure of, and how to read, a case report, in this instance from the Court of Appeal; and
- the challenge of adapting old precedents to the modern day.

9.1 Introduction

Judges, case law and precedent are old friends. They are not quite The Three Degrees – a vocal trio from the 1960s – but they have spent a lot of time together, providing legal entertainment of a sort for centuries.

Although in theory judges are meant to limit themselves to the interpretation of the law, in reality they end up either creating it, or at least expanding on it. Imagine you own a house with a friend. Unexpectedly your friend gets into debt. They then die. Your friend's creditor obtains a court order allowing seizure of property within the house. As you are, or at least were, co-owner with your friend you, quite understandably, resist this idea. Enforcement officials come knocking on the door. You refuse entry.

 These were, broadly, the facts of Semayne's Case (1604) KB 5 Co Rep 91, *one of a line of decisions involving Sir Edward Coke in the early part of the 17th century. Sometimes Coke judged. At other times he reported. This appears to be an instance of the latter.*

The justices in the Court of the King's Bench faced some tricky issues. First, the officials represented powerful interests, and challenging their power required courage. Second, a combination of legal principles interacted, requiring the law to be unpicked. On the one hand the creditor had an entitlement. On the other, the friend of the debtor, the co-owner, was wary of giving way when he had done no wrong. Third, any underlying law lacked clarity, there being a reference to a repealed statute and other old legislation, which left people wondering as to the exact position.

Coke's report contains several crucial statements reinforcing the rights of property owners. He recites the famous phrase that a person's home is their castle, meaning an individual acting lawfully should be entitled to protection from interference within their own property. Coke says entry to another's land, even if requested by the Crown, requires the correct permissions. He also states, even when there is lawful authority to enter, the arrival and intention to break down the door should be properly announced. In the absence of the appropriate procedures, the owner can lock the door and refuse entry. The justices here decided in favour of the defendant homeowner, and against the claimant creditor.

This case illustrates the fine line between interpretation of the law and its creation. Which of the two, exactly, happened here? No doubt the judges believed they were interpreting the law as best they could, balancing different principles to arrive at the correct result. The officials seeking entry probably took the alternative view, that the Court was arriving at a conclusion inconsistent with legislation and previous rulings.

It really does not matter whether we conclude the Court in *Semayne's Case* was interpreting or creating law. Either way, the judgment resulted in something called *precedent*. In other words, the Court made a statement of law subsequently followed by other courts. This chapter explores the nature of precedent, its place within the court system, and its significance to the legal system and sources of law. We examine how precedent is created, and its relationship to the hierarchy of the courts. We will consider how judges use, and adapt, precedent to achieve what they believe to be the correct result. We will also look at the structure of a case report, which we need to understand in order to identify, and utilise, precedents.

9.2 The concept of precedent: three questions

It is all very well for the judiciary to tell us their decisions should be followed. But a number of questions arise.

- First, where did this idea come from?
- Second, which courts are the leaders, and which are the followers, so to speak?
- Third, what aspects of any given decision should be subsequently adopted?

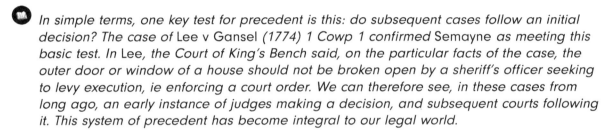 *In simple terms, one key test for precedent is this: do subsequent cases follow an initial decision? The case of* Lee v Gansel *(1774) 1 Cowp 1 confirmed* Semayne *as meeting this basic test. In* Lee, *the Court of King's Bench said, on the particular facts of the case, the outer door or window of a house should not be broken open by a sheriff's officer seeking to levy execution, ie enforcing a court order. We can therefore see, in these cases from long ago, an early instance of judges making a decision, and subsequent courts following it. This system of precedent has become integral to our legal world.*

Let us now consider the three questions posed.

9.3 The first question: the origins of the doctrine of precedent

The concept of precedent, ie the idea the sayings of one court should influence others, took root in a meaningful manner in the era of Sir William Blackstone (1723–1780). The germ of the principle no doubt existed well before that. But he certainly espoused the matter with great clarity. Jo Ann Boylan-Kemp in her excellent *English Legal System*, 4th edn (Sweet & Maxwell, 2018) reminds us of the statement in Blackstone's *Commentaries* of 1769 of a judge

> being sworn to determine not according to his private sentiments ... not according to his own private judgement, but according to the known laws and customs of the land: not delegated to pronounce a new law, but to maintain and expound the old one.

This statement means that judges should put aside their personal preferences and make decisions based on the law of the land. Further, they shouldn't make new law, but instead continue and build on the existing law. Here, Sir William is articulating the traditional role of the judge as someone with an essentially conservative approach. The question remains whether his views reflect the reality of judicial action over time. Do judges merely state the law, or are they more assertive?

There is much to be said for the concept mentioned by Sir William. Most obviously, precedent is efficient, in the sense that building on existing law removes the need to reconstruct the basics every time a judge considers a dispute. The joy of precedent lies in its ability to cut corners in an entirely legitimate manner.

Courts appreciated this from an early stage. The case of Hanslap v Cater *(1673) 1 Ventris 243 involved a dispute over the sale of goods. There was mention of a broken promise, and jurisdictional queries. The matter was fiercely contested. At the case's conclusion one of the learned participants is recorded as submitting to a key principle. They:*

consented that (an earlier statement) should be reversed according as the later precedents have been, for he said it was his rule 'Stare Decisis'.

Thus the Court confirmed something should be reversed to comply with precedent. The rationale for this, the case report says, was the previous decision in the Barnstaple Court, in Devon, of Parsons and Muden, *a case that now appears to be lost in the mists of time.*

What exactly was the Court saying in *Hanslap*? First, it states the importance of precedent, saying decisions should be consistent. In this instance it involved reversing an earlier, incorrect, statement. Second, it reinforces this by referring to a previous case – *Parsons* – which it was now following. Third, it referred to something called '*Stare Decisis*'. This is Latin for 'the previous decision should stand', meaning the Court accepted the importance of following earlier rulings. There are references before 1673 to *Stare Decisis*, but this case, and the subsequent ponderings of Blackstone, represent a reasonable place to start when detecting precedent's growing maturity. The doctrine of *Stare Decisis* has a double relevance today. It confirms previous court decisions can and should be relied on. And it hints at the need for lower courts to take note of higher ones.

To illustrate the development of precedent, **Figure 9.1** explains the starting point as, usually, the need for some sort of ruling on a matter important to society. Traditionally, and to an extent still the case today, a preponderance of cases stem from the agendas of those with money and influence. Courts will then take a particular issue, deal with legislation which

Figure 9.1 How precedent developed

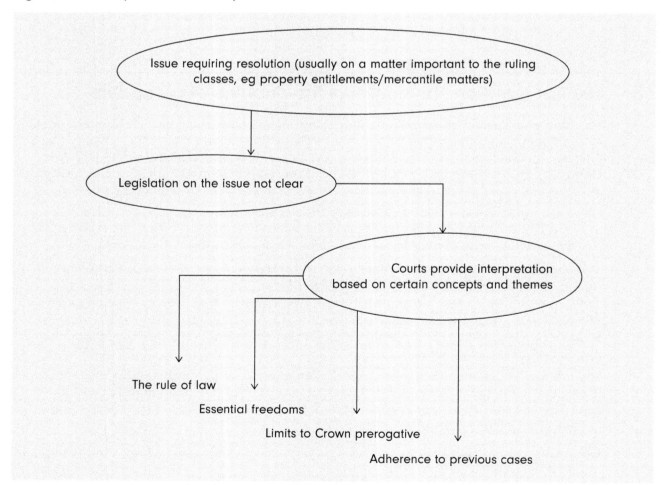

perhaps is unclear or requiring some formal updating, and then arrive at an interpretation. If the court ruling on the matter is sufficiently senior, the precedent train then leaves one station and arrives at another.

9.4 The second question: precedent and the hierarchy of courts

The next question to consider, therefore, is: which courts should bow down before the others? If we pause here for a moment, it clearly cannot make sense for every court to command loyalty from the rest. Utter confusion would reign, with judges tying themselves in knots attempting to follow their colleagues.

In the first place, there are too many decisions being made. Courts have always been proportionately busy to the societies they serve, and, now as much as in the past, the flow of judgments can only make sense if there are rules that identify the important ones worth observing. Additionally, you would not expect a senior judge to take note of rulings by, say, a humble justice of the peace in some remote county. There clearly must be a court hierarchy within which the system can sensibly operate.

9.4.1 The role of the Supreme Court

Let us therefore start at the top of the tree, at the Supreme Court, or, as it used to be called, the House of Lords. Putting to one side the influence of European Union law, the Supreme Court is the highest court of the land. You would expect all courts beneath it – ie the Court of Appeal, the High Court, the County Court, the Crown Court, the magistrates' courts and so on – to acknowledge and follow their decisions. And this is indeed the case. This, therefore, is the simple rule: lower courts must take heed of the higher. That basic proposition is well worth remembering.

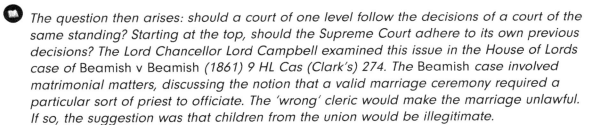 *The question then arises: should a court of one level follow the decisions of a court of the same standing? Starting at the top, should the Supreme Court adhere to its own previous decisions? The Lord Chancellor Lord Campbell examined this issue in the House of Lords case of* Beamish v Beamish *(1861) 9 HL Cas (Clark's) 274. The* Beamish *case involved matrimonial matters, discussing the notion that a valid marriage ceremony required a particular sort of priest to officiate. The 'wrong' cleric would make the marriage unlawful. If so, the suggestion was that children from the union would be illegitimate.*

You can see why this matter required scrutiny. Lord Campbell referred to a royal decision of 940 (yes, that long ago – before the Norman Conquest) and a later court case. He made it clear, if it were down to him, he would rule against the law as it stood, hinting he found it 'tyrannical'. But he then went on to say:

> it is my duty to say that your Lordships are bound by this decision ... and that the rule of law which your Lordships lay down as the ground of your judgment, sitting judicially, as the last and supreme Court of Appeal for this empire, must be taken for law till altered by an Act of Parliament ...

He referred to something called the *ratio decidendi*, ie the decided *ratio*, or the central reasoning of the case, being binding on all inferior tribunals. Put into today's language, the Court was saying it was bound by its earlier decisions, unless and until Parliament changed the law by passing a new statute. We will look at *ratios* shortly.

The significance of the Beamish *decision lies in its assumption the House of Lords, now the Supreme Court, should follow its previous judgments. Their Lordships confirmed this in the case of* Jones v South West Lancashire Coal Owners Association Limited *[1927] Ll L Rep 259 where Lord Chancellor Viscount Cave stated:*

> My Lords, when a question of law has been clearly decided by this House, it is undesirable that the decision should be weakened or frittered away by fine distinctions.

Viscount Cave here was quite direct in reminding the House of Lords not to undermine – or to use his phrase 'fritter away' – essential principles previously established. But society changes, and the law with it. The judiciary took the view the House of Lords should have flexibility to change it its mind should circumstances require. On 26 July 1966 the House of Lords issued the Practice Statement 3 All ER 77 with the heading 'departure from previous decisions when appearing right to do so'. The Lord Chancellor Lord Gardiner's text said:

> Their Lordships regard the use of precedent as an indispensable foundation upon which to decide what is the law and its application to individual cases. It provides at least some degree of certainty upon which individuals can rely in the conduct of their affairs, as well as a basis for orderly development of legal rules. Their Lordships nevertheless recognise that too rigid adherence to precedent may lead to injustice in a particular case and also unduly restrict the proper development of the law. They propose, therefore, to modify their present practice and, while treating former decisions of this House as normally binding, to depart from a previous decision when it appears right to do so.

The Statement explained the vital role of precedent, describing it as indispensable, and saying it provided certainty to lawyers and their clients. But it went on to remark on the possibility of too rigid an application of the concept leading to possible injustice.

In conclusion, the House of Lords recognised the need for it to have a certain discretion in adapting its views over time. Interestingly, it impliedly accepted the potential inflexibility of precedent, at least insofar as it related to the House of Lords. This hints at something we see regularly throughout the judicial process: the ability of courts to traverse away from a dogmatic loyalty to previous rulings. As we shall see, there are various techniques available to judges to tweak, resist or circumnavigate precedent.

Having said that, we should note the Practice Statement does not apply to lower courts. It relates purely to the House of Lords and its ability to bind itself.

What then is the position today in the Supreme Court? The Statement did not release a flood of decisions controverting earlier rulings. In *Miliangos v George Frank Textiles* [1976] AC 433 Lord Cross said the Statement

> does not mean that whenever we think that a previous decision was wrong we should reverse it.

This appears to represent the current approach of the Supreme Court. It is generally accepted it should use the power to go against itself sparingly. It requires something more than a previous decision being wrong. Rather, it should be used where a previous decision causes injustice, or impedes the development of the law, or itself causes uncertainty. Even where it concludes the law should be changed, it should perhaps consider whether departure from the previous decision is preferable to legislation from Parliament.

We can conclude as follows:

- The Supreme Court is not invariably bound by its previous decisions; this is as a result of the 1966 Practice Statement.

- However, departure from a previous precedent by the Supreme Court will be an unusual event.

- You can therefore have a robust discussion as to the continuing significance of statements by Lord Chancellors in cases such as *Beamish* and *SW Lancashire*.

- The Practice Statement hints at occasional rigidity in the concept of precedent, and we should be alert to the various judicial tools that allow courts up and down the land to operate flexibly.

- Of course, the entire concept remains subject to the caveat that UK law remains subject to European Union law influences, at least until any departure timetable (following the 'leave' vote in 2016) has run its course.

Incidentally, decisions of the Judicial Committee of the Privy Council are persuasive rather than binding. This means courts can refer to Privy Council advice if they wish, but are not compelled to do so.

9.4.2 The Court of Appeal and precedent

Immediately below the Supreme Court sits the Court of Appeal. Naturally, it is bound by the Supreme Court, and of course it binds the courts below it: the High Court, County Court, magistrates, tribunals and the rest. But does it bind itself?

The presumption is yes, following the case of *Young v Bristol Aeroplane* [1944] KB 718, which stated the key principle. But in that case the Court also outlined three exceptions to the basic rule. *Young* decreed the Court of Appeal could depart from its previous stance where its own previous decision:

- conflicts with another one from it; or

- has been implicitly overruled by the Supreme Court; or

- was made *per incuriam*, ie through carelessness.

Let's look at these three exceptions. First, it would be unusual for Court of Appeal decisions to conflict. You would expect the Court to be aware of its previous judgments. However, in limited circumstances a conflict could happen where the earlier judgment happened just a few days before, or perhaps was not reported. It is also possible that an earlier decision was not cited to the Court, or – and this is very unlikely – it was cited but misunderstood.

Second, you might wonder how the Supreme Court could implicitly, rather than expressly, overrule a decision. This could happen where a case bypasses the Court of Appeal and goes straight from, say, the High Court to the Supreme Court through the leapfrog procedure, or where the Supreme Court overrules another Court of Appeal decision without reference to a relevant alternative ruling.

Third, it is again unusual for the Court of Appeal, or indeed any court, to make a decision through carelessness. Note this is not the same as a decision being wrong, in the sense of the Supreme Court reversing a decision. Incidentally, we shall look at court terminology, such as 'reversing', in a moment.

In Morelle v Wakeling *[1955] 2 QB 379 Lord Evershed MR said the* Young *point about carelessness only applied to 'decisions given in ignorance or forgetfulness of some inconsistent statutory provision, or of some authority binding on the court concerned'. According to Lord Donaldson in* Duke v Reliance *[1988] QB 108 a decision is* per incuriam *if the court* must *have reached a different conclusion, rather than just* might *have done so.*

There is also a further category of decision where the Court of Appeal can depart from earlier statements by it. In *Boys v Chaplin* [1968] 2 QB 1 the Court of Appeal said decisions by two judges, on an interlocutory basis, where the decision was wrong, were not binding on the full court.

9.4.3 Precedent in the High Court and other courts

The High Court has a dual function both as a court of first instance and an appellate body. In its appeal function, in the Administrative Court for instance, the High Court is bound by its own decisions, subject to the exceptions applicable in the Court of Appeal. By contrast, decisions of individual High Court judges in first instance cases are not binding elsewhere in the High Court. However, in the interests of certainty, where possible judges try not to depart from previous decisions. High Court decisions are of course binding on lower courts, which within the civil hierarchy means the County Court.

The County Court and Family Court are considered inferior courts. They do not bind each other, nor are they capable of setting precedents in the traditional sense for other courts to follow. Their decisions can be referred to by other courts as persuasive only. There are several reasons for this. First, they are simply too low on the judicial ladder. Second, the level of activity, which for lower courts and tribunals is considerable, means it is impossible to keep track of, and log in any meaningful way, the decisions that emerge. Third, most lower cases are not reported, and so the details are either unknown or cannot be relied on (important tribunal cases are reported, however).

When we say lower courts are not followed in the 'traditional sense', we need to appreciate, once again, the human element. It is not unknown for advocates to make a note of cases in which they were involved. They might then produce that note to a judge in a subsequent hearing, with the appropriate permission of course, or simply refer to their previous experiences by way of giving a judge additional information. Such references generally carry little formal weight, but they illustrate an interesting aspect of 'storytelling' as part of legal process.

To end this section of the manual, **Figure 9.2** presents a flowchart on the hierarchy of courts and precedent. It starts at the very top with the ECJ, and progresses downwards through the Supreme Court, Court of Appeal and lower courts. There is a process of binding until you arrive at the High Court (in its first instance guise), Crown Court, County Court, and magistrates'. You need to 'watch this space' in terms of the ECJ, of course.

Figure 9.2 Hierarchy of courts and precedent

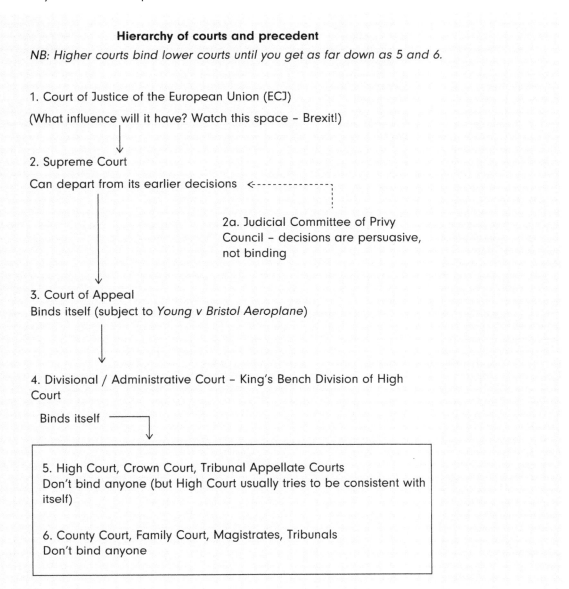

Hierarchy of courts and precedent
NB: Higher courts bind lower courts until you get as far down as 5 and 6.

1. Court of Justice of the European Union (ECJ)

(What influence will it have? Watch this space – Brexit!)

2. Supreme Court

Can depart from its earlier decisions

2a. Judicial Committee of Privy Council – decisions are persuasive, not binding

3. Court of Appeal
Binds itself (subject to *Young v Bristol Aeroplane*)

4. Divisional / Administrative Court – King's Bench Division of High Court

Binds itself

5. High Court, Crown Court, Tribunal Appellate Courts
Don't bind anyone (but High Court usually tries to be consistent with itself)

6. County Court, Family Court, Magistrates, Tribunals
Don't bind anyone

9.5 The third question: what aspects of a decision can become 'precedent'?

The conventional approach to precedent states one case is binding in a later case if it meets the following four requirements:

1. There is a proposition of law.

2. That proposition is part of the *ratio decidendi* of a case.

3. The proposition is decided in a court whose decisions are binding on the present court.

4. There are no relevant distinctions between the two cases. A more 'legal' way of stating this final point is that the later case is not capable of being *distinguished* from the earlier one, ie the facts are sufficiently different to allow the judge to arrive at an alternative conclusion.

9.5.1 Propositions of law

It is not always easy to detect a precedent. To start with, a proposition of law might not be immediately apparent. Sometimes the law can be easily mixed with fact. Some judgments are lengthy, and deal with an awful lot of detail. Somewhere there may be a relevant proposition, but it could be tricky putting your finger on it.

What exactly is a proposition of law? Broadly, it is a judicial statement confirming a legal principle, derived either from statute or case law, or perhaps both, or indeed stemming from other sources such as custom or academic commentary. It is not uncommon for judges to proffer propositions of law stemming from statements by advocates in other cases, sometimes hundreds of years ago; or from law textbooks by established authors; or even speeches by prominent legal figures. In fact, the judiciary, certainly at a senior level, has considerable freedom to seek out and state the law from a wide range of possibilities.

Having said that, most propositions of law are based purely on statute or common law. That doesn't mean they are necessarily straightforward. In *Qualcast Ltd v Haynes* [1959] AC 743 an employer made available to workers what is now classed as personal protective equipment (PPE). But it did not compel them to use it. The claimant in the case declined to use spats covering his legs and was injured when molten metal splashed on to his feet. He then alleged negligence.

The House of Lords held that whether use of PPE should have been enforced was not a question of law. Rather, it was one of fact. Their Lordships were stating something that we can all appreciate: each case turns on its own circumstances. In some instances failure to require use of PPE would be negligent. In other situations it would not be.

Here are some examples of propositions of law, and their particular areas of application. These may have developed further since their judgments. You can learn more about these when exploring the subjects in more detail:

- Business law: *Salomon v Salomon* [1897] AC 22 – the House of Lords held that a company was a separate legal entity to its shareholders.
- Contract law: *Pinnel's Case* (1602) 5 Co Rep 117 – Lord Coke held that part payment of a debt cannot be satisfaction for the whole.
- Administrative law: *Associated Provincial Picture Houses Ltd v Wednesbury Corporation* [1948] 1 KB 223 – local authorities could have their actions challenged if their decisions were so unreasonable that no reasonable authority would ever consider making them.
- Tort law: *Wagon Mound No 1* [1961] AC 388 – the House of Lords held that a party can only be liable for loss that was reasonably foreseeable.

9.5.2 *Ratio decidendi*

Second, you may find it difficult to identify the *ratio decidendi* of a case. So what is it? In essence, it is the central legal reasoning of a case, capable of creating precedent. To find it you need to identify the material facts. As we shall see, it is not always easy to detect a *ratio*.

Alternatively, if you are in a creative mood, you might be able to find several *ratios*. You could even be tempted to find a *ratio* to suit your particular situation. There is nothing wrong in this. The law is a living breathing entity, and is capable of many nuances.

9.5.3 Other parts of the test for precedent

The third limb of the test – the earlier decision being made by a higher court whose views are binding – can usually be established without difficulty.

Finally, concerning the fourth point, a judge may think the later case can be distinguished from the earlier case. If so, the later case will escape the clutches of precedent. The earlier case remains a precedent, but it won't apply to the later scenario.

You can appreciate, from these four requirements, a court might have something of a dilemma in seeking to establish whether an earlier decision should be followed or not. Sometimes healthy doses of common sense are needed. Most judges take a practical approach by asking whether the earlier decision, from a higher court, has a key ruling, and if it does they then decide whether it can sensibly be applied in the instant case.

Commentators believe this approach to precedent meets and achieves two basic principles of justice: consistency and proportionality. The first of these is essential in the rule of law. Litigants need to know that courts will apply a uniform approach when dealing with the issues. Society also needs the flexibility inherent in proportionality, which allows judges to take note of the specific facts of a case. This can lead to the distinguishing process, which allows a judge to work around a precedent without contradicting it or undermining the underlying principle.

9.6 The concept of *ratio*

Assuming the four elements inherent in the concept of precedent are satisfied, it would still be a 'fool's errand' (ie an impossibility) to follow everything said by the higher court. Lower courts therefore need the ability to detect which aspects of a decision require their obedience. This means establishing the *ratio*.

9.6.1 An example of an important *ratio*

Imagine you are out shopping. You buy a bottle of ginger beer. You drink it with gusto, and very refreshing it is too. But unknown to you it is polluted. There is a dead snail at the bottom. You then suffer terrible gastric illness.

 These are the outline facts of Donoghue v Stevenson *[1932] AC 562. This is a leading case in the law of negligence, confirming the concept of neighbourhood. The ruling states we should take care of those close to us, and in the context of a ginger beer manufacturer that means consumers who might drink the product. Here, the House of Lords held the consumer could claim damages.*

The Supreme Court today would not be bound to follow this decision, but in the normal course of things it would not expect to deviate from this important ruling. The principle now is too well established. Failing to follow it would cause a legal earthquake. But let's transport ourselves back in time to the 1930s. Imagine you are a judge in a lower court. What exactly would you be bound by? Are you obliged to follow that bit of the judgment about bottles, or ginger beer, or snails or illness? It would seem a little odd for precedent to be based too closely on individual facts or a collection of them. Courts need guidance to identify which part of a ruling creates subsequent obligations.

9.6.2 Narrow and wide *ratios*

Over time, commentators have come to accept there are two sorts of *ratio*: the wide, and the narrow. The wide one has broad applicability. The narrow has a more limited and specific impact.

Let's say you hold shares in a company as an investment. An accountant audits the company. The audit understates the company's financial position. It is in a much worse state than originally thought. The shares drop in value. You decide to make a claim against the accountant.

These are the outline facts in *Caparo Industries v Dickman* [1990] UKHL 2. The House of Lords decided the auditor owed no duty to provide the shareholder with financial information to assist an investment. This would be an example of a narrow *ratio*. It is the key legal reasoning on the specific accountancy relationship between two participants in the business world. Their Lordships went on to explain how a novel duty of care would arise in circumstances where there was no clear previous duty.

Lord Bridge of Harwich confirmed the Court of Appeal's analysis on this point. He said there should be first forseeability, second proximity, and third justness and reasonableness in all the circumstances. This can be seen as a wide *ratio*. It is the key legal reasoning applicable to a wider range of situations. It is now referred to as the three-stage '*Caparo* test', highly relevant as to the existence of a novel duty of care.

In the *Donoghue* case there are also generally considered to be two *ratios*. The wide one is a person owes a duty to take reasonable care of their neighbours, ie people who could be in the reasonable contemplation of others as likely to suffer injury in the event of a breach. You can see that this has very general application, and quite correctly so. It means we all need to be careful. Whether driving a car, or walking the dog, or doing a job of work, we should take care not to cause damage or injury.

There is also a narrower application that still has value and relevance: a manufacturer should take care to prevent injury from its products to consumers.

9.6.3　How to identify a *ratio*

It is quite a skill identifying the *ratio* of a case. A reported decision could cover many pages. There may be judgments by several judges. One or more of those judgments could be dissenting, ie they disagree with the majority. Within any one judgment there could be different strands to the argument. There could be lengthy discussions of the law, maybe covering many issues, previous cases and statutes, sometimes going back centuries. How, then, is the reader, or another court, meant to arrive at a *ratio*? In fact, there could be a number of *ratios* in a case. They could derive from the following:

- a sentence or a collection of sentences by one judge; or

- a passage constituting several paragraphs from one judge; or

- different passages, appearing at various places within the views of one or more judges; or

- a theme or themes within the judgment from various judges; or

- (and this is perhaps the least likely) the tenor of the case as a whole.

In the case of *Rylands v Fletcher* (1868) LR 3 HL 330 the facts were as follows. The defendant had a reservoir built on his land. The contractor who did the work was negligent. As a consequence water escaped and flooded the claimant's mine. The outcome of the case was the defendant was liable to the claimant.

Why should this be? The reason relates to ownership of property. If you own property you have a source of wealth, usually, and there are responsibilities that go with that privilege. Here, the courts say a property owner should have strict liability – ie be automatically responsible – for an escape from their land.

The facts considered to be material by the court, and hence relevant to a *ratio*, were:

- the defendant had a reservoir;

- water escaped; and

- the mine flooded.

This formed the basis for a narrow *ratio*: an escape of water from the defendant's land to the claimant's land created a cause of action. The wider *ratio* in this instance was not vastly different: it was, in the words of the judgment:

a person who for his own purposes brings on his land and collects and keeps there anything likely to do mischief if it escapes must keep it at his peril and if he does not do so is prima facie answerable for all the damage which is the natural consequence of its escape.

These are examples of discernable *ratios*. But it is not always straightforward finding one. Conversely, the case could be structured in such a way there could be several possible options. Whichever it is, we can agree finding an appropriate *ratio* can sometimes take time.

This is for various reasons.

- First, old cases often gave obscure justifications for their decisions, or no guidance at all. It is therefore difficult to decipher the thought process of the judge.

- Second, vast parts of many judgments are irrelevant in terms of the final decision. This could be because there is a focus on the facts or a discussion of matters that, over time, subsequent courts would consider to be peripheral or irrelevant.

- Third, a judge may give reasons for a decision but those reasons have little subsequent significance or application to later cases.

- Fourth, some *ratios* may be readily apparent, and significant, at the time of the judgment, but rapidly lose relevance as time goes on.

- Fifth, something that is not obviously a *ratio* at the time may gather significance in later years, a bit like a snowball gathering pace down a hill.

- Sixth, there may be several statements, or passages, or themes, which could constitute different *ratios*, and it then becomes a matter of choice as to which is subsequently relied on and followed in later years.

An example of a court arriving at a decision, but with different *ratios*, is *Esso v Commissioners for Customs and Excise* [1976] 1 All ER 117. Here the issue was whether Esso had to pay purchase tax on commemorative coins that it gave away with fuel. Five judges gave judgments. Four were in the majority, but they gave a range of reasons for their decisions. In this situation, lower courts have a range of reasoning at their disposal. They can almost 'pick 'n' mix' a *ratio* to suit.

9.7 Obiter statements

Once the *ratio* has been identified, you might think the rest of the judgment becomes somewhat irrelevant. But this is not always the case. Sometimes courts make statements unimportant to the outcome but with significance for the future. These are called obiter dicta (ie other things said). The classic definition of an obiter dictum (singular rather than plural) is:

- a proposition of law not necessary for a case's conclusion.

Alternatively, it can be considered as:

- a statement that is not *ratio* but is significant for the future.

You can see identifying an obiter statement represents something of a moving target. It can be difficult, and indeed a redundant exercise, to attempt to spot an obiter statement at the time it is made. You could certainly identify it as not relevant to the immediate outcome of the case, but how can you tell that it will have significance for other cases later in time? The short answer is in most instances you cannot. You might have to wait months, years or decades before any such a remark achieves significance later.

9.7.1 Examples of obiter dicta

There are two types of obiter. First, a proposition may be obiter if it is wider than necessary to decide the particular case. This could be a series of statements, or a lengthy discussion, by a judge to explain their reasoning that is not, however, crucial to the final outcome. Second, a judge may make a decision on a case, and then speculate as to what alternative judgment they may have given had the facts, or some aspect of the case, been different.

Crossley v Rawlinson [1982] 1 WLR 369 provides an example of an obiter statement being used by a judge to assist in the overall outcome of the case, whilst not being central to the result. Here, Mr Richard Tucker QC, sitting as a deputy High Court judge in the QBD, decided a claimant failed in a negligence action against a defendant lorry driver whose vehicle had caught fire. The judge stated the defendant to be not liable and then went on:

> If I had awarded damages I would have awarded the plaintiff £3500 for pain and suffering and loss of amenities. I accept that his complaints are genuine.

Here, we see the role of obiter as part of the human process of arriving at a result. The judge was at pains to categorise the claimant's actions, on the facts, as praiseworthy and valuable. Unfortunately, in the eyes of the law there was no valid claim. The obiter statement helped soften, admittedly in a non-financial way, the harsh result.

The *Crossley* case also illustrates the influence of High Court decisions. In *Sparrow v Andre* [2016] EWHC 739 (QB), the QBD referred to it in deciding a claimant could succeed in a negligence claim where injuries stemmed directly from the defendant's breach of duty in allowing their car to roll backwards in a car park. The High Court doesn't bind itself, but the judge in *Sparrow* referred to *Crossley* as being both helpful and well known.

The case of RG Securities (No 2) Ltd v Allianz Global Corporate and Specialty CE and others [2020] EWHC 1646 (TCC) illustrates the flexible approach of the courts to obiter statements. Here, Fraser J, sitting in the Technology and Construction Court of the QBD, noted observations by Lord Nicholls in the House of Lords case of Sheldon v Outhwaite [1996] AC 102.

Those statements related to the principle of limitation – ie the period of time available to a party to commence proceedings, failing which they will be barred from claiming – in insurance matters. Mr Justice Fraser said the statements, 'if obiter would be of powerful effect'. He said they were capable of being binding rather than just persuasive. He was stating an important point: obiter statements in one setting can become ratios elsewhere. This is an indication of the judiciary's ability to convert one thing into another, a bit like a potter taking wet clay and remodelling it into a fine earthenware plate.

9.7.2 An older example of obiter and something more recent

Cases such as *RG Securities* confirm an established, if not exactly common, process. In *Central London Property Trust Limited v High Trees House Limited* [1947] KB 139 Mr Justice Denning, as he then was, in the High Court stated a property landlord who agreed to accept half rent for a given period from a tenant could not later claim the balance. Denning J's comment was obiter because the landlord in fact was only claiming full rent for the future.

But the Court of Appeal in *Combe v Combe* [1951] 2 KB 215 considered the point and was persuaded by it, and embraced it as an important principle of contract law. The statement by Denning J therefore moved from one realm to another.

The case of *London Steam-Ship Owners' Mutual Insurance Association Ltd v Kingdom of Spain* [2020] EWHC 1582 (Comm) provides a further insight into the life and times of an obiter statement. This was a dispute over jurisdiction and the role of an arbitrator. Mr Justice Henshaw heard the matter in the Commercial Court of the QBD. The judge needed to consider a particular phrase, namely 'proceedings relating to the transaction', in the context of enforcement of an arbitration award.

Henshaw J embarked on a paper chase of different cases in converting a supplementary comment into something with greater force. First he referred to a High Court case, *Svenska Petroleum* [2005] EWHC 2437 (Comm). That case in turn considered another High Court judgment, *AIC v Federal Government of Nigeria* [2003] EWHC 1357 (QB). That case had considered a statement by Lord Millett in the House of Lords case of *Holland v Lampen-Wolfe* [2000] 1 WLR 1573.

Mr Justice Henshaw in *Steam-Ship Mutual* noted, through his reading of *Svenska*, which had itself considered *AIC*, which had then pondered *Holland,* that the relevant passage was strictly obiter at the time of its original statement. Yet in *Svenska* the same passage was given greater status. Crucially, Henshaw J also noted the Court of Appeal had endorsed the approach of the first instance judge in *Svenska*, thus giving the matter further gravitas.

To illustrate the process, **Figure 9.3** starts at the top with the 2000 House of Lords decision. There, an obiter statement was made. You can then see how that statement was treated in 2003, 2005, 2017, and then in 2020.

Figure 9.3   The life and times of an obiter statement

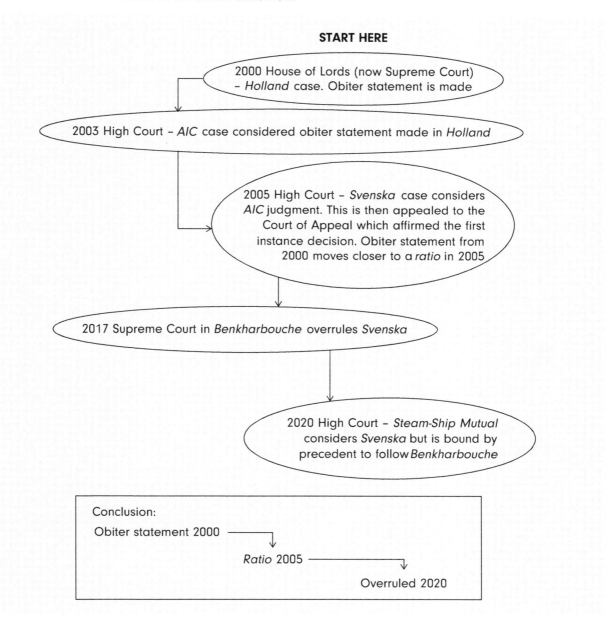

The chain of events was therefore this.

- The House of Lords in 2000 made an obiter statement.
- The High Court in 2003 gave that statement significance.
- The High Court in 2005, although not bound to follow itself, gave increased weight to the statement.
- This was something the Court of Appeal approved.

Over a period of five years, therefore, an obiter statement had achieved something close to a *ratio*. This sequence of events illustrates a number of points as follows:

1. It demonstrates the extraordinary lengths judges go to to get to the nub of an issue, digging deep into one case after another.

2. It shows how an obiter statement can transform itself into something more central.

3. It indicates this may only happen over a period of time, in this instance several years.

4. It reinforces the hierarchy of decision-making, in that, in the *Svenska* case, the Court of Appeal validated the High Court approach.

5. It indicates the human nature of judging. The metamorphosis of the House of Lords statement in 2000 into something more meaningful in 2005 could only happen with judges giving their views. That takes us back to an earlier point: were they simply applying the law, or making it? This is something for you to ponder.

The *Steam-Ship Mutual* case also contained another element of hierarchical decision-making. Henshaw J noted the Supreme Court case of *Benkharbouche* [2017] UKSC 62 had rendered *Svenska* old law. The relevant contention, therefore, having travelled from the margins to the centre, had now been judicially neutered.

This therefore illustrates another basic point relevant to the legal system, and this publication: the power of the Supreme Court to overrule lower courts. It also indicates the requirement of the High Court to follow a Supreme Court precedent. Ultimately, this is what Henshaw J did.

9.8   How precedents can be used flexibly

Precedents have the potential to be inflexible. The 1966 Statement from the House of Lords confirmed that. The judiciary has therefore developed certain tools to navigate around rulings. Judges would not say, at least openly, they are getting around inconvenient precedents, but in a sense that is what is happening. It is an inevitable aspect of effective justice.

 The Supreme Court, being the top dog, can alter precedents set by the Court of Appeal by overruling them. The colourful case of Ivey v Genting Casinos (UK) Ltd (trading as Crockfords Club) *[2018] 2 All ER 406 illustrates this. Mr Ivey won £7.7m at a casino through a specialised technique he had devised for playing the card game Baccarat. The casino refused to pay. Messy litigation resulted.*

The Supreme Court upheld the Court of Appeal's decision that Mr Ivey should not receive his winnings. In so ruling, the Law Lords reviewed the previous Court of Appeal decision in R v Ghosh *[1982] 2 All ER 689. The Supreme Court decided a key aspect of the test for dishonesty in* Ghosh *did not correctly represent the law. They therefore overruled it. We should make it clear this was a civil case and in no way is it suggested here Mr Ivey thought he was doing something either criminal or dishonest.*

Two other methods of moving away from, or watering down perhaps, a precedent are as follows:

- treating a statement as obiter, as discussed above; and

- distinguishing the instant case from a previous ruling. This is where a court finds reason to disagree, on the facts, with a decision from a higher court that would otherwise operate as a precedent and bind it. Judges take an absolute delight in doing this.

  - For example, in the Court of Appeal case of *365 Business Finance v Bellagio Hospitality WB* [2020] EWCA Civ 588 Lord Leggatt explored the case law on who comes first in the pecking order when several creditors are seeking satisfaction from a debtor.

  - Lord Leggatt considered the leading case from the 1700s, the Kings Bench ruling of *Hutchinson v Johnston* (1787) 1 Term Rep 729. This case indicated creditors should take precedence on a first come, first served basis.

  - The Court went on to say *Hutchinson* distinguished two earlier cases, one from 1697 and the other undated, but by implication from the same era (roughly).

  - This is a fascinating example of the durability of legal decisions, and an instance of how far back in time judges may go to ensure they are drawing the necessary conclusions.

9.9 Terminology

Courts have a number of other tools to assist them in coming to a decision. These are sometimes used purely to arrive at a judgment. But they also assist a student in finding their way around precedents, *ratios* and other matters relevant to the hierarchy of the legal system. It is useful to be aware of the relevant terminology. Here is a selection of the main terms – we do not represent this as being an exhaustive list:

- Affirming. This is when a higher court confirms it agrees with the appeal before it from a lower court. For instance, in the *Ivey* case, the Supreme Court affirmed the Court of Appeal decision, ie the casino should indeed obtain judgment.

- Applying. This happens when a court indicates it is adopting statements or reasoning from other decisions. For instance, in the *Ivey* case the Supreme Court applied statements – or 'dicta' – from two cases: *Royal Brunei Airlines* [1995] 3 All ER 97 and *Barlow Clowes* [2006] 1 All ER 333.

- Departing. This happens where a court of one level disagrees with a previous decision, in another matter, by an equal court. In *Pepper v Hart*, the House of Lords (now the Supreme Court) held courts could refer to parliamentary material recorded in Hansard where a statute is ambiguous or obscure, and the material consists of clear statements by a minister. This was a departure from *Davis v Johnson* [1979] 2 WLR 553, where Lord Scarman stated:

  > such material is an unreliable guide to the meaning of what is enacted. It promotes confusion, not clarity. The cut and thrust of debate and the pressures of executive responsibility, essential features of open and responsible government, are not always conducive to a clear and unbiased explanation of the meaning of statutory language.

- Overruling. This is where a higher court comments on a previous unrelated decision by a lower court and declares it to be wrong. This is what happened to *Ghosh* when considered in *Ivey*.

- Reversing a judgment. Here, a higher court disagrees with the earlier decision, in the same proceedings, of a lower court. Effectively this is what happens whenever an appeal succeeds. There are plenty of examples of this. One mentioned in this publication, for instance, is the decision of the Supreme Court in *R (on the application of Privacy International) v Investigatory Powers Tribunal and others* [2019] UKSC 22. There, in a case about computer intercept operations – hacking, to you and me – by the security services, the Supreme Court decided by a majority of 4 to 3 that the Court of Appeal's decision was wrong.

Figure 9.4 briefly states the way in which the *ratio* in one case can be changed subsequently. Ultimately these methods are all tailored towards one outcome: the need for some sort of sensible and appropriate ruling which meets the needs of contemporary society.

Figure 9.4 How courts treat precedents flexibly

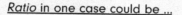

Ratio in one case could be ...

- Distinguished in another (a popular way of traversing a precedent)

- Or overruled (if considered later by a higher court)

- Or departed from (can be by an equal court)

- Or reversed (if a higher court)

9.10 How to read and make sense of a reported case

To get a feel for precedent, *ratios*, obiter dicta and their friends, it helps to read cases. You should therefore develop an understanding of the layout of a typical case report.

Usually, a judge, if sitting with others, will give a leading judgment. They will outline the facts and sequence of events leading to the case being heard. Then they will consider the relevant law, which could include a considerable analysis of legislation or previous cases or both. The judgment will then apply the facts to the law and come to a decision. This process could be repeated by other judges on the panel. A *ratio* could appear almost anywhere within the judgment, although the most likely setting is when applying the law to the facts, ie in the later stages.

Let's use *Ivey* to illustrate the layout of, and how to read, a case. The High Court found for the defendant casino. The claimant card player appealed. The Court of Appeal dismissed the appeal 2-1. Remember here the Supreme Court had the final say, agreeing with the Court of Appeal. A reminder, therefore: you should always update your research.

We will look at the Court of Appeal decision as it is a fine example of reasoning, structure and layout. Incidentally in the modern internet age you can read a case online without commentary. Important cases are, however, brought to us by skilled lawyers – law reporters – and adopt a particular format. They appear as case reports. These have 'added value', to use a phrase, beyond the pure judgment as delivered by the court.

Figure 9.5 Case report for *Ivey v Genting Casinos UK Ltd*

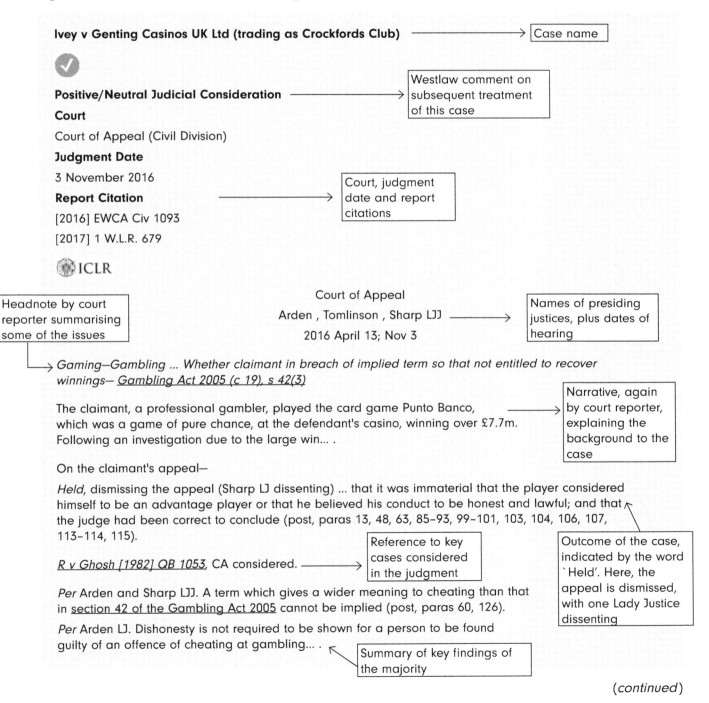

Figure 9.5 (*continued*)

Per Tomlinson LJ. The content of the implied term ... On the facts found the judge ← | Summary of the judgment of the Lord Justice agreeing with Arden LJ
should have concluded that the claimant had brought about a physical interference
with the cards ... conduct falling within the ordinary and natural meaning of the word... .

Decision of Mitting J [2014] EWHC 3394 (QB); [2015] LLR 98 affirmed on different grounds.

The following cases are referred to in the judgments:

- Lyons v State of Nevada (1989) 775 P 2d 219; 105 NR 317 ← | Cases referred to in judgment

- *Pepper v Hart [1993] AC 593; [1992] 3 WLR 1032; [1995] ICR 291; [1993] 1 All ER 42*, HL(E)

- *Practice Direction (Hansard: Citation) [1995] 1 WLR 192; [1995] 1 All ER 234*, SC

- *R v Ghosh [1982] QB 1053; [1982] 3 WLR 110; [1982] 2 All ER 689*, CA

- Richmond's Case see Moo KB 776

- *Seay v Eastwood [1976] 1 WLR 1117; [1976] 3 All ER 153*, HL(NI) | Cases referred to by advocates in argument

The following additional cases were cited in argument:

- *Barlow Clowes International Ltd v Eurotrust International Ltd [2005] UKPC 37; [2006] 1 WLR 1476; [2006] 1 All ER 333; [2006] 1 All ER (Comm) 478; [2006] 1 Lloyd's Rep 225*, PC

- *Royal Brunei Airlines Sdn Bhd v Tan [1995] 2 AC 378; [1995] 3 WLR 64; [1995] 3 All ER 97*, PC

APPEAL from Mitting J

By a claim form the claimant, Phillip Ivey, claimed against the defendant, Genting Casinos UK ← | Confirmation this is an appeal from Mitting J
Ltd, trading as Crockfords Club, for the recovery of moneys which he had won while playing
Punto Banco at the defendant's casino. The defendant denied liability on the grounds that ... .

By an appellant's notice filed on 29 October 2014 and pursuant to the permission | Reference, by court reporter, to the procedural background to the case, mentioning the appellant and respondent notices
of the Court of Appeal (Lewison LJ) granted on 2 February 2015 the claimant ←
appealed on the following grounds. (1) The judge had erred in holding that ... .

By a respondent's notice the defendant sought to uphold the judge's decision ... .

The facts are stated in the judgment of Arden LJ, post, paras 6–12.

Richard Spearman QC and *Max Mallin* (instructed by *Archerfield Partners LLP*) for the claimant.

Christopher Pymont QC and *Siward Atkins* (instructed by *Kingsley Napley LLP*) for the defendant.

The court took time for consideration. ← | Date of the handing down of judgment

3 November 2016. The following judgments were handed down.

ARDEN LJ ← | Justice providing the leading judgment. The verbatim judgments begin here, indicating the end of the section drafted by the court reporter

| Use of headings to organise the judgment, which is lengthy – so headings assist the reader by making things more accessible

Core issue: is edge-sorting legitimate play or cheating if used when playing Punto Banco? ←

1. The principal issue on this appeal is whether a method of play called "edge-sorting",
which involves exploiting design irregularities on the backs of playing cards, results
in cheating when playing Punto Banco, a variant of Baccarat ... . ← | Paragraphs are numbered throughout, which facilitates ability to locate different arguments/ sections across the decision

Punto Banco and the meaning of edge-sorting

6. Mitting J helpfully described Punto Banco and edge-sorting as follows ... .

Overview of this judgment

13. After carefully considering the arguments and numerous cases relevant to this appeal, I conclude, ← | Overview section helps readers understand what follows
for the reasons developed below, that Mr Ivey's challenge to the judge's conclusion must fail ... .

Figure 9.5 (*continued*)

My conclusion: there may be cheating without dishonesty ←

> This is a key conclusion and would be considered a possible *ratio* of the case

37. For the reasons given below, I consider that <u>section 42</u> does not require dishonesty to be shown ... .

Summary of my conclusions

99. I now summarise my conclusions ... . In my judgment, this section provides that a party may cheat within the meaning of this section without dishonesty or intention to deceive:

TOMLINSON LJ

104. I agree with Arden LJ that this appeal should be dismissed... . ←

> Judgment by second justice, agreeing with Arden LJ

114. For these reasons the judge in my view reached the correct conclusion as to the disposition of the claim and I too would dismiss the appeal.

SHARP LJ

116. I gratefully adopt Arden LJ's recitation of the facts and ← analysis of the law, save in relation to the issue of the mens rea ... .

> Dissenting judgment. This means the overall decision is 2-1 in rejecting the appeal

139. The test has undoubtedly come in for considerable academic criticism ... . Leveson LJ ← expressed (obiter) his concern if the concept of dishonesty for the purposes of civil liability were to differ to any marked extent from the concept of dishonesty as understood in the criminal law ... .

> Reference to obiter statement

In my opinion, the judge in this case was wrong to construe the issue of cheat in the way that he did, and I would allow this appeal.

Appeal dismissed. ←

> Reporter's confirmation of overall decision

Nicola Berridge, Solicitor

The main elements of the Court of Appeal report in *Ivey* are, starting at the top and working down:

- The case name. Here, it is *Ivey v Genting Casinos UK Ltd (trading as Crockfords Club)*.

- The case reference. Here, it is [2017] 1 WLR 679. This indicates the report is from the Weekly Law Reports. Cases can also have a neutral citation suitable for the internet age. Here, it is [2016] EWCA Civ 1093.

- There will then be some dates. These refer to the dates of the hearing and handing down of the judgment.

- The justices will then be named. Here, they are Lady and Lord Justices Arden, Tomlinson and Sharp.

- There is then an italicised summary of the case, consisting of key words and findings.

- There is then a headnote, consisting of various components. First, there is a summary of the facts. Second, there is a section entitled 'held', indicating the Court's judgment. This gives a summary of the various views of the Justices. There is also a mention of cases considered and affirmed. Third, there is a list of cases considered in the judgments, and cases cited in argument by the advocates. Fourth comes a summary of the proceedings so far, explaining the original claim, appellant's notice and the appeal. Finally, the headnote mentions the advocates who appeared, and their instructing solicitors.

- Then we have the real meat of the report, ie the judgment itself. Lady Justice Arden gives the leading judgment. It is beautifully organised, reminding us of the need for suitable headings as a means of clarifying complicated matters. She starts with the core issue.

She then defines and explores the gambling issues involved. She gives an overview of her judgment. There are sections on the parties' submissions, applicable statutes, dictionary definitions of certain words, various conclusions, earlier authorities and the use of Hansard. At every stage her findings are signposted and headlined. It is a model of clarity. She has also read the judgment of Sharp LJ and refers to that. She finishes with a summary of her conclusions and states she would dismiss the appeal. Within this lengthy judgment you would find one or more *ratios*.

- Lord Justice Tomlinson then gives his judgment in agreement. His judgment is altogether shorter, as Lady Justice Arden has already fully explored most points.

- Lady Justice Sharp then gives her dissenting judgment. She considers the submissions of the advocates, and the relevant legislation, from a different perspective. She concludes by stating she would allow the appeal.

- The overall result, therefore, is 2–1 in rejecting the claimant appellant's appeal.

The disappointed claimant appealed again to the Supreme Court and was once more rebuffed.

9.11 How old precedents can be used in a modern setting

How do precedents adapt to the modern day? Let's consider *Pharmaceutical Society of Great Britain v Boots Cash Chemists (Southern) Ltd* [1953] 1 QB 401 (CA). This was a case that flirted with a criminal element, but for our purposes the relevant law related to formation of contract. When you study contract law you will see a contract can only be formed with a suitable offer and acceptance. The crucial *ratio* in *Boots* is a shopper only enters into a contract in a self-service environment when offering to pay for goods at the till. A contract duly forms when the retailer accepts the customer's offer and receives payment.

It is interesting to speculate on the operation of this decision in the modern day world of online purchases. You can imagine the situation: you surf the net, identify a desirable product, visit a website, select the item, and click on 'purchase now' (or something similar). You then enter your credit card details, encrypted of course, and conclude the purchase.

How does this correspond to the *Boots* case? At what stage does the customer offer, and retailer accept? When exactly is the contract concluded? You can see there are a number of problems in matching this precedent with the modern world. It is tricky updating a retail issue from the 1950s to the high tech environment of today. This example is purely for illustration, but you can be sure courts would find a way of dealing with it should the matter come before them – as it almost certainly has in one guise or another.

9.12 Conclusion

This chapter gives an insight into the flexible nature of judicial decision-making. The conventional approach would be to say judges should have merely a limited role of interpretation.

But the pace of change in society, and the range of decision-making required by the courts, tends to militate against a restricted role for judges. An element of law creation seems increasingly inevitable. Perhaps it always has been. Society appears to require decisions to be made on a range of issues. Who would have thought, for instance, courts would be asked to rule on the lawfulness of proroguing Parliament, as happened in the second Supreme Court case of *Miller* [2019] UKSC 41?

This was part of the Brexit story. The level of judicial activity has increased as the years roll on, Brexit being an example, but the core principles remain the same. Higher courts should be followed by lower courts; precedents carry weight; and *ratios* continue to be applied.

Summary

This chapter has travelled a considerable distance in time. Precedent has its origins in Norman times, probably, but we have chosen to start the story in the 1600s when judgments, particularly those relating to personal freedoms, become more obviously discernible. We then explain the development of precedent, its component parts, the way in which higher courts influence lower courts, and the various techniques that judges use to adapt, shape and grow the decision-making process. The UK constitution has a high degree of flexibility, which explains its durability. The process of precedent is equally adaptable and enduring.

Sample questions

Question 1

A supermarket is judicially reviewing refusal of permission by the local authority for a new site. There is disagreement over access arrangements through a local park. The matter is being heard in the Administrative Court of the King's Bench Division of the High Court. The judgment states as follows: 'The Claimant is a supermarket operative. The Defendant is the local council. The Claimant's case is as follows. It says people in the local area can only drive to shops elsewhere. People could walk to this site. That would be environmentally friendly. They would go through the local park. That is important: a park is a public space. Easy access is a material matter.'

Which of the following statements by the judge is most likely to be a *ratio decidendi*?

A   The Claimant is a supermarket operative.

B   People could walk to this site.

C   That would be environmentally friendly.

D   A park is a public space.

E   A park is a public space. Easy access is a material matter.

Answer

Option E is correct. This option represents a proposition of law within some key reasoning. The judge is stating a park is a public place, and then says this fact is important to the dispute. As such, it is capable of being a *ratio*.

Option A is wrong because it is purely confirming the status of one of the parties to the litigation. Option B is wrong because it is a statement of fact, without sufficient context for it to become a *ratio*. Option C is wrong because it is an observation, and indeed an opinion, by the judge without any key legal significance on the facts. Option D is wrong because, although it is capable of being a *ratio* in the sense it confirms the nature of a park, and thus could be relied on in subsequent cases, it does not say as much as option E, and on its own does not convey the central legal reasoning of the matter.

Question 2

A large travel agent is claiming damages for breach of contract against a hotel chain that has provided unsafe play areas for children. The claim is in the High Court. The travel agent's advocate refers the judge to a Court of Appeal case from five years earlier. The extract is as follows: 'I find the hotel is not liable. However, I would have decided differently if it could be shown risk assessments were not followed, as proper risk procedures are essential'.

What advice should be given to the travel agent about the Court of Appeal extract?

A   The statement 'the hotel is not liable' is a precedent.

B   The whole extract is a *ratio*.

C   The High Court can depart from the Court of Appeal decision.

D   The reference to risk assessments and procedures was obiter, and is capable of becoming a *ratio* in your this case.

E   If the High Court in this client's case decides risk assessments had not been followed it would be reversing the Court of Appeal.

Answer

Option D is correct. The extract from the Court of Appeal was an obiter statement. It was an additional comment to the main judgment finding the hotel not liable. It is possible for an obiter statement to become a *ratio* in subsequent cases: see *Combe v Combe* [1951] 2 KB 215. Here, the High Court would be able to rely on the statement to reinforce the hotel's responsibilities.

Option A is wrong because a simple statement of liability is not enough to be a precedent – there needs to be some reasoning as well. Option B is wrong because the extract is not a *ratio*. It is a statement of liability together with an obiter remark. Option C is wrong because the term 'depart' applies to a court disagreeing with a previous decision of a court of the same level, which is not the scenario here. Option E is wrong because the High Court, if it gave judgment for the travel agent, would be placing emphasis on effective risk procedures, something consistent with the Court of Appeal extract. The term 'reversing' means a higher court disagreeing with a lower court in the same case, which is not what is happening here.

Question 3

A broadcast company is contesting a decision by the broadcasting regulator to fine it for lack of impartiality. The case is being heard in the Administrative Court of the King's Bench Division of the High Court. The judge in your client's case finds for the regulator, saying: 'It is the duty of the regulator to consider very few facts. Its duty is purely to protect the public from misinformation'. Commentators have expressed surprise at this ruling and some have suggested it is incorrect law.

Which of the following statements as to hierarchy and precedent is correct?

A   An appeal is possible to another Division of the High Court.

B   Decisions of the High Court in the Administrative Court are binding on the Court of Appeal.

C   A County Court would not be bound by the High Court's ruling, as it may be incorrect.

D   The High Court in the future could depart from the finding on the basis it was 'per incuriam', ie through carelessness.

E   The comment about protecting the public from misinformation is obiter. It can be relied on in the future by other courts as necessary.

Answer

Option D is correct. Although the High Court in its appellate role usually binds itself, it can depart from previous decisions where they are made through carelessness. This follows the principle adopted by the Court of Appeal in *Young v Bristol Aeroplane* [1944] KB 718. The court appears to have relied on incorrect law and so the 'per incuriam' principle would apply. Incidentally there is no presumption the High Court in its first instance role binds itself. Option A is wrong because an appeal from the High Court lies to the Court of Appeal. Option B is wrong because the system of precedent, and the hierarchy of the courts, does not allow the High Court to bind the Court of Appeal. It is in fact the opposite – the Court of Appeal binds the High Court. Option C is wrong because the County Court is bound by the High Court, even if it disagrees with its decisions. Option E is wrong because the ruling in this case is not obiter. It is in fact a *ratio*, albeit apparently a wrong one.

10 Criminal Case Law and Precedent

SQE1 syllabus

This chapter will enable you to achieve the SQE1 assessment specification in relation to functioning legal knowledge concerning criminal case law and precedent.

Note that, for SQE1 candidates are not usually required to recall specific case names or cite statutory or regulatory authorities. Cases are provided for illustrative purposes only.

Learning outcomes

By the end of this chapter you will be able to apply relevant core legal principles and rules appropriately and effectively, at the level of a competent newly qualified solicitor in practice, to realistic client-based and ethical problems and situations in the following areas:

* society's need for lawyers to be clear as to what constitutes a crime, and the obligation on the state to prove any criminal case beyond reasonable doubt;

* the role of case law in determining murder and manslaughter, and the difference between the two;

* the development of case law on assault and theft;

* the nature of sentencing, and the place of case law in arriving at the appropriate punishment for any given crime;

* the importance of case law in interpreting issues relating to the admissibility of evidence;

* gaining an insight into the significance of case law on confessions, unlawfully obtained evidence, and a defendant's character;

* the legal system's attitude towards the obligations of prosecuting authorities, and how judges deal with supervening principles of national security; and

* the place of professional conduct principles in criminal practice.

10.1   Introduction

Everyone knows crime is bad. We are taught from an early age the difference between right and wrong. But as lawyers we need to probe further. For a start, it is useful to understand the origins of certain crimes, and how courts develop consistency in dealing with them. In other words, we need to understand the system of precedent and case law in identifying crimes and dealing with the accused.

It is also important for lawyers to question the nature of crime. Imagine you are a protester on a city street. You walk with others. You wave banners. You chant slogans. In some jurisdictions that might be a crime for challenging authority, or destabilising society, or denigrating the state, or questioning traditional values. But in the UK, providing you have communicated with the authorities, peaceful public protest and marching along streets in a group are entirely lawful. And you can hoist emblems and voice statements without fear, providing they are not obscene or in some way inciting disorder.

A crucial aspect of being a criminal lawyer, therefore, is the ability to question authority, challenge the notion of unlawfulness, and seek proof from the state, beyond reasonable doubt, that an alleged crime has indeed been committed.

This chapter examines case law in the criminal context. It considers some types of crime and their origins, development and treatment by the courts. We examine the link to Acts of Parliament, because politicians tend to legislate heavily in this area. We consider sentencing, and the courts' approach to certain aspects of evidence. We briefly consider the rule of law and international elements. We end with a reminder of some essential conduct principles.

Note we are not providing a detailed critique of the criminal law, merely an introduction to some aspects of it. You can discover more when you study the subject in detail elsewhere.

10.2   Case law, manslaughter and murder

Many people, including some of us who study law, are intrigued as to the distinction between manslaughter and murder. Together these crimes attract the somewhat American-sounding label of homicide. Most of us, whether lawyers or not, can grasp they are extremely serious offences, whichever one you are considering. You would expect to go to jail if found guilty.

In view of their importance they are a logical place to start when considering the way in which judges deal with criminal offences. We will therefore ponder the origins of the two, see how they differ and consider their treatment by the courts. We will thus see how case law and precedent provide a platform for their interpretation.

As we have seen in earlier chapters, in the Crown Court juries decide on innocence or guilt. They do not provide written or indeed any reasons for their verdicts. Criminal jurisprudence is accordingly different to civil. The vast bulk of cases in the criminal sphere go unreported. Hence principles can generally only be derived from appellate decisions. These are by their very nature a restricted source of intelligence, as most criminal verdicts are not appealed. However, the more serious crimes, such as homicide, are more likely to be referred upwards, and thus be capable of creating precedent. We can look at some cases now.

10.2.1   Murder

Society has recognised murder as something fundamentally wrong for many centuries. John Chrysostom (347–407), Archbishop of Constantinople, believed one of Christ's fellows at the crucifixion was a murderer. If this is so, and regardless of your view of biblical events, it would confirm the act of taking someone's life unlawfully has been a crime for at least two thousand years.

Perhaps this is unsurprising, but in any event oriental scholarship supports the notion. Cary Bricker and Michael Vitiello of the McGeorge School of Law in the USA wrote a 2013 paper entitled 'Chinese Homicide Law, Irrationality and Incremental Change' for the *Temple International and Comparative Law Journal*. There, they noted the Tang Dynasty in 653 codified capital punishment, ie the death penalty, in China for murder and indeed many less serious crimes.

10.2.2 Murder and manslaughter – some early cases

What is murder, and manslaughter, and how do they differ? A good place to start is a report from proceedings at the Old Bailey, or the Central Criminal Court to give it its formal name.

 There, on 7 July 1675, it was reported 'a Dutch gentleman was arraigned for murder of a Frenchman'. The two had quarrelled. The victim boxed the ears of the defendant. The latter drew his sword and, presumably as a response to this slight, 'unhappily killed the Frenchman'. The verdict was manslaughter.

No reasons were given, but the implication is there was no specific intent to kill. This decision also envisages something that would become commonplace in due course, namely the plea of self-defence, which would negate any suggestion of criminality, whether murder or manslaughter, and result in an innocent verdict if accepted by the court.

The decision in favour of the Dutchman can be contrasted with the case on 9 September 1674 of John Randal. Here, an Old Bailey report states that 'amongst the criminals John Randal may be reckoned one of the most notorious'. He entered a residence to steal some valuable plate and killed the housekeeper. He did this by knocking her down with his fists. He was convicted and sentenced to death. Again, we can only speculate as to the jury's reasoning, as is indeed the case today when a jury returns a verdict, but the implication is Randal deliberately and callously killed someone who was in no position to resist. As such we have a clue to the variables between manslaughter and murder: the latter involves a more positive and clinical intent.

10.2.3 Definition of murder and comparison with manslaughter

The nature of murder, and its distinctive character, became clearer with the writings of Chief Justice Coke (1552–1632). In his *Institutes of the Laws of England*, published between 1628 and 1644, Coke defined murder as being

> when a man of sound memory and of the age of discretion unlawfully killing within any County of the realm any reasonable creature ... under the Kings peace with malice aforethought ... so as the party wounded or hurt die of the wound or hurt.

In plain English, this means someone commits murder if, being in charge of their mental faculties, they kill someone maliciously. You might be forgiven for pondering the reference to 'aforethought', as this suggests some degree of planning is required. But that is by no means the case. It is very much possible for a murder to take place (pretty much) spontaneously.

Coke then provided a somewhat gory list of possible killings, starting with poison and mentioning weapons sharp or blunt, use of a gun, strangling, suffocating, and, intriguingly, inciting a dog or bear to bite.

Coke by way of alternative touches on manslaughter. He deals with this in the negative, saying the defining nature of the act is the absence of malice aforethought.

These early cases, and Coke's writings, indicate the formative approach of the authorities towards murder and manslaughter in England and Wales. First, we should note neither offence has a statutory basis. They are what we call common law offences. There was a 1751 Murder Act but it dealt with peripheral matters and was repealed some years later. Likewise, the Homicide Act 1957 merely amends some common law elements.

Second, the mindset of the villain, together with the immediate circumstances of the event, are important considerations. For murder, there must be 'malice aforethought'. Third, either offence can happen in the blink of an eye, in as long as it takes someone to flash a knife. Juries often spend days or even weeks mulling over an event that occupied just seconds of real time.

10.2.4 Some more recent cases

There are many manslaughter and murder cases each year. We can look at a few to track the sense of continuity from the 1600s to the present. In *R v Goodfellow* (1986) 83 Cr App R 23 the Court of Appeal considered the case of a man who set fire to his council house in the hope of obtaining housing elsewhere. In the resulting conflagration the man's wife, girlfriend and child all died. There was no suggestion this was murder. Instead, the question before the Court was whether it was manslaughter or some lesser offence. In finding the defendant guilty of manslaughter, the Lord Chief Justice stated:

> Where the act which a person is engaged in performing is unlawful, then if at the same time it is a dangerous act, that is, an act which is likely to injure another person, and quite inadvertently he causes the death of that other person by that act, then he is guilty of manslaughter.

This confirms a key aspect of what we today call involuntary manslaughter: conduct taking the form of an unlawful act involving a danger of some harm that results in death, to quote the CPS website as of December 2019.

In *R v Bristow* [2013] EWCA Crim 1540, the Court of Appeal considered a burglary that went badly wrong. A group entered a workshop on a farm. The property owner discovered them in the dark of night. In escaping in various vehicles, including a Land Rover taken from the premises, the burglars ran down the owner and killed him. In confirming the conviction of the defendants, the Court stated there was an unlawful act that a reasonable bystander would inevitably realise would subject any person intervening to the risk of some harm. The Court confirmed the death of the owner as manslaughter.

How then does this contrast with verdicts of murder today? In *R v Wilson* [2018] EWCA Crim 1352 the Court of Appeal refused leave for the defendant to appeal against both conviction and sentence. The defendant, a serial offender, was in a relationship with a vulnerable woman. There was evidence he was controlling, possessive and a bully. She suffered violence from him. When he was absent in prison, which was often, she flourished, to use the court's words. But when they were together she had a perilous existence.

One day they argued. The defendant fractured her larynx, and also stabbed her in the stomach with a kitchen knife. She died at the scene. If ever there was evidence of 'malice aforethought', this was it.

10.2.5 Learning points on this area of law

Some learning points from this brief analysis of manslaughter and murder would be as follows:

- They are ancient crimes, and arguably the most heinous.
- The essential elements of them both have broadly remained the same for centuries.
- The law is considerably more forgiving when the verdict is manslaughter.
- Chief Justice Coke's definition of murder retains validity today. The presence of malice aforethought, ie some sort of evil intent, remains a key ingredient.
- Court cases and judicial decisions remain the main source of this area of law.

10.3 Case law and assault

For many years the law embraced a broad definition of assault. Reports from the Old Bailey in the 17th and 18th centuries identify the following as assaults: running someone through with a sword, attempting to murder them, stabbing with a knife, strangling, destroying partially or entirely someone's sight, and much more. Today these would be classed as more serious offences. Conversely, 'ye olde' reports also mention lesser crimes, such as hitting someone with your fists, and these have a greater parallel with the offence as we know it today.

10.3.1 A successful prosecution ...

 For instance, in 1697 William Norman was indicted following an insurrection of weavers. He and others broke into part of East India House on Leadenhall Street in the heart of the City of London. The protesting weavers eventually dispersed. An official shut the gate to the property, with Norman still inside. He therefore struck the official several blows on the arm with a stick.

Norman suggested in his defence the East India Company had a financial obligation to him, but this cut no ice. You could easily see this defence being dismissed in similar manner today: just because someone owes you money does not allow you to beat them up. The jury found him guilty of assault.

10.3.2 ... And one that failed

It is insightful to note an instance where a prosecution for assault failed. In November 1716 Robert Peel (no relation to the fellow who founded the Metropolitan Police) was indicted for assault on three men. They alleged Peel had 'clapped his hand on his sword and thrust them downstairs' as they proclaimed their loyalty to the King. They suggested Peel had come from a meeting of non-jurors, ie those who refused to swear an oath of allegiance to the Crown. Peel in his defence said he drank the health of King George frequently, and had only peeped into the meeting of non-jurors out of curiosity. Witnesses provided character evidence as to his loyalty to the monarch. The jury believed Peel's version of events, and he left the court a free man.

10.3.3 The nature of assault throughout the ages

The *Norman* and *Peel* cases represent an early version of what today we would regard as allegations of assault occasioning actual bodily harm. They indicate the presence of violence together with some minor injury. Of course, the concept of an injury being minor is a relative one, and something low-key to an observer can be upsetting to the victim, so we need to be careful about diminishing the significance of supposedly 'low level' crimes. That is even truer today than in earlier centuries, when brutality lurked below the surface of much of society. One thinks of the paintings of William Hogarth (1697–1764) whose works such as Beer Street and Gin Lane, and the Election Series, are laced with violent undertones.

We all condemn major acts of aggression, but English society has a somewhat conflicted relationship with minor violence. The antics of undergraduates in an Oxbridge setting are considered high jinks. Similar behaviour of unemployed youths in a northern town, by contrast, is considered a breakdown of society.

Middle England routinely frets about violence on the streets. Police stations and hospitals are indeed busy on Friday and Saturday nights with individuals who have clashed and bashed at sporting events, on public transport, and in pubs and bars.

We all frown on this behaviour, conveniently forgetting the way our society validates behaviours responsible for such problems: accepting the use and abuse of recreational drugs and alcohol, deifying material wealth, and prioritising superficiality. Whatever the cause of routine disturbances on our streets, courts are awash with people confronting, usually in a remorseful manner, the fruits of their behaviour from the previous weekend. Such is the place of assault within our legal system.

10.3.4 Legislation on assault

As we have seen, courts in the past interpreted assault on a broad canvas. Near death by stabbing? Assault. Pummelled with a fist? Also assault. Parliament eventually decided to offer some assistance. The Offences Against the Person Act 1861 provided a statutory basis for various types of the offence. In particular, s 47 of the Act states:

> whosoever shall be convicted upon an indictment of any assault occasioning actual bodily harm shall be liable to be kept in penal servitude.

 As you can tell, this wording didn't clarify matters a great deal, and like a clucking hen the courts came to the rescue with successive interpretations of the section. The 1934 case of R v Donovan *said bodily harm includes any hurt calculated to interfere with the health or comfort of the victim, which must be more than transient and trifling.*

As time progressed, and society developed a warmer feel, the concept of harm was extended to include less physical, but equally traumatic, matters such as cutting off someone's hair without consent, as in DPP v Smith *[2006] EWHC 94 (Admin). The courts have also confirmed bodily harm includes psychiatric injury.*

10.3.5 A recent case exploring various assaults

How does this translate to the modern era? The case of *AB* [2017] EWHC 1694 (Admin) examined the troubled history of a young offender. They had a long history of assaults. The court confirmed the following as falling within the definition: pushing and grabbing a teacher; biting a prison officer; punching another prison officer several times in the side of the head; kicking a prison officer; punching kicking and kneeing people in the face; and spitting.

In conclusion, we can see the steady development of case law on assault. In the 1600s assault encompassed a broad range of crimes. By the 19th century it was shaping up as a more minor categorisation. Court decisions in the 20th century confirmed it as the crime we recognise today.

10.4 Case law and theft

Society places a disproportionate emphasis on the value of property and, by association, personal possessions. You might say it has always been thus. Religious tracts, philosophy, myth and history all bulge with examples of retribution for taking unlawfully the items of another. Perhaps we should value other things more highly: artistic endeavour, caring behaviours, sharing, tolerance and so on. We do, generally, but even so there are few sanctions for denying someone artistic opportunities, or for ignoring someone in need, or declining to share your wealth, or belittling someone's views and making them feel inadequate. Yet when someone steals from another, the legal system sits bolt upright and becomes massively focused.

10.4.1 Some old cases

Cases illustrate the fairly consistent approach of the courts towards theft. On 29 April 1674, proceedings from the Old Bailey tell of a woman tried for stealing a silver cup. She went into a 'victualling house', ie an old style tavern or establishment selling refreshments. There, she distracted the owner by asking for a chamber pot, took the cup from a shelf, and ran away with it. At the trial she suggested she was intending to return it. The court did not believe this story and handed down a sentence of transportation, ie removal to one of England's colonies for service of the jail term.

The defendant's defence in this case highlights a common ploy in a theft case. The suspect often says something along the lines of: 'I wasn't intending to take this item permanently. I was simply borrowing it. I wasn't stealing. I am innocent.'

Juries of course are not born yesterday. They are alert to this sort of trickery. If the defendant here had intended to return it, why had she distracted the owner, and then run away with the item? Only the truly naive would accept this as a plausible explanation.

As with assault, the courts developed a certain philosophy relating to the treatment of theft cases. For centuries the system operated to a certain standard. Once again, however, legislators considered it desirable to codify the offence. It was translated into statute by the Theft Act 1968. Section 1 defined the offence, confirming the essential elements that had grown up over time:

> A person is guilty of theft if he dishonestly appropriates property belonging to another with the intention of permanently depriving the other of it.

You can see why the woman taking the cup was found guilty. She fooled the owner, thus indicating dishonesty. She took the cup off the shelf and left the premises, and in so doing appropriated the item. She ran off, seeking speedily to put some distance between her and the victim. This gives support to the idea she was intending to deprive. The possibility she was simply borrowing the item was swiftly discounted by those sitting in judgment.

10.4.2 A modern case of theft

The case of *R v Ibrahim* [2011] All ER (D) 167 (Mar) illustrates the modern approach of the courts. A woman was using a cash machine in Mitcham, Surrey. A man distracted her. She looked away. On turning back to the cash machine her card was missing. She saw the man talking to someone else 25 yards away. When she challenged them, they ran.

The jury found the defendant guilty of theft. It decided, beyond reasonable doubt, the defendant had taken someone else's property dishonestly with the intention of permanently depriving them of it. The defendant appealed against the trial judge's refusal to allow a submission they had no case to answer, but the Court of Appeal found the conviction to be safe.

In conclusion, there are many sorts of theft offences, and we have concentrated on the most basic. There is a pleasing consistency in the courts' interpretation of the crime over the years. A lady in a tavern in the 1600s runs off with someone's silver cup. A chap at a cashpoint in the 2000s makes off with someone else's cash card. They have both appropriated the property of another with the intention of permanently depriving the other of it. Accordingly they are guilty of theft.

By way of summarising matters on assault and theft in the case law context, below **Figure 10.1** presents a flowchart with some considerations. Some of these points refer back to earlier chapters – for instance, the reference to procedural matters.

10.5 Sentencing and case law

A large part of criminal law involves dealing with those who accept they have transgressed. A great many wrongdoers tend not to plead their innocence. Particularly with minor crimes where you are caught 'red handed', the criminal fraternity take the view it is better to admit guilt and proceed swiftly to sentencing.

Figure 10.1 Overview of case law considerations for 'everyday' crime (ie assault and theft)

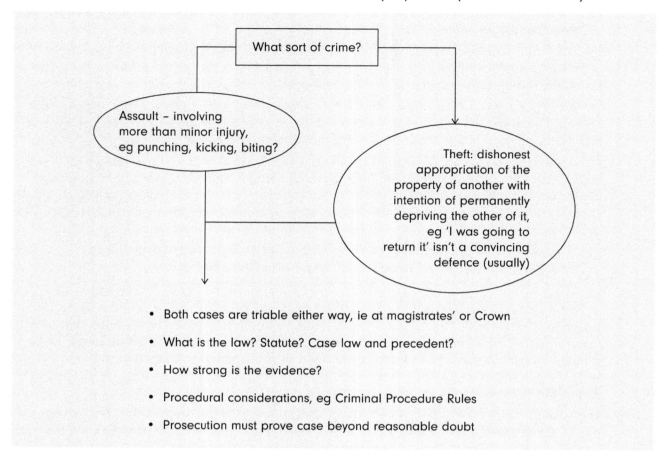

- Both cases are triable either way, ie at magistrates' or Crown

- What is the law? Statute? Case law and precedent?

- How strong is the evidence?

- Procedural considerations, eg Criminal Procedure Rules

- Prosecution must prove case beyond reasonable doubt

This has several benefits: it makes you look good in front of the judge who is handing down the sentence; it reduces the time you spend with lawyers and other 'stuffed shirts' discussing the details of trial; and it increases the chance of a light punishment by way of a community sentence, something that essentially allows you to remain in charge of your own life rather than delegating it to a prison guard.

10.5.1 The sentencing culture

The question therefore becomes: how do we hand out, systematically and fairly, punishments that are proportionate? The modern starting point is the five purposes of sentencing, as articulated by the Sentencing Council. These are:

- Punishment of offenders
- Reduction of crime
- Reform and rehabilitation
- Protection of the public
- Making good to victims.

These principles are accompanied by the idea you should, in any sentencing process, consider imposing a lesser punishment first before working up to something more drastic. This is the so-called sentencing ladder. This functions as follows. A court should consider whether a discharge of the defendant is appropriate. If not, the court should then ponder a fine. If the matter is too serious for that, the courts should impose a community sentence. Lastly, a custodial term – jail – should be ordered only if the matter is too serious for a community sentence.

Partly because much of the criminal justice system is presided over by magistrates, who are laypeople, and partly to encourage a systematic approach, there are guidelines to assist the process. A body called the Sentencing Council provides written guidance for both the magistrates' courts and the Crown Court. The guidelines require an assessment of two further elements:

- Culpability (ie the amount of blame to be shouldered by the defendant)
- Harm (ie the impact on the victim)

So, taking theft as an example, the guidelines suggest greater *culpability* for a defendant who takes a leading role in a group activity, or coerces others into involvement in the theft, or breaches a high degree of trust, or engages in sophisticated planning. Similarly, the guidelines measure *harm* through the value of stolen goods to the loser, inconvenience to the victim and others, emotional distress, fear and loss of confidence caused by the crime, impact on a business and so on.

The question then arises as to how the courts interpret these guidelines. As you can imagine this is fertile ground for guilty parties and their lawyers. It is one thing to be convicted, and quite another to achieve punishment that is appropriate in all the circumstances.

10.5.2 Theft and the sentencing culture: an example

The case of *R v Maxwell* [2017] EWCA Crim 1233 provides an insight into the operation of the sentencing regime in England and Wales. As the term suggests, the guidelines are by no means mandatory, and are there to offer a framework rather than an absolute answer.

In *Maxwell*, the defendant committed a series of offences over 10 days in early November 2015. Two 'counts' – another term for a charge – involved theft. The first was stealing a quantity of meat from a store in Barry, South Wales. The second involved stealing clothing valued at about £240 from Tesco in Barry. There were numerous other offences as well.

The Court of Appeal quashed the sentence of two months for the first count, on the basis the conviction was unlawful (we need not concern ourselves here with the reason why; you can read the case report if interested in discovering more). Had it not been so quashed, the implication is the sentence itself was satisfactory. The court confirmed a separate sentence of two months for the second count.

10.5.3 Sentencing: a discussion

Maxwell provides an insight into the operation of the punishment regime for lesser theft offences. Some of us might think two months behind bars is too severe for an amount that would buy a return flight to Croatia. Alternatively, you might think the jail term is completely feeble. There has been significant dishonesty, and the sum in question is three-quarters of a claimant's monthly entitlement to Universal Credit. In other words, decent and honourable people up and down the land eke out a living for several weeks on the sum under scrutiny here.

Further, you could be forgiven for thinking a limited jail term is insufficient when considering the damage and stress to the victim, even if the complainant is a corporate entity. There is a human and financial element to every crime. Only clothes were stolen, but there is more to it than that. A member of the sales staff might feel responsible, shaken up and vulnerable; blame might be allocated to the security guard on the exit door; the closed-circuit TV (CCTV) system might need to be overhauled; and the finance department's projections might require reassessment.

These are valid views on either side, but both lack the full perspective. The whole point of the punishment regime, including the sentencing guidelines, is to put any given crime in context. Naturally it is serious. All crimes are. The dishonesty is lamentable.

To progress the matter, the court should consider the five principles mentioned above. It should also assess the totality of a victim's offending as presented to the court at the time of sentencing. In *Maxwell*, this would include other offences committed over the same period by the defendant, including burglary, attempted robbery, aggravated vehicle taking and more. The court should then consider mitigating factors – a sceptical layperson might call this the perpetrator's 'sob story' – which would result in a lower sentence than would otherwise appear obvious at first sight: the defendant's personal and family circumstances, their remorse, out-of-character behaviour at the time of the crime, perhaps an early guilty plea and so on.

10.5.4   Conclusion on sentencing

In conclusion, the state has routinely attempted to flex its muscles on sentencing matters. It has legislated voluminously on punishment, and strives endlessly to corral the legal system into passing sentences that meet the wishes of Westminster and therefore, one presumes, society. But the nature of criminality, and indeed the proliferation of complex factors within the criminal justice system, mean courts continue to have an active role in deciding on punishment. It is simply impossible to create a strict statutory regime for punishing criminals. The human element inevitably intervenes. Case law therefore remains a key aspect of dealing with the reform of offenders.

Incidentally, judges comment regularly on the complexity of the sentencing process. There is an abundance of laws, procedures, agencies, guidance and agendas for a judge to consider when dealing with the convicted. The entire process lends itself to challenge and appeal. It is little wonder sentencing remains a fertile area of case law.

In **Figure 10.2** we have a flowchart attempting to summarise case law and sentencing. It starts with the crime, and a reminder we lawyers, whatever our role, should not lose sight of the human process. Victims, defendants and witnesses all deserve decency and consideration. There is then a triangle of considerations: previous case law, sentencing guidelines, and the 'pure law', which is multifarious, but which we have symbolised through the Criminal Justice Act 2003 and its various principles and so on.

We have created at the nexus of these three a 'sentencing zone', which represents the perfect combination of factors in any sentencing process. At the bottom we have added the softer – or perhaps harsher, given the views of many people on the ineffectiveness of the rehabilitation culture in our jurisdiction – elements of societal involvement in the process.

10.6   Crime, legislation, the treatment of evidence and case law

Legislators thrive on crime. They don't approve of it, naturally. But the existence of crime, its changing nature, and the dynamic nature of offenders all offer an electoral opportunity to MPs seeking victory at the ballot box. Politicians can win and lose elections on the basis of a manifesto promising to curb crime, increase police numbers or impose harsher punishments. This translates into a mass of legislation aimed at dealing with criminal behaviour.

You might think these laws would remove the need for court involvement, or at least reduce the amount of interpretation required by judges. But this is far from the case. As the physicist Sir Isaac Newton (1643–1727) suggested, every action has an equal and opposite reaction. Every Act of Parliament creates a judicial reaction. This has nothing to do with the judiciary's natural inclination to tweak the nose of the Government. It is simply that defendants, prosecutors, witnesses, lawyers and others with a stake in the criminal justice process expect, and require, laws to be given an interpretation. A court is the only place where a definitive ruling on a statute can be handed down.

Figure 10.2 Case law and sentencing

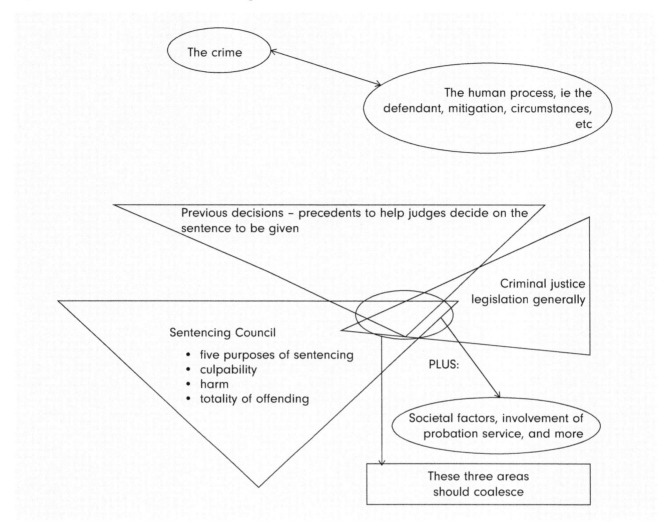

There is accordingly much case law interpreting criminal statutes. We now examine a fundamentally important area of criminal case law: how courts deal with evidence when deciding on the innocence or guilt of a defendant. Courts are well versed in developing law that interprets, and sometimes extends the ambit of, legislation. Let's look at some important areas now.

10.6.1 Confessions

A defendant can be convicted through a confession. After all, if a supposed criminal says 'yes, I did it' when asked about a crime, that usually makes the prosecution an 'open and shut' case. At a subsequent trial you would expect a guilty verdict to result.

The Police and Criminal Evidence Act 1984 devotes considerable wordage to the definition of a confession and its impact on the trial process. There are sections on retracting or contesting a confession. You can imagine the scenario. You might say something you regret and wish to withdraw it. That is a retraction. Alternatively, an overeager police officer might suggest you said something when in fact you didn't. In that situation you would contest the words were ever said.

10.6.1.1 Retracting confessions

The 1984 Act is particularly fascinating on retracting a confession. It can be done where the confession was, or may have been, obtained either by oppression or in consequence of anything said or done that was likely to render unreliable any confession that might be made.

The unreliability point raises a curious possibility. It could be the confession was entirely true. The suspect might have said: 'Yes, I did indeed steal those items on the day in question'. And yes, they did steal. But if you made that statement, even if true, in circumstances that make it or any confession unreliable, the court will be required to exclude your statement as evidence. Without that evidence the prosecution could well be terminally weakened. It could result in a not guilty verdict. How about that for a result?

How have the courts interpreted this provision, ie where a defendant wishes to withdraw a confession?

> *Example one*: Someone with a drug dependency is kept in custody for 18 hours, interviewed several times without rest, and denied access to legal advice. Their confession is excluded as being unreliable.

> *Example two*: Someone confesses to a robbery having been denied legal advice. At trial they confirm they understood their legal rights. The court refused to exclude the confession, as there was no evidence there were circumstances that made that, or any, confession unreliable.

Note in both these cases the court did not ask itself if the confessions were true. They were instead concerned with the circumstances surrounding the making of the relevant statement. If the prosecution could not refute the suggestion of unreliability, the confession was excluded, as with example one. Where there was no unreliability, the confession stood, as with example two.

10.6.1.2 A case on excluding confessions

Any number of reported cases confirm this approach. In *R v Roberts (Neil)* [2011] EWCA Crim 2974 the Court of Appeal considered a conviction at Woolwich Crown Court for theft of an iPod. Mr Roberts worked in a second-hand electronics store. In October 2010 the owner accused him of theft. The owner in his initial conversation with Mr Roberts said words to the effect: 'you can admit to this crime and the matter will go no further, or if you deny it the police will be involved'.

Mr Roberts in evidence stated he had indeed said to the owner he had taken the device, but only because of the owner's promise. Also, he said he felt threatened. Broadly, he said he was stampeded into making remarks he regretted. Despite the promise, the police were called, the matter did go to trial, and the jury found Mr Roberts guilty on the basis of his admission to the owner. At paragraph 7 of their judgment the Court of Appeal described the owner in his initial conversation as 'lying'.

The Court held Mr Roberts had been induced – ie improperly encouraged – into making a confession to his employer. The Court decided the confession should be excluded on the grounds of unreliability.

A number of points arise from this decision as follows:

- first, the Court of Appeal confirmed a confession does not need to be made to the police at the police station. It is entirely possible for a suspect to confess elsewhere to someone – such as the owner – who has no official role;

- second, the provisions of the 1984 Act, and the accompanying case law, can and must apply to such a confession;

- third, the burden is on the prosecution to show any confession was not made in circumstances that would render it, or indeed any confession, unreliable. Here, they were unable to do this;

- fourth, the Roberts appeal shows some essential consistency in the judicial approach to individual freedoms. The decision impliedly validates principles going back centuries. It confirms the rule of law, in that a conviction can only stand if it complies with legal requirements. It places the onus on the authorities not only to prove their case beyond reasonable doubt, but to confirm the relevant procedures – in this case the confession process – were appropriate. And it highlights the judiciary's concern – indeed, obsession with the idea – that trials should be fair in all respects, expressing disdain for the idea that someone should be tricked 'by lying' into confessing guilt.

10.6.2 Unlawfully obtained evidence

Courts have an essentially simple approach to wrongdoing, or unlawfulness, by authority. They will, generally, take the view evidence should be admitted if it would be fair so to do. Equally, they will exclude it if, on balance, its admissibility would somehow render the proceedings unfair. This is the thrust of the 1984 Act. As with any legislation, and as we have seen with confessions, such provisions require interpretation.

What is the status of unlawfully obtained evidence, we wonder? In some jurisdictions, for instance the USA if we are to believe TV drama and some parts of the media, you would expect police to be chastised, evidence declared inadmissible and vast sums of money paid to the innocent party.

10.6.2.1 A case on unlawfully obtained evidence

But in this jurisdiction the situation seems to be different. In *R v Stewart* [1995] Crim LR 500 a utility company, backed by the police, entered the defendant's premises unlawfully to investigate what the court described as irregularities in the consumption of electricity. Evidence was gathered. The Court of Appeal confined itself to a narrow issue. It referred to s 78 of the 1984 Act and concluded the question was not whether evidence was obtained unlawfully, but whether the admission of the evidence would have an adverse effect on the fairness of proceedings. It decided there would be no such adverse effect in this instance.

10.6.2.2 Conclusion on this area of law

In conclusion, certain points arise relating to unlawfully obtained evidence:

- Courts will give great thought to all the facts of the case. Clearly, if a defendant is held incommunicado, and subject to undue pressure, and makes an incriminating statement as a result, that is one sort of evidence, and the courts will be quick to declare it inadmissible.

- Obtaining some sort of document from outside someone's home, however, or even inside it where it is perhaps lying on a desk, would be considered in a different light. It may well be it was obtained as a result of some nefarious behaviour. But the context would be altogether different and may well not be a bar to its use.

- Usually, on the basis that someone's home is their castle, to use another expression from Chief Justice Coke (who is mentioned elsewhere in this publication), you would not expect officialdom to be able to enter private premises unlawfully. Equally, you would therefore not expect evidence gathered in such circumstances to be allowed to be used at trial.

- The *Stewart* case, however, shows the nature of case law. Judges must take note of supervening, and pre-eminent, legislation. Parliament is of course supreme. So the relevant sections of any given Act should be given the necessary consideration, and that is what happened in *Stewart*, with respect to the provisions of the 1984 Act.

- The Court of Appeal usually binds itself subject to the exceptions in *Young v Bristol Aeroplane*. You would expect *Stewart* to remain good law. But it would still be open to the Supreme Court to revisit the matter. And of course there are many situations where it could be distinguished if the facts allow it. Such are the joys of case law.

10.6.3   A defendant's character: previous convictions

Many defendants, sadly, are only too familiar with the inside of a criminal courtroom. Your average defendant has a good chance of being a repeat offender. They routinely get into trouble, and appear incapable of reform. The posh term for this is recidivist, ie seemingly unwilling, or unable, to extract themselves from a cycle of criminality and punishment.

Some members of the general public tend to believe, perhaps inadvertently, a defendant in court who has previously committed crime is generally likely to be guilty of the current charge. We all have stories of people who regularly get into trouble with the police. No doubt you have heard someone say: 'They've got a criminal record as long as your arm'. This indicates someone has been found guilty not just on several occasions but many times.

10.6.3.1   The golden thread

Courts do not presume someone's past convictions mean they are guilty of the current charge. The case of *Woolmington v DPP* [1935] UKHL 1 confirmed the 'golden thread' of justice in this jurisdiction. There, the House of Lords stated a defendant is innocent until presumed guilty. So, no matter how many times you have previously offended, you are entitled to be considered blameless in court for the current offence unless and until a magistrate or the jury decides otherwise.

10.6.3.2   Previous convictions: the arguments

The question then arises: should your bad character – which generally relates to previous convictions, but can be 'other reprehensible behaviour', such as actions resulting in arrest, even if there are no subsequent charges – be revealed to the court as part of the prosecution case? You can imagine the impact this might have. Let us say a defendant is on trial for shoplifting. They have previous convictions for theft, burglary and robbery. The defence are likely to object to these convictions being revealed to a jury, because the jury might jump to conclusions, and think the past is a suitable guide to the present. There is a risk the defendant will be found guilty purely from their past record rather than the current evidence.

The prosecution, however, would respond in this manner:

> This defendant's previous convictions indicate the nature of their character. They have a propensity, or tendency, to commit crimes of this sort. They might also have a propensity to be untruthful. This is part of the makeup of the defendant. It is part of the reason why the crime was committed. The jury needs to have this information in order to come to a conclusion on innocence or guilt.

Traditionally, courts were reluctant to allow a defendant's previous convictions to be adduced in evidence. It would usually only happen if the defendant ran their defence in a particular way, or had behaved in a particular manner at some stage of the criminal investigation and prosecution.

But today the situation has changed. The Criminal Justice Act 2003 gives the prosecution various grounds for requesting the defendant's character to be presented as evidence. In other words, the jury is entitled to know about suspect behaviour, as well as confirmed convictions, of the defendant as part of understanding the overall nature of the evidence.

It is of course possible for the defence to argue against the admission of such evidence, but the crucial point for us to grasp now is the reversal of the previous presumption. Not long ago, it would be a departure from the norm for a defendant's record to be revealed. Now, it is becoming increasingly common.

In R v Hassan Mohammed [2020] EWCA Crim 761 the Court of Appeal examined the admissibility of not just a defendant's previous conviction but also related behaviours attracting no charges. On 19 March 2018 Hassan killed Balbir Johal in Southall, London. Hassan told the Old Bailey he confronted the victim out of somewhat altruistic motives, hoping to dissuade him from dealing drugs in the local area. He then acted in self-defence when Johal attacked him.

The prosecution applied to present a previous conviction for cannabis possession as evidence Hassan himself was involved in the drugs trade. They also applied to adduce in evidence two other instances where Hassan was arrested on drug-related offences but not charged.

The prosecution suggested these three events were relevant because they contradicted Hassan's version of events concerning Johal. Rather than being concerned to prevent drugs being dealt near his home, it was said, Hassan in fact was an active participant in drug criminality. The Crown Court judge allowed the prosecution application, and thus the jury were informed of the three incidents. Those events therefore became part of the evidence for them to consider in rejecting Hassan's plea of self-defence and declaring him guilty of murder.

The Court of Appeal decided the conviction was entirely safe. They confirmed as correct the trial judge's decision to allow in evidence Hassan's three previous involvements with drugs.

10.6.3.3 Some conclusions

The points to note from this case, and they are indicative of the judiciary's approach to a defendant's character generally, are:

- For decades precedent and case law developed a specific approach to evidence of a defendant's character. Legislation by Parliament – here, the 2003 Act – changed this at a stroke. The courts have had to adjust accordingly.

- You might think there is a danger a defendant, under the 2003 Act, could be convicted simply because a jury places undue weight on previous convictions, rather than considering the evidence relating to the trial at hand. There are, however, numerous protections against this.

- The fact remains these provisions of the 2003 Act represent a perfect example of the will of Parliament. Legislators wanted defendants to reveal to juries their previous criminality. That is what now happens on an increasingly frequent basis.

- In a sense, therefore, the wheel has been reinvented since the 2003 Act in this area of law. There is now a body of case law and precedent on character evidence under the 2003 Act. You can learn more about this, and indeed a wide range of other topics, when you study criminal law as a dedicated subject.

To remind you of the three areas we have just discussed, indicative of the way in which judges and their decisions are heavily influenced by criminal justice legislation, **Figure 10.3** presents a simple flowchart.

Figure 10.3 Interesting areas of case law/statute in criminal matters

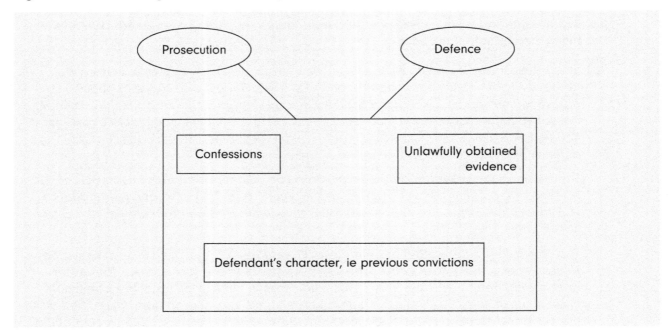

10.7 Criminal case law, obligations to prosecute crime and international matters

 In Corner House Research [2008] UKHL 60 the House of Lords, now the Supreme Court, was required to consider case law and precedent on a sensitive matter of national security. The Serious Fraud Office (SFO) in 2006 was in the process of investigating allegations of corruption against a well-known British defence contractor. One aspect of the investigation involved a valuable contract between the UK Government and Saudi Arabia. The latter threatened to withdraw cooperation in certain operational, weapons and security areas, should the investigation continue.

10.7.1 The arguments from both sides

The director of the SFO somewhat reluctantly, and against the backdrop of intense political activity, decided it was in the national interest to discontinue the investigation.

Corner House and Justice, two organisations promoting social reform and human rights, requested a judicial review of the decision. Judicial review takes place when there are suggestions a body exercising a public function has acted unreasonably or irrationally. Corner House and Justice believed there was an obligation on the SFO to continue the prosecution. They thought the authorities owed a duty of sorts to society to pursue the company, and the Saudi gambit should be resisted.

The Divisional Court of the King's Bench Division agreed, quashing the SFO's decision. The SFO appealed by way of the leapfrog procedure to their Lordships. The leapfrog arrangement allows a case to jump from the High Court to the Supreme Court if there is an urgent need to obtain an authoritative interpretation on a particular matter.

10.7.2 *Corner House*: the issues

This case is a blend of the criminal and civil jurisdictions. The matter began as a criminal prosecution, albeit by the SFO rather than the CPS. As such, had the matter progressed, there would have been a trial in the Crown Court. But it never got that far. The decision to discontinue the criminal investigation metamorphosed into another question in the judicial review arena: was it fair, just and reasonable for matters of national security to block a probe into alleged international corruption? The High Court said it wasn't. From there it progressed to the highest court of the land.

The House of Lords allowed the SFO's appeal. They confirmed as lawful the SFO decision to discontinue their enquiries in favour of smoothing relations with a foreign power.

10.7.3 Learning points on this area

A number of points relevant to the criminal matters, the rule of law, and the operation of our legal system become apparent through this case:

* First, the director of the SFO gave great consideration to the rule of law when deciding to discontinue the investigation. Ultimately the law and procedures relating to national security trumped any law relating to the investigation of alleged corruption. This was not, therefore, as the tabloid media might have you believe, a simple instance of governments and wealthy interests getting their way. It was a decision subject to due legal process.

* Second, it illustrates some basic aspect of precedent and case law. At least one earlier case – *Phoenix Aviation* [1995] 3 All ER 37 – was considered as part of the House of Lords deliberations, and it was distinguished. That means the principles there were discussed and considered correct, but on the facts of *Corner House* a different conclusion could be drawn.

* Third, the case highlights one aspect of appeal procedure. It is a reminder of the leapfrog process, whereby a matter can 'hot-key', so to speak, from the High Court to the Supreme Court. This leaves the Court of Appeal with gooseberry status, ie metaphorically twiddling its thumbs while the other courts interact.

* Fourth, the case has echoes of other decisions in which the courts are reluctant to impose prosecutorial duties on the authorities. Whether you are the police, the SFO or some other enforcement agency, the presumption is you should be allowed to get on with your job to the best of your abilities. The courts are uncomfortable with the idea you should be fettered unduly with too many duties to victims, witnesses and in particular the general public. More recently the courts have started to consider obligations under the Human Rights Act 1998, and it is interesting to speculate on the result of any similar dispute should something akin to *Corner House* come before the courts today.

* Fifth, and returning to the rule of law, the case reinforces the international outlook of the courts. Throughout the process the judiciary took it for granted the entitlement to scrutinise events beyond these shores. Yes, there were public interest limits to any scrutiny of Saudi–UK relations, but broadly it was accepted that allegedly underhand dealings in other jurisdictions could and should be litigated.

* Finally, and most obviously, the case is an example of a higher court reversing a lower court. The House of Lords examined the High Court judgment and rejected it.

10.8 Lawyers, professional conduct and criminal case law

It is apt to end this chapter, and indeed this publication, with some words as to professional conduct.

Solicitors, barristers and by implication other lawyers too have certain key obligations. We must uphold the rule of law and the proper administration of justice; uphold public trust and confidence in the legal profession; act with independence, honesty and integrity; encourage equality, diversity and inclusion; and act in the best interests of each client. To the extent there is any conflict between these concepts, the public interest prevails. There are other duties too: ensuring you do not mislead the court, maintaining client confidentiality and so on.

10.8.1 A possible scenario

Imagine you act for a defendant in a fraud matter. They ask you to shred certain incriminating documents. That may well be in the client's best interests, but it would clearly be contrary to the proper administration of justice. You would therefore politely decline your client's request, and indeed insist on taking the documents from them.

10.8.2 Defending someone who says 'I did it'

Let's look at one aspect of professional conduct that routinely generates debate among students. What are a lawyer's obligations where a defendant client, charged with a criminal offence, either deliberately or inadvertently tells you they have committed the crime? Can you act for the client at all? If so, how do you go about your job? Are you allowed to represent them at trial if they insist on pleading not guilty?

Clearly very few criminal clients would ever deny a crime to the police, proceed with a not guilty plea, and then tell their legal advisers something to the contrary. Generally the criminal fraternity keep their guilt to themselves, on the basis that all officialdom, including their own 'briefs', as lawyers are sometimes called, are not to be trusted.

10.8.3 The solution (of sorts)

But assuming they do share the truth with their lawyer, yet continue to plead not guilty, what should be done? In fact it is surprisingly straightforward:

1. It is an essential element of a properly functioning democracy for every defendant to be allowed legal advice. So you must continue to act unless your professional conduct obligations mean you should cease for some reason.

2. The duty of confidentiality requires you to tell no one, except colleagues within your law firm if you are a solicitor, of your client's statement to you.

3. A client who tells you 'yes, I did it' has not confessed in the formal sense. Nor are they guilty. The pure definition of a confession is: a statement adverse to the interests of the maker. You can argue it is not adverse to the interests of a client to confide in their lawyer. So there is no confession at this stage. Equally, only a court can decide on guilt. The client who says to their lawyer 'I did it' is simply making a statement, rather than being confirmed as guilty in the pure sense of the word. The finding 'Guilty!' is something said by a magistrate, jury or appellate judge at appeal, no one else.

   ○ Incidentally, lawyers have a professional conduct duty to ensure a client isn't falsely admitting to a crime they didn't commit. It sounds strange, but there are people out there who for a variety of reasons might pretend they have offended when in fact they are entirely innocent. As a lawyer you need to have your wits about you at all times.

4. It is entirely appropriate for a lawyer to act for a client who suggests they have indeed committed a crime to which they intend to plead not guilty. Guidance to the Code of Conduct for barristers states the position:

   if your client were to tell you that they have committed the crime with which they were charged ... you would not be misleading the court if, after your client had entered a plea of 'not guilty', you were to test in cross-examination the reliability of the evidence of the prosecution witnesses and then address the jury to the effect that the prosecution had not succeeded in making them sure of your client's guilt.

This passage, the thrust of which would apply equally to solicitors, says lawyers can put the prosecution to proof. Allowing a plea of 'not guilty' to be made, where the client had indicated to their legal advisers they committed the crime, in no way constitutes misconduct. This reinforces a number of basic principles, such as requiring the state to make the running in any prosecution, and allowing a defendant to decline any cooperation with the prosecuting authorities, generally.

In a similar vein, someone arrested and taken to the police station is under no obligation to answer police questions. Declining to cooperate may be mentioned in court at trial, as a hint that you have something to hide, perhaps, but it is an absolute entitlement, going back many centuries, for a suspect to maintain silence in the face of official inquisition.

10.8.4 Conclusion on conduct

In conclusion, therefore, where a client tells you they have committed the crime, you can continue to act for them, and they can continue to plead not guilty at court, and you can defend them, providing you do not mislead the court by actively suggesting your client's innocence. You would be forbidden, for example, from allowing your client to 'take the stand' and give evidence.

Figure 10.4 Ethical and conduct considerations where a client says 'I did it'

- Confirmation of solicitor–client relationship

- SRA Code of Conduct and principles

- Can the client give coherent instructions?

- Is the client telling the truth?

- Every defendant is entitled to legal representation, no matter how horrible they are, and no matter how heinous the crime

- Defendants are innocent until proved guilty in court

- Defendants can put the prosecution to proof of its case – a defendant can plead 'not guilty' and let the prosecution make the running

- Lawyer cannot allow defendant to mislead the court

- Case must be proved beyond reasonable doubt

- Other considerations too

10.9 Overall conclusion to this chapter

This chapter continues the theme of this manual as a whole, which is to deal with the legal system of England and Wales and sources of law. In this chapter we have discussed criminal matters, the role of the courts in adjudicating on crime, and case law. There is no attempt to provide detail, nor do we attempt to cover things comprehensively. We have been deliberately selective in our approach.

The key points for the reader to appreciate remain constant. They are the importance of the rule of law; the need for the state to prove its case beyond reasonable doubt; the importance of case law and precedent; the primacy of parliamentary legislation; and the ever-present desire of the judiciary to arrive at a fair and just outcome.

Summary

In this chapter you have considered criminal case law and precedent. In particular, we have discussed:

- the importance of challenging the state when it accuses an individual of a crime;

- certain crimes from long ago, and how they are handled today;

- why courts have a vital role in deciding evidential matters in criminal cases, even if, or perhaps because, there are Acts of Parliament dealing with the underlying areas of law;

- the complexities of sentencing, and the courts' role in ensuring the appropriate punishment is handed down to a wrongdoer;

- the somewhat unusual conflicts that arise within the legal system when prosecuting corruption, on the one hand, and maintaining international relations, on the other; and

- the pervasive importance of codes of conduct, and ethical standards, for lawyers, without which our legal system would be infinitely diminished. In particular we have established all defendants are entitled to legal advice; every defendant is entitled to put the prosecution to proof; the state must prove its case beyond reasonable doubt; and a lawyer can continue to act for a client on a 'not guilty' plea, even if that client has indicated to the lawyer, privately and confidentially, they committed the crime in question.

Sample questions

Question 1

A not-for-profit organisation judicially reviews the decision of a government agency for failing to prosecute a company for breach of environmental law. The case is heard in the Administrative (Divisional) Court of the King's Bench Division of the High Court. The underlying law is novel and unclear.

The judge finds in favour of the agency. The judge certifies there is an urgent need to obtain an authoritative interpretation on the matter in dispute.

Which of the following is the most likely route of appeal for the organisation?

A   The Crown Court, because this is a criminal matter.

B   Another part of the King's Bench Division, because judicial review is a civil matter.

C   The Administrative Court again, by way of case stated, as there is point of law to be decided.

D   The Court of Appeal, because it is the next court up within the hierarchy.

E   The Supreme Court by way of the leapfrog procedure, as there is an urgent need to obtain authoritative interpretation on the matter.

Answer

Option E is correct. The leapfrog procedure allows an appeal from the High Court to the Supreme Court where there is an urgent need to obtain authoritative interpretation of the matter in dispute.

Option A is wrong because, although breaking the environmental law in question might well be a criminal offence, judicial review is not a criminal process. It is an administrative one. In any event, it is not possible to appeal from the High Court to the Crown Court. Option B is wrong because it is not possible to appeal from one part of the High Court to another. Option C is wrong because it is not possible to use the case stated procedure from the High Court. It must be from a lower criminal court (although it is indeed correct that appeals by way of case stated are heard in the King's Bench Division). Option D is wrong because an urgent need to obtain authoritative interpretation results in an appeal to the Supreme Court – through the leapfrog procedure – rather than the Court of Appeal.

Question 2

Police arrive at a man's house. They knock on the door. He opens the door and they enter without his permission. They take a bank statement from his desk. They ask him to accompany them to the police station, without giving a reason why. The man refuses. They arrest him. In so doing there is no violence and the man is not intimidated.

At the police station they put him in a room. They take his house keys for safe keeping, indicating they will be returned later. The police refuse to explain why they are holding the man. After several hours the police allow the man to see his solicitor.

Which of the following best explains what the solicitor should do and why?

A Explain to the man the law relating to the possible offences he has committed, so the man understands his situation.

B Object to the man's arrest on the basis the bank statement is unlawfully obtained evidence and thus inadmissible.

C Object to the man's arrest on the basis it contravenes the rule of law.

D Object to the man's arrest because the police have assaulted him.

E Object to the man's arrest because the police have stolen his keys.

Answer

Option C is correct. The police behaviour is in breach of the rule of law. They have entered the man's house without reason, arrested him without explaining why, and held him in a form of isolation without explaining what offence, if any, he has committed. It is a fundamental and basic aspect of the legal system for the authorities, here represented by the police, to act on the basis of established laws. Here there is no evidence the police have behaved lawfully. The onus is on the state to explain its actions.

Option A is wrong because, without the police confirming the alleged offence, if any, the solicitor is not able to explain the relevant law. A solicitor cannot speculate as to the reasons for a client's arrest. They should be told by the police. Option B is wrong because case law and statute suggest unlawfully obtained evidence can still be admissible, unless it has an adverse effect on the fairness of proceedings. Option D is wrong because there is no evidence of assault by the police, and in any event that is a relatively minor argument to make compared to the 'bigger picture' of the overall wrongdoing. Option E is wrong because there is no evidence of the police intending to permanently deprive the man of his keys, and thus there is no theft.

Question 3

A man with 12 previous convictions is on trial in the Crown Court for theft of a pedal bike. When arrested the man protests his innocence. At the police station he feels unwell and tells the police he had indeed stolen the bike. He says this not because he had committed the crime but because he thought it would allow him to leave the police station as soon as possible.

At trial the prosecution obtain permission to adduce evidence of the man's previous convictions.

Can the jury find the man guilty of theft?

A   Yes, because the man made a confession.

B   Yes, because of the man's previous criminal record.

C   Yes, if the prosecution proves their case beyond reasonable doubt.

D   No, because the man only confessed on account of feeling unwell.

E   No, because the man protested his innocence when arrested.

Answer

Option C is correct. The jury can convict the man if they believe the prosecution has proved its case beyond reasonable doubt. As per *Woolmington v DPP*, the golden thread of British justice is that a defendant is innocent until presumed guilty.

Option A is wrong because a court can exclude a confession, and the fact that the man stated he had stolen the bike would not on its own be conclusive. Option B is wrong because basic principles of justice do not allow a jury to convict a defendant on the basis of previous criminality. Rather, the jury must establish guilt in relation to the offence charged. Option D is wrong because the fact of the man being unwell is itself not conclusive. The defence must prove that any illness at the police station made the confession, or indeed any confession made in those circumstances, unreliable. In addition, the man could be convicted on the basis of other evidence. Option E is wrong because many suspects protest their innocence on arrest, so that would not, on its own, be a reason for the jury to find the man not guilty.

11

SQE1 Consolidation: The Legal System of England and Wales and Sources of Law

SQE1 syllabus

The purpose of this final section is to review discrete topics explored in this manual. This is to consolidate your knowledge and understanding. We have chosen these topics by reference to the SQE1 assessment specification in relation to functioning legal knowledge. This is a focused guide for students, but you should note that it does not purport to set out exhaustively matters that could be examined in those assessments. You will need to undertake your own review of the preceding chapters, and take heed of the SQE1 specification, as part of your preparation.

Learning outcomes

By the end of this chapter you will be able to consolidate relevant core legal principles and rules appropriately and effectively, at the level of a competent newly qualified solicitor in practice, to realistic client-based and ethical problems and situations in the following areas:

- The courts (structures, judges and rights of audience);
- The development of case law and the doctrine of precedent;
- Primary legislation and the structure of an Act of Parliament; and
- Statutory interpretation, including presumptions and aids to interpretation.

11.1 The courts

The modern court structure is set out in **Figure 11.1**. You will see it starts at the top with the Supreme Court, previously the House of Lords, and travels down through the Court of Appeal to the High Court and Crown Court. The courts at the very bottom of the ladder are inferior courts, the Family Court being a somewhat more recent addition to the category.

Figure 11.1 The modern court structure

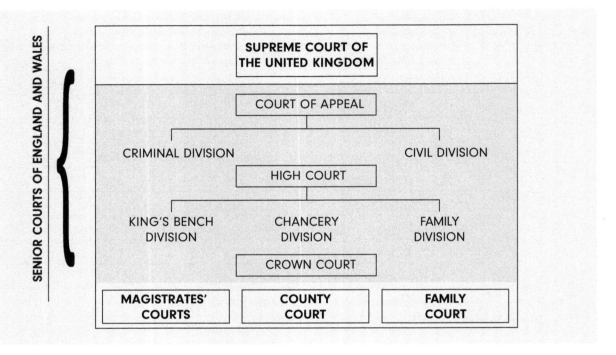

As mentioned in **Figure 11.1**, courts can be divided into superior and inferior courts:

(a) Superior courts have unlimited jurisdiction both geographically and financially, and generally try the most important and difficult cases.

(b) Inferior courts have limited geographical and financial jurisdiction, and deal with less-important cases (although they address significantly more cases than the superior courts and therefore play a crucial role in the legal system).

Table 11.1 lists the superior and inferior courts of England and Wales.

Table 11.1 Superior and inferior courts

Superior courts	Inferior courts
Supreme Court	County Court
Court of Appeal	Magistrates' courts
High Court	Family Court
Crown Court	

Courts can also be divided into trial and appellate courts:

(a) A trial court hears cases at first instance (ie for the first time). A trial court will rule on issues of fact and law.

(b) An appellate court will reconsider the application of legal principles to a case that has already been heard by a lower court. This appeals process allows errors of law – and occasionally fact and procedure – to be corrected.

Figure 11.2   Which courts hear trials and which hear appeals

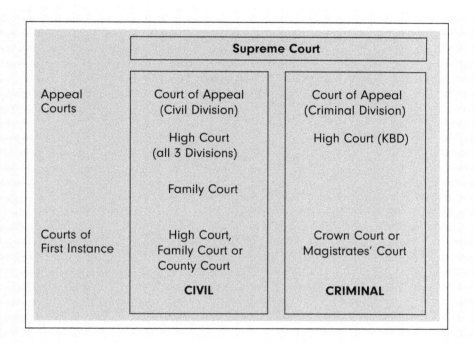

11.2   Civil court structure

The court system is divided into civil and criminal. The civil court structure is set out in **Figure 11.3**.

Table 11.2 summarises some key functions of these courts. The key distinction for most litigants is that between the County Court and the High Court. The former generally deals with lower value claims.

Figure 11.3   Civil court structure

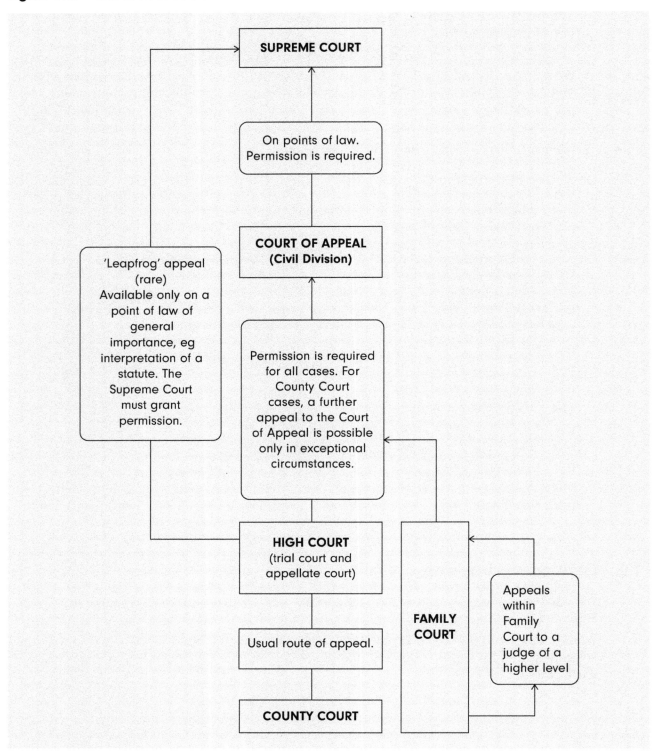

Table 11.2 Summary of the main courts involved in civil proceedings

Court	County Court	High Court	Court of Appeal	Supreme Court
Where?	All over the country	In London (The Royal Courts of Justice) and in District Registries in major cities	In London (The Royal Courts of Justice)	In London (Parliament Square)
Who?	Circuit judges and district judges	High Court judge (usually sitting alone)	Lord Justices of Appeal (usually 3 sitting at once)	Justices of the Supreme Court (usually 5 sitting at once)
What? (Civil jurisdiction)	Unlimited financial jurisdiction (although mainly deal with claims of lower value) General types of work include: Contract/tort claims Equity jurisdiction, eg mortgages Disputes over wills Recovery of land Disputes under the Consumer Credit Act	Claims must generally be valued at £100,000+ (£50,000 for personal injury) to be commenced in the High Court King's Bench Division Contract/tort claims Specialised courts, eg Technology and Construction Court Chancery Division Disputes over wills and administration of estates Trusts Land and mortgage actions Company law Bankruptcy Family Division	Appeals in civil cases from: High Court County Court Certain tribunals	Appeals from: Court of Appeal High Court (leapfrog appeal)

NB: this table does not address the Family Court being the national court in which nearly all family cases must be commenced

11.3 Criminal court structure

In order to understand the hierarchy of courts in the criminal system, it is essential to understand the classification of criminal offences:

(a) Summary only offences (eg driving without insurance or common assault). These are minor offences and must be dealt with in the magistrates' court.

(b) Indictable only offences (eg murder or robbery). These are the most serious offences and can be tried only in the Crown Court (in front of a jury).

(c) Either way offences may be dealt with in either court. These are typically offences that are capable of being more or less serious depending upon the way in which they were committed (eg theft, which may involve taking a chocolate bar from the local shop or a sophisticated fraud involving millions of pounds).

An overview of criminal procedure is set out in **Figure 11.4**. This chart presumes that the police wish to prosecute, in which case there is a first hearing in the magistrates' court. Depending on the nature of the offence, the matter will be tried either there or in the Crown Court.

Figure 11.4   An overview of criminal procedure commenced by the police

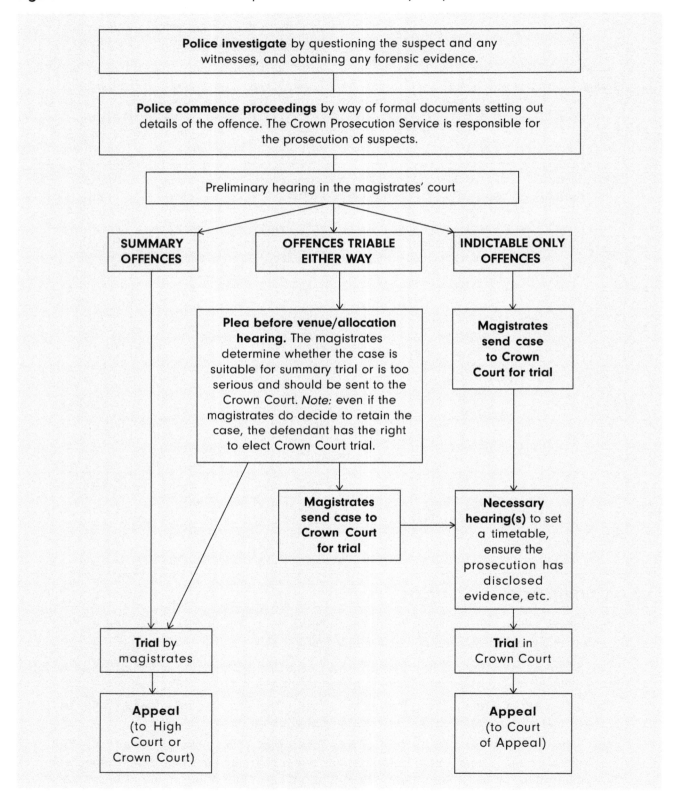

Guilty defendants in magistrates' trials may wish to appeal either the verdict or sentence or both. The route of appeal following a summary trial is set out in **Figure 11.5**.

Figure 11.5 Summary trials: appeals

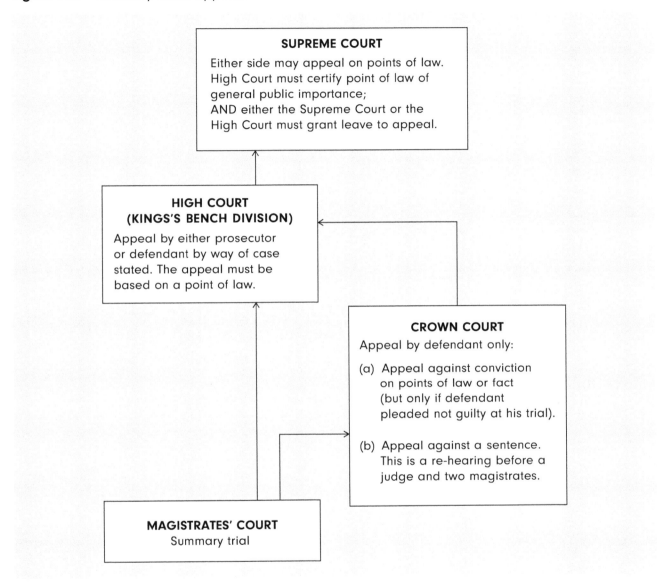

Appeals from the Crown Court are rarer, as the test for allowing an appeal is stiffer. The route of appeal following trial on indictment is set out in **Figure 11.6**.

Figure 11.6   Trial on indictment: appeals

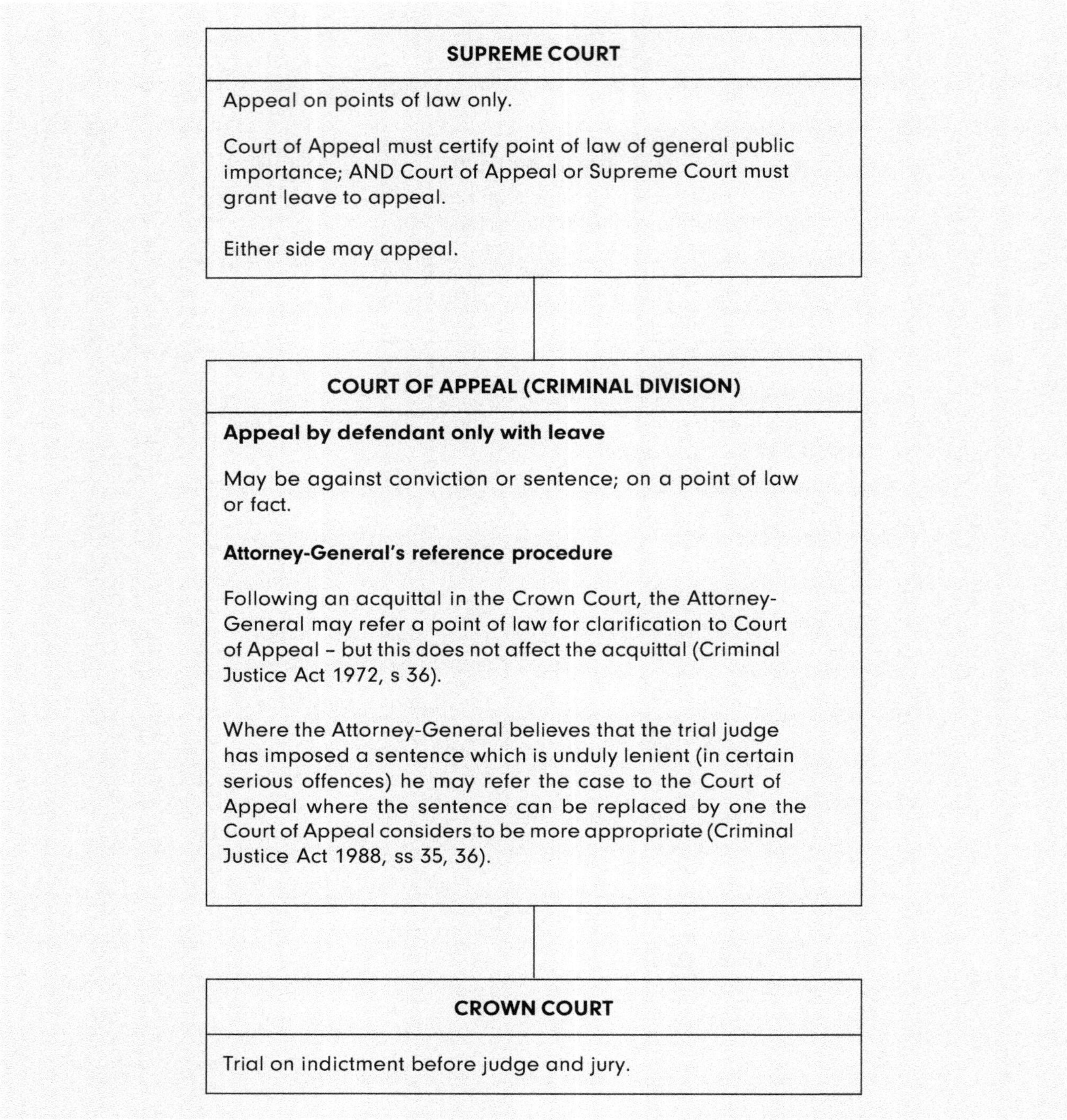

SUPREME COURT
Appeal on points of law only.
Court of Appeal must certify point of law of general public importance; AND Court of Appeal or Supreme Court must grant leave to appeal.
Either side may appeal.

COURT OF APPEAL (CRIMINAL DIVISION)
Appeal by defendant only with leave
May be against conviction or sentence; on a point of law or fact.
Attorney-General's reference procedure
Following an acquittal in the Crown Court, the Attorney-General may refer a point of law for clarification to Court of Appeal – but this does not affect the acquittal (Criminal Justice Act 1972, s 36).
Where the Attorney-General believes that the trial judge has imposed a sentence which is unduly lenient (in certain serious offences) he may refer the case to the Court of Appeal where the sentence can be replaced by one the Court of Appeal considers to be more appropriate (Criminal Justice Act 1988, ss 35, 36).

CROWN COURT
Trial on indictment before judge and jury.

A summary of the courts mentioned in these routes of appeal is set out in **Table 11.3**. This table states the court in question, where they are located, who presides and the nature of their jurisdiction.

Table 11.3 Summary of the main courts involved in criminal proceedings

Court	Magistrates' courts	Crown Court	Court of Appeal	Supreme Court
Where?	All over the country	In various centres across the country	In London (The Royal Courts of Justice)	In London (Parliament Square)
Who?	Lay magistrates (not legally qualified – usually 3 sitting at once) or district judge (usually sitting alone)	High Court judge, circuit judge or recorder (usually sitting alone) Jury for trials	Lord and Lady Justices of Appeal (usually 3 sitting at once)	Justices of the Supreme Court (usually 5 sitting at once)
What? (Criminal jurisdiction)	Issue of summonses and warrants for search / arrest Bail applications Trials of summary offences Mode of trial procedure to decide whether case should be tried summarily or on indictment	Trials on indictment Committals for sentence from magistrates' courts where the magistrates sentencing powers are inadequate Appeals by defendants convicted summarily in magistrates' courts	Appeals in criminal cases from: Crown Court by defendant References by AG on points of law or against lenient sentences Cases referred by the Criminal Cases Review Commission	Appeals from: Court of Appeal (Criminal Division) KBD (Divisional Court)

Note: Appeals by way of case stated go to the High Court KBD

11.4 Other courts

The law of England and Wales is also affected by the Privy Council, the European Court of Justice and the European Court of Human Rights. The main features of these courts are summarised in **Table 11.4**.

Table 11.4 Summary of the other courts whose judgments can impact on English law

Court	Privy Council	European Court of Justice	European Court of Human Rights
Where?	In London (Parliament Square)	Luxembourg	Strasbourg
Who?	Justices of the Supreme Court and Commonwealth judges who are members of the Privy Council (usually 5 sitting at once)	Judges appointed with agreement from Member States Assisted by Advocates-General	Judges appointed from each state that is a party to the 1950 Convention
What? (Jurisdiction)	Appeals from certain Commonwealth countries	Preliminary rulings on EU law and the actions of EU institutions Actions against Member States to determine whether they have failed to fulfil their Treaty obligations NB: influence reduced/ removed by repeal of the European Communities Act 1972	Hears cases on alleged breaches of the European Convention on Human Rights

11.5 The judiciary

Figure 11.7 summarises the various judges who sit in England and Wales, their roles and how they fit into the court system. The Lord Chief Justice, who is eminent and highly qualified, sits at the top of the structure, and at the very bottom we find the magistrates, who are ordinary people doing an extraordinary job.

11.6 Rights of audience

A right of audience is the right of a person to appear and conduct proceedings in court.

Solicitors have the right to appear in the magistrates' courts and county courts. If they wish to exercise such rights in the higher courts (the Crown Court, the High Court, the Court of Appeal and the Supreme Court), they must have completed the appropriate higher courts advocacy qualification:

(a) the Higher Courts (Civil Advocacy) Qualification, which entitles the solicitor to exercise rights of audience in all civil proceedings in the higher courts; and/or

(b) the Higher Courts (Criminal Advocacy) Qualification, which entitles the solicitor to exercise rights of audience in all criminal proceedings in the higher courts.

More detail on higher rights of audience can be found on the SRA's website (www.sra.org.uk).

Figure 11.7   Who's who in the judiciary?

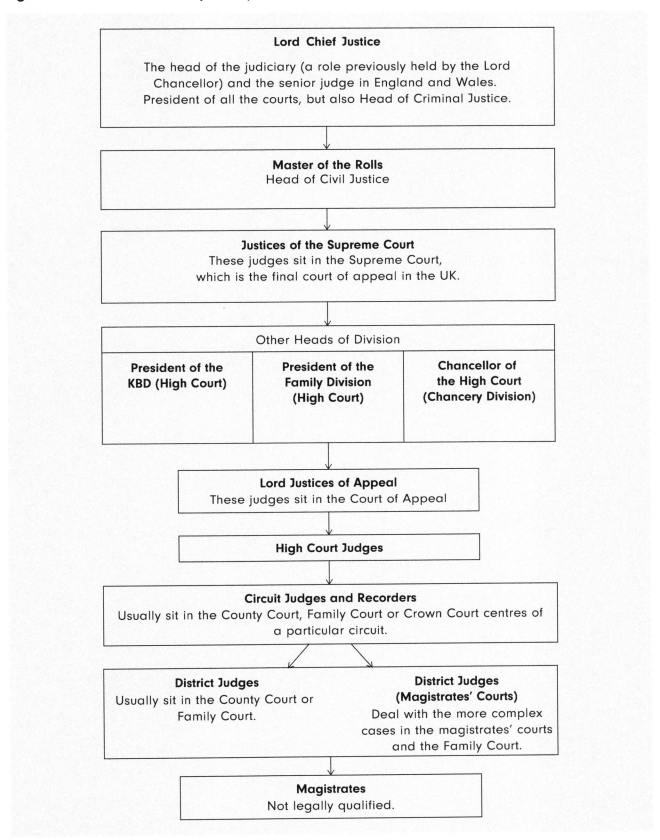

11.7 Development of case law: the doctrine of precedent

A proposition stated in one case is binding in a later case if it is:

(a) a proposition of law (not fact);

(b) part of the *ratio decidendi* of a case (ie the central legal reasoning of a case). Statements that are unimportant to the outcome (but which might have future significance) are obiter dicta – persuasive but not binding. Generally obiter involves:

    (i) the judge speculating about the decision they would have given if the facts of the case had been different;

    (ii) the judge addressing submissions that were made in legal arguments but that are no longer relevant given the *ratio* of the case; or

    (iii) dissenting judgments;

(c) decided in a court whose decisions are binding on the present court – see **Figure 11.8**; and

Figure 11.8 Who binds whom?

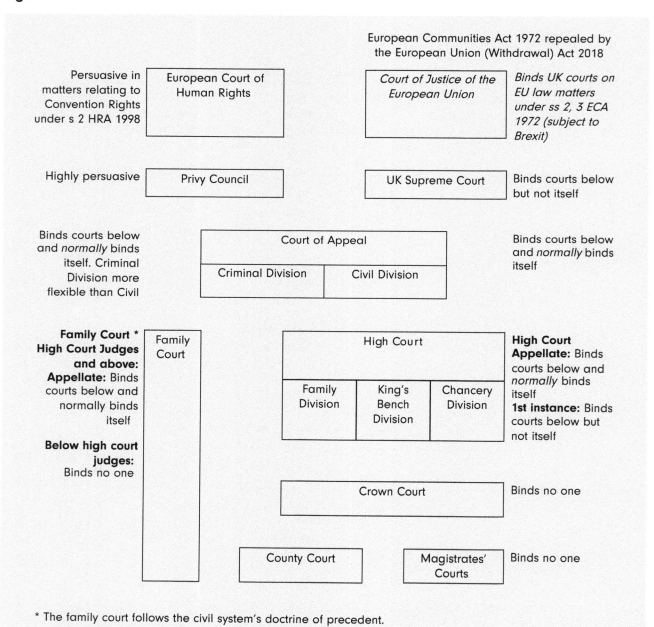

* The family court follows the civil system's doctrine of precedent.

(d) there are no relevant distinctions between the two cases.

Figure 11.8 presents a chart indicating the court hierarchy, and which courts bind other courts, and this helps you decide on an important aspect of the precedent process (from (c) above). For the Crown Court, magistrates' courts and the County Court there is no system of precedent – there are too many decisions, coming thick and fast, for judgments to be faithfully followed in any sensible way.

11.8 Can courts depart from their own previous decisions?

The general presumption is the Supreme Court and the Court of Appeal would expect to follow their own previous decisions. But this is not an inviolable rule. Note that the inferior courts do not bind themselves and this is in line with the idea their decisions have no precedent value. A summary of the current status is set out in **Table 11.5**, and as you can see this links in with **Figure 11.8**.

Table 11.5 Do courts bind themselves?

Court	Does it bind itself?
Supreme Court	No – see Practice Statement (HL: Judicial Precedent) [1966] 1 WLR 1234 – although ordinarily it will follow its own decisions
Court of Appeal	Yes, subject to the following exceptions (the first three come from the case of *Young v Bristol Aeroplane Co Ltd* [1944] KB 718): • Where there are two conflicting decisions of the Court of Appeal, it may choose which to follow • Where the previous decision of the Court of Appeal, even if not expressly overruled, conflicts with a Supreme Court (or House of Lords) decision • Where the decision was made *per incuriam* (ie the court neglected to consider a statutory provision or a binding precedent) • Where it was an interim decision by two judges (an exception added by *Boys v Chaplin* [1968] 2 QB 1) • Where one of its previous decisions is inconsistent with a subsequent decision of the European Court of Human Rights • In criminal matters, where a decision is obviously wrong and would lead to the appellant remaining in gaol
Divisional Court of the High Court (appellate jurisdiction)	Yes, subject to the same exceptions as the Court of Appeal
The High Court (first instance/trial jurisdiction)	No, although in the interests of certainty judges try not to depart from previous decisions
The Crown Court	No, although in the interests of certainty previous decisions are highly persuasive
Inferior courts (County Court, Family Court, magistrates' courts)	No

11.9 Distinguishing cases

The *ratio* is an application of the law to material facts. If a court considers a case before it to be different in some material way from the precedent cited, either on the facts or the law, the earlier case need not be followed. The present case will be distinguished.

11.10 Other ways in which courts deal with other judgments

(a) Affirming – a higher court confirms it agrees with the appeal before it from a lower court.

(b) Applying – a court adopts statements or reasoning from other decisions.

(c) Departing – a court of one level disagrees with a previous decision, in another matter, by an equal court.

(d) Overruling – a higher court comments on a previous unrelated decision by a lower court and declares it to be wrong.

(e) Reversing – a higher court disagrees with the earlier decision, in the same proceedings, of a lower court.

11.11 Primary legislation: the structure of an Act of Parliament

An Act of Parliament is structured as follows:

(a) The Royal Coat of Arms.

(b) A short title, being the name by which that statute is commonly referred. For example, the short title of the 2015 statute that currently sets out many protections afforded to consumers is known as the 'Consumer Rights Act 2015'.

(c) A year and chapter number, being that statute's unique reference number. From 1962 onwards, each statute has been given a sequential number to identify what order the statute was passed in any calendar year. For example, the chapter number of the Consumer Rights Act 2015 is 'Chapter 15' (or c 15) identifying that this Act was the 15th statute that was passed in 2015.

(d) A long title, which serves to describe the purposes of the Act (which might serve to assist judges when interpreting the Act). For example, the long title of the Consumer Rights Act 2015 is: 'An Act to amend the law relating to the rights of consumers and protection of their interests; to make provision about investigatory powers for enforcing the regulation of traders; to make provision about private actions in competition law and the Competition Appeal Tribunal; and for connected purposes.'

(e) The date of Royal Assent, being the final part of the process to enact legislation. Royal Assent to the Consumer Rights Act 2015 was granted on 26 March 2015.

(f) The enacting formula, being a formally worded paragraph to confirm that the statute has passed all the relevant legislative processes. The common wording is: 'BE IT ENACTED by the King's most Excellent Majesty, by and with the advice and consent of the Lords Spiritual and Temporal, and Commons, in this present Parliament assembled, and by the authority of the same, as follows:—'

(g) Many statutes are long documents, and bits of an Act are often parcelled together into different parts and chapters to promote understanding as well as consistency in approach and interpretation. Each part/chapter will be described by a note (on electronic versions of legislation, these notes often appear as headings).

(h) Each provision of a statute is known as a section. Many statutes will have various sections that list definitions or help the reader to interpret different provisions. Such sections often appear at the beginning or ends of relevant Parts/Chapters of the statute. It is important to know where these definitions appear in the Act. Each section is also accompanied by a 'marginal note'. In paper versions of the statute, these notes appear in the margins of the text; in electronic versions, these notes tend to appear as headings.

(i) Towards the end of the statute, there will be sections addressing matters of general interpretation as well as commencement of the statute, its application and extent.

(j) Many statutes also have a number of schedules. The content of such schedules is specific to each statute, but a common purpose is to list amendments and repeals to other Acts of Parliament that must be made as a result of (consequential to) this statute coming into force.

11.12 Statutory interpretation

There are various methods that judges can use to interpret statutory provisions. The most common ones are summarised in **Figure 11.9**. As you can see it deals with the literal, mischief and golden rules and the purposive approach.

Figure 11.9 Methods of statutory interpretation

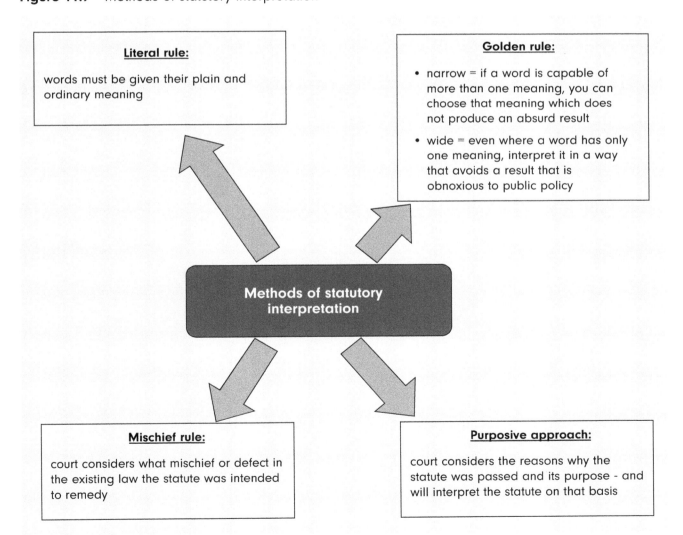

Literal rule:

words must be given their plain and ordinary meaning

Golden rule:

- narrow = if a word is capable of more than one meaning, you can choose that meaning which does not produce an absurd result

- wide = even where a word has only one meaning, interpret it in a way that avoids a result that is obnoxious to public policy

Methods of statutory interpretation

Mischief rule:

court considers what mischief or defect in the existing law the statute was intended to remedy

Purposive approach:

court considers the reasons why the statute was passed and its purpose - and will interpret the statute on that basis

11.13 Presumptions

Courts also use various presumptions when interpreting statutes. These include presumptions:

(a) against alteration of the common law. Unless the statute expressly states an intention to alter the common law, the interpretation that does not alter the existing law will be preferred;

(b) against the retrospective operation of statutes. Where an Act of Parliament becomes law, a presumption arises that it will apply only to future actions, unless the legislation is specifically stated to have retrospective effect;

(c) against criminal liability without guilty intention (*mens rea*). If a statute creates a new criminal offence, it is presumed that the defendant must have a 'guilty mind' to be convicted of that offence, unless Parliament makes it clear that the offence is one of strict liability;

(d) against deprivation of the liberty of the individual. If there are two possible constructions of a statutory provision – one that is in favour of the defence and the other that is in favour of the prosecution – the construction that favours the defence should be used, unless Parliament intends the opposite;

(e) against deprivation of property or interference with private rights;

(f) against binding the Crown. Unless there is a clear statement to the contrary, legislation is presumed not to apply to the Crown; and

(g) against ousting the jurisdiction of the courts.

11.14 Aids to statutory interpretation and construction

Common aids used by judges to interpret a statute when its meaning is not clear are summarised in **Figure 11.10**.

Figure 11.10 Examples of aids to statutory interpretation

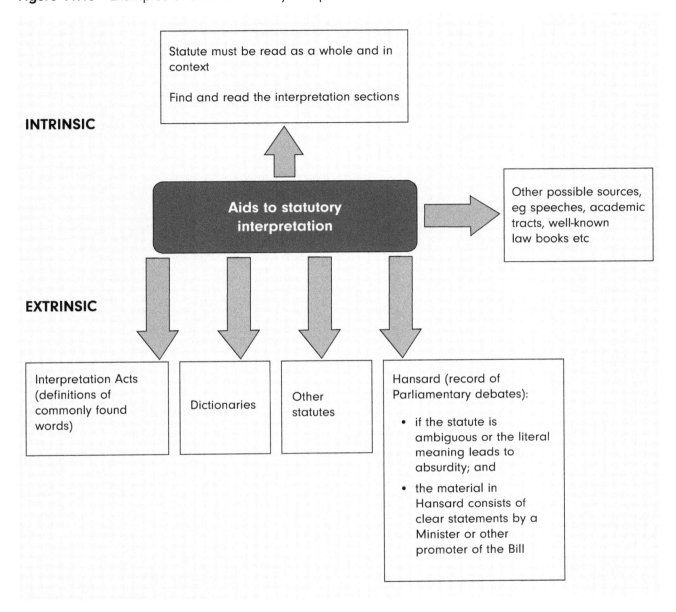

INTRINSIC

Statute must be read as a whole and in context

Find and read the interpretation sections

Aids to statutory interpretation

Other possible sources, eg speeches, academic tracts, well-known law books etc

EXTRINSIC

Interpretation Acts (definitions of commonly found words)

Dictionaries

Other statutes

Hansard (record of Parliamentary debates):

- if the statute is ambiguous or the literal meaning leads to absurdity; and

- the material in Hansard consists of clear statements by a Minister or other promoter of the Bill

Glossary

Here is a glossary, or brief explanation, of some words and terms appearing in this Manual. In general we have attempted to expand on things as we go along. Therefore this list does not pretend to be all embracing. Rather, it fills in some gaps. For more details, you should refer to the specific subjects in other publications when you come to study them in greater depth.

Acquittal	The process of finding a defendant not guilty at the end of a trial.
Arraignment, or being arraigned	The old-fashioned way of saying someone has been charged with a crime.
Asylum	The process of seeking shelter in another country from, usually, your own hostile government.
Burden of proof	The nature of the requirement to succeed in a legal case. The burden in a criminal matter is beyond reasonable doubt. The burden in a civil matter is on the balance of probabilities.
Commissioner of Police of the Metropolis	The boss of the Metropolitan Police. This is the top officer in 'the Met', ie the policing body for the Greater London area. The Met answers to the Home Secretary in the Government of the day. Police forces outside London are answerable to their local police and crime commissioners (and note these 'commissioners' are elected officials, ie not at all the same as the Met Commissioner, who is a serving officer).
Common law	The traditional form of judge-made law. This has been seen as having some inflexible aspects, which therefore led to the development of equity (see below).
Constitution	In most countries this is a written document setting out a combination of citizens' rights, institutional powers, and government obligations. In the UK, it is a blend of tradition, legislation, legal principles, conventions, judge-made law, history ... the list goes on. It is not codified (ie written down in any one place).
County Court Money Claims Centre	The court hub where the majority of lower value civil claims commence.
Credibility	Whether a witness is believable. Dressing smartly, combing your hair, etc to impress a judge or jury visually can also make an impact here. A credible witness can make the difference between a court case being won or lost.
Declaration of incompatibility	A statement by a court that legislation does not comply with the European Convention on Human Rights (ECHR). Note this is not a European Union (EU) law matter, being instead the preserve of the ECHR arena.
Devolution	The process of central government allowing regions more autonomy. The most obvious examples of devolution are the settlements for Wales and Scotland. Traditionalists see devolution as a way of staving off overt independence.

Equity	The legal principle of treating litigants fairly in all circumstances. Traditionally this means moving away from a strict interpretation of the law and replacing it with broader concepts. Over time, principles of equity have become as predictable as any other area of law.
European Council	The body representing governments of the EU. It acts in a coordinated manner with the European Parliament and the European Commission.
Fiscal burden	The financial cost to a government – and thus all of us – of running the country.
Franchise	In constitutional terms this means the entitlement to vote. A significant extension of the franchise, ie broadening the voter base, took place in the 19th century.
Gross income	The amount of money someone earns, or receives, before tax, National Insurance, and other deductions are made for the benefit of the public purse. The word 'gross' is to be contrasted with 'net' – see below.
Hansard	Publication service providing verbatim reports of proceedings in Parliament.
Indictment	The means of charging someone with a more serious crime, which, if it progresses, would be tried in the Crown Court.
Insolvency	The process of being unable to pay your debts as they fall due. An individual insolvency, if it comes to a conclusion, results in bankruptcy. Corporate insolvency would lead to liquidation or some similar form of company death knell.
Jurisdiction	This can mean different things depending on the context. Broadly, the term implies the administrative reach and powers available to a given body. Governments have jurisdiction, ie influence and control, over citizens and the general population. They also have jurisdiction in terms of foreign relations. Courts have a different sort of jurisdiction – meaning their powers and rules in terms of judgments they are able to hand down.
Jurisprudence	The somewhat lofty name given to the combined concept of law and philosophy. Reduced to its basics, it embraces what the law means and how it is applied.
Jury	The group of men and women who decide on innocence and guilt at a Crown Court trial. A jury can also sit at an inquest, ie the coronial process of establishing the identity of someone who has died unexpectedly, and how, where and when they came by their death.
Leasehold reform	The somewhat vexed, and ongoing, process of establishing the rights of (usually residential) leaseholders as against their freeholders. A leaseholder owns an estate in a piece of land for a given period of years, at the end of which the land reverts to someone else, usually leaving the leaseholder with nothing of financial value.
Lords spiritual	The term given to archbishops and bishops who sit in the House of Lords.
Lords temporal	The somewhat outdated term for other people who sit in the House of Lords. 'Temporal' implies something more obviously worldly and material than the word spiritual.

Monarchs	Those who rule over us, at least in theory. These days governments have replaced them in terms of practical power. In the past they had considerably more punch. Those mentioned in this publication include William I, who landed in Sussex in 1066, and saw off Harold; John, who signed the Magna Carta in 1215; the Tudor Henry VII, who had certain Welsh connections in the late 1400s; his son, Henry VIII, who prompted the English reformation, ie the break from obedience to the Pope in the 1530s; and George I who was from Hanover in Germany and became King in 1714.
Magna Carta	Latin for the Great Charter. It is an important constitutional source.
Monopoly	A business stranglehold on a particular aspect of the market.
Moot	An old-fashioned word for a debate or discussion. Law schools still hold them, however.
Mortgage	The financial instrument whereby a lender, typically a bank, ensures it can regain its loan through taking a charge over, typically, a property.
Neighbourhood	The concept of being responsible for, and owing obligations to, those you come across. It is most obviously apparent in the field of tort.
Net income	The amount of money left over once deductions have been applied to a gross figure.
Parole	Allowing a serving prisoner to enter the community subject to conditions of good behaviour.
Patent	Legal protection for a novel invention (yes, we appreciate this could be a tautology – ie a form of repetition – in that all inventions presumably are novel – but you get the idea).
Privilege	This has different applications. Parliamentary privilege means the ability of our Westminster chambers to control their own affairs. Privilege as it applies to lawyers means the sanctity of advice received by a client from their legal advisers, or alternatively the privacy of communications where the sole or dominant purpose of the communication is for the purposes of litigation.
Probation	The process of supervising an offender for the purposes of rehabilitation.
Quashing, or quashed	The process of a (usually senior) court overturning a judgment or conviction.
Retracting a confession	Taking back a damaging statement in a prosecution which, if left in evidence, could result in your being found guilty.
RSPCA	Royal Society for the Prevention of Cruelty to Animals. An immensely powerful charity. All politicians know you should never criticise pet-owners.
Shareholder democracy	The idea, which emerged in the 1980s, that ordinary people should have a stake in big, previously state-owned, companies.
Sovereignty	The ability of a nation state to flex its muscles, if necessary ignoring the views of other countries. Alternatively, it denotes the impulse towards self-determination.

Index

Note: page numbers in italic type refer to
Figures; those in bold type refer to Tables.